TESTIMONIALS

"When we thought that there was nothing more that we could do, he always would help us find that next level, that other level. And that has influenced my work today — breaking barriers, breaking some of the mental barriers that we did not even know we had."

Timothy G. Benson, M.D.
Harvard Medical School, Assistant Psychiatrist
Medical Director, McLean Residence at the Brook

◆

"He was a mentor and a father figure to most. I'm truly blessed that he gave me a scholarship that allowed me to come play for him. There should be a statue of Joe T at the Hampton University campus."

Marcus Dixon
NFL — N.Y. Jets, Defensive End

◆

"I definitely give a lot of credit to Joe Taylor's program and Hampton University. I can't say enough about the man. He was there for all his players and everyone appreciated and loved him."

Kendall Langford
NFL — St. Louis Rams, Defensive Tackle

◆

"I am most honored to have been asked to provide a paragraph of reference to this book which reflects the life work of a dear friend and colleague of thirty years, Coach Joe Taylor. The subtitle, "Success Is an Inconvenience" is most fitting and appropriate. If you know Joe, you understand how the title of this book has guided his personal and coaching life in so many wonderful ways. By reading this book, such statements as "...treat a man as he is and he will be; treat him as he can be and he will become..." will paint the portrait of a dynamic and genuine mentor of young people from all backgrounds and demographics. It will reveal how accountability, faith based virtues and a goal oriented structure became the metal that forged his life's armor. The book is filled with memorable axioms substantiated with real life examples from Coach Taylor's rich coaching background and experiences of four decades of young people who have benefited from his leadership. Reading "The Making of a Champion" will become a daily journey until you reach the final chapter; then you will want to start all over again!"

Floyd Keith
Executive Direction
Black Coaches Association of America

"I have to give a lot of credit for anything that I was able to overcome to Coach Taylor's philosophy that he instilled in me. He is living proof of his philosophy. You are what you teach and he is going to live forever in us. You would be a fool not to pass this down or pass it forward. You just cannot let it go. You have got to give it to somebody else, whether it be coaching youth football or baseball or anything else. It is all relative to life."

Corey Swinson
NFL — St. Louis Rams
Director of Security, Bay Shore School District

♦

"It was another one of those moments where it was a window, although it was in my youth, it was a window where I saw some clarity. I said this man, this coach, and the coaches he has around him are doing something different. This is something different that I have never experienced before in my football career."

Jonathan Hunt, Attorney
McKenna, Long, and Aldridge — Atlanta Georgia

♦

"As I look back, I realize that the time I would have spent wondering why 'I can't,' he took the time and showed me how 'I can.' I am very grateful for what he did for me."

Coach Don Hill-Eley
Head Football Coach, Morgan State

THE MAKING OF A CHAMPION

THE MAKING
OF A
CHAMPION

Success is an Inconvenience:
The Hard Truth About What it
Takes to Be Successful.
Not Just on Game Day, but Every Day!

COACH JOE TAYLOR

with

Ronald L. Mann, Ph.D.

Waterfront Digital Press

THE MAKING OF A CHAMPION

Cover Design: Ron Mann
Cover Photo: Mega Ace

ISBN-13: 978-1984012586

ISBN-10: 1984012584

Waterfront Digital Press

ACKNOWLEDGMENTS

Writing a book is a monumental project. Although, my name is on the book with Dr. Ron Mann, it took a team of former players, coaches, administrators and mentors to make the undertaking a success. As I have learned over my forty year career, few significant accomplishments can even be completed alone, and this book is no exception. Though it would be virtually impossible to list all the people who have influenced me and contributed to *The Making Of A Champion*, I want to recognize a special few who helped make this book possible.

First, Mr. James Cox who helped to get this journey started back in 1968. He was instrumental in the admission process to Western Illinois University. Thanks to Robert Headen and Darrell Mudura, my high school and college coaches for inspiring me to coach.

Thanks to my parents, whose unconditional love and support allowed me to chart my own course and follow my dream. Thanks to my sister and brother, Mary and Leroy for being there throughout. Thanks to my extended families on both sides of uncles, aunts, cousins, and neighbors for their encouragement and compassion. Thanks to Ms. Jenny Bury for her timeless re-writes.

Boundless thanks to my wife, Beverly and sons Aaron and Dennis. Your understanding, support and many sacrifices allowed this project to manifest into a reality.

Foremost, I want to thank God for my special combination of caring, perseverance, dedication and life experiences that pushed the inspiration necessary to complete this book.

CONTENTS

Chapter 8

Chapter 9

Chapter 10

Chapter 16

Chapter 17

FOREWORD
Coach Bobby Bowden

The Making Of A Champion: Success is an Inconvenience is a book about football and life. As the title implies, success does not come easy. Coach Taylor shares the real hard facts of what it takes to succeed in life on and off the field. Coach Taylor is a legend in his field and is respected with the likes of Eddie Robinson and my close friend Jake Gaither (Deceased). I have known Joe Taylor for more than twenty years and consider him one of my close friends as well. We served together on the Board of Trustees of the American Football Coaches Association, in which he became president in 2001. He brings great respect to the coaching profession and I am honored to support him and recommend this book. Joe and I share similar values and a philosophy about life, God, and football. We both believe in the importance of mentoring young men with our coaching profession. Many of our coaches went on to obtain positions as head football coaches across the county.

The Making Of A Champion provides a blueprint and a roadmap for the development of a successful football program. He lays out his successful plan that addresses both the path for individual greatness and the organizational plan required to be a champion. He shares the key elements required for personal development at a physical, academic, and spiritual level. He discusses the organizational success within a university environment, and some great information about basic football strategy. Joe Taylor is giving away the kitchen sink here. He holds nothing back. His generosity of spirit is revealed by the amount of information he is willing to share, even while he is still competing with others.

Joe won 21 Conferences championships, 3 National championships and has a present win/loss record of 229 wins and 89 losses. More important than his coaching success, is the fact he mentored thousands of young men from teenagers to manhood. He has coached in Historically Black Colleges and led many young men who may have gone down the wrong path to becoming college graduates and successful contributors to society. He is so loved by his former players that they don't hesitate to come forward and share the stories about their Coach. The addition of these personal memories brings a lot of heart to this book. You will be inspired as well as educated. NFL players such as Marcus Dixon (N.Y. Jets), Kendall Langford (St. Louis Rams), and Corey Swinson (St. Louis Rams) provide personal insight into Coach Taylor's success and methods. Harvard Professor Timothy Benson, M.D., Attorney Jonathan Hunt, Orthopedic Surgeon Tim Frazier, M.D., Head Football Coach Michael Bailey, and Coach Donald Hill-Eley plus others share stories about the demands and rewards of playing for Coach. Dr. Frazier is a navy Doctor assigned to USMC, and just returned from Afghanistan. When asked what was most difficult: Being in the Marines or playing ball for Coach Taylor? He replied "it is not even close, playing ball for Coach Taylor."

Joe Taylor believes in the total person, mind, body, and spirit in order to create a winning athlete as well as great human being. His work is a ministry and he has devoted his life to developing and transforming these young men. He believes in 'Tough Love'. As Corey Swenson said, "Many will come, but only a few will be chosen, and those that are chosen will make the choice themselves." Those who stuck it out with Joe found a level of greatness that changed their lives. Their testimonies provide the proof and documentation for Coach Taylor's Blueprint.

Both Joe and I are very involved in The Fellowship of Christian Athletes. We firmly believe that having a strong faith is important in life. We are both convinced that The Lord has played a central role in our success and the success of our student-athletes. The Reverend Jerome Barber details his time with Coach Taylor's team over the years at Hampton University. Reverend Barber shares the bible verses and inspirational teachings that were given to these young men. Once again, Joe takes you inside the locker room by inviting you to learn directly from Revered Barber. You will be touched by this important discussion.

The final section, football 101 provide a 'Behind the Scenes' understanding of football from defense, to offense to special teams. If you love to watch football and want to learn more about the game you will find value in this discussion.

Coach Taylor is an inspiration and an asset to our coaching profession. Everyone can learn valuable lessons from this book. *The Making Of A Champion* is a must read for football fans, coaches, and athletes. I am proud to recommend this book. If you want to take your life to the next level, Joe Taylor will help you get there! Coach Taylor has been inducted into three separate Hall of Fames. He is a 'Living Legend'....... Read this Book!

PREFACE

Writing *The Making Of A Champion* with Coach Joe Taylor has been one of the highlights of my life, and I have not lived a boring life. I do not say this lightly. Joe Taylor is one of the most honest and inspiring men I have ever met. My life was taken to a higher level after the first three days I spent with him at the beginning of this project. Be prepared for a life changing experience through this book.

I want to give you some perspective on my life so you can appreciate how much I respect Joe Taylor. Shortly after I received my Ph.D. in psychology and was working in Beverly Hills, California, I expanded my private practice to include terminally ill children. I had the good fortune to meet and become close friends with Elizabeth Kűbler-Ross, M.D., known for her work on death and dying. She wrote the foreword to my book, *Sacred Healing*. While on retreat with her in one of her seminars in Hawaii, I had a spontaneous spiritual awakening. I felt the Christ presence enter my heart and awaken my soul and my life was changed. I became consciously aware of God's healing power and dedicated my life to serving humanity. During the 1980's, I founded and directed Projects for Planetary Peace, which was engaged in Citizen Diplomacy exchanges between the Soviet Union and the United States. During those intense years, it seemed like the United States was moving in the direction of a nuclear war with the Soviet Union. I and other Americans created NGO programs to bring ordinary people together. It is easier to bomb someone when they are demonized. It is more difficult to wage war and destroy people you know and like. This was the premise of our program. We had a variety of people working with us: actors Dennis Weaver and Mike Farrel; singer Shelly Fabares; Swami Satchidananda, founder of Integral Yoga; Barbara Marx Hubbard; and hundreds of wonderful ordinary citizens. I attended high-level meetings in the Soviet Union with Russian Generals and gave presentations to our FBI in San Francisco. This program brought us in contact with many spiritually minded individuals like the Dali Lama, Mother Teresa, and Sri Daya Mata, former President of the Self Realization Fellowship. I attended the National Prayer Breakfast with the Reverend Billy Graham. I have been on national TV, radio, and taught worldwide regarding personal development, spiritual awakening and peak performance.

I have written three books, traveled and lectured around the world and have had the good fortune to meet many wonderful people who are contributing to humanity. My first book, *Sacred Healing: Integrating Spirituality with Psychotherapy*, was on the Los Angeles Times Healthy Bestseller list. My latest book, *Bouncing Back: How to Recover When Life Knocks You Down*, is based on interviews with world-class athletes. I was able to interview football legend Jim Brown; boxing legend Jose Torres; baseball great Doug DeCinces; Dick Fosbury, the creator of the Fosbury Flop, Lee Brandon, Women's World Long Drive Champion, and others. Each had important contributions to make. I have been around some great people in my life.

I maintained a private practice in clinical psychology for over thirty years. I left the mental health world and transitioned into corporate consulting with leadership development and executive coaching. I had the good fortune to help brilliant and very successful people like the executive team at EBay.

My own professional work places a high value on authenticity. My psychological training made me very sensitive and aware when someone is presenting a façade or a false sense of self. It is the power of one's being that changes people, not what they say. There are too many people preaching and lecturing without a depth of unconditional love. There are a limited number of people offering a genuine experience of love, wisdom and integrity. My spiritual life has revealed to me the power and presence of the Christ energy. The best teachers embody all these qualities. Joe Taylor is one of these special people who is dedicated to serving others.

I was very fortunate to be able to speak to a number of his previous student athletes. Some of these fine men came from difficult backgrounds with little if any family support. I was often moved to tears from their stories about playing under and being guided by Coach Joe Taylor. I felt the love, respect, and appreciation that these young men had for him. He was like a father to them, but much, much more. He gave them hope, direction, purpose, and meaning. He helped them achieve what would have been impossible without him. Joe Taylor does not revel in pride nor does he seek admiration. He is humble and grateful for the opportunity to help and serve others. I know from the many interviews I conducted, how much he has helped transform the lives of these men. As you read through the stories presented here, you will learn a lot about life, love, dedication, discipline, strength, and wisdom. Joe Taylor is a man's man. He has a heart of gold and the inner strength to withstand life's test and challenges. His profound relationship with the Lord Jesus Christ gives him a depth of understanding and impact that is beyond words.

I have been asked by others to help them write their book. Up till now, I have declined. Coach called me out of the blue and asked if I would help him write his book. I had no idea who Coach Taylor was. After three minutes on the phone, I felt the depth of his heart and wisdom and knew this was a project worth doing. I knew I would personally benefit from my association with him and his life and message were worth sharing. I now value him as a friend and colleague. This is a book worth reading. You will learn from him and be better from the experience. It will touch your heart and inspire you to take your life to the next level.

Ronald L. Mann, Ph.D.

INTRODUCTION

My friends and colleagues have been telling me for years to write a book. I always thought it was a great idea, but I never had the time to write a book. As with all coaches, we work 24/7, thirteen months a year from early in the morning to late at night. I know there are only twelve months in a year. Coaching is unending — it is all consuming. How could I possibly find the time to write a book. During the summer months, I always read a new book(s). I recently read a good book by Dr. Ron Mann, *Bouncing Back: How to Recover When Life Knocks You Down*. I really liked this book and the way it was written. I had a feeling about the author, so I gave him a call. I asked if he could help me write a book. After a couple phone conversations we found a way to make it happen. I have come to trust those gut feelings in my life. I believe it is the Lord guiding me in the right direction. I believe in Obedience to His will and it is my duty to know his will through prayer and study of the scriptures. I am constantly moved by his presence in my life and the responsibility He has entrusted me with to help these young men. All my players are like my own children. I am proud to see them succeed and grow up to be successful fathers, doctors, lawyers, teachers and businessmen who have successfully gone through our program.

I start my day by 5:00 am (sometimes 4:00 am) with a cup of coffee and reading scripture. Coaching is a ministry because our goal is to improve the lives of others. I hope this book carries this message regarding His work through my life and in our football program. We are dedicated to developing men of character, honor, integrity and excellence. I know our blueprint works. You don't have to believe me, just look at the fruits of our work— twenty-one conference championships with a seventy-five percent winning percentage (three wins per four games for twenty-nine years), an eighty percent graduation rate, and many men successfully contributing to society in various respected professions! The results speak for themselves.

The Lord is not an abstraction to me. He is a living reality that manifests everyday in little and important ways. He has guided my life and my work. For example, when Dr. Ron Mann was visiting us in Tallahassee in January, we were talking about this book and developing a plan, he suggested that my spiritual convictions should be honored and represented. He thought quoting some scripture might be a good way to do that. We contacted Reverend Jerome Barber; team Chaplain when I was at Hampton University, that you will read about later. He was honored to be apart of this book because he saw the growth and development of the young men that came through the program. He incorporated the NFL phase of the program — Necessary For Life. It was awesome!

It is my experience that the Lord is near and loves us so much, that every need is fulfilled. The Bible says, "Ask and you shall receive." The Lord knows what we need, before we ask. I felt this was a good sign that we were on the right track with this book, when so many was willing to share their success stories.

I felt that Dr. Mann and I shared a deep spiritual connection and were motivated from the same source. My life is dedicated to being obedient. I believe that through my obedience I have been blessed in my life. If I tried to do it on my own, things would have turned out differently. I believe there is a Higher Being at work here. In those first days, I decided to trust that feeling and let the process unfold. I want to make it clear that I am no saint but doing what's right is important to me. I enjoy seeing young people grow and become happy productive citizens.

Throughout this book you will often see the term "we" instead of "I." We are in a team sport. And in a team sport, there is no "I." We all know that in T-E-A-M, Together Everyone Achieves More. I often tell my staff to never think less of yourself, but think of yourself less, because we are interdependent on each other for success.

We always want to promote, and let it permeate in their inner fiber, that in a team sport, you have to be able to depend on others and others must be able to depend on you. And I do not think that is any different in life. It is about being accountable and dependable — relationships and purpose are essential for success in life.

I think one of the greatest lessons that comes out of participation in athletics is socialism. You learn that you must be a dependable person and a caring person. I always ask my players — if a group of people are sitting talking and they see you walk up, what do they say? "Oh, I am so glad you are here. Come join us, have a seat." Or do they say, "Oh, here comes that pessimistic, you know... let's go!" You want to be that guy that everybody cannot wait to see and feel that way because of you. You want to be an asset. We are better because you are a part of this. I met you, I am a better person. You met me and you are a better person.

My blessing in this profession is for forty years, thirty years as a head coach, there have been so many good people in my life. I have been around great administrators, great coaches, and great athletes. And every time I speak, I am always careful to include them. I do not ever want anybody to think that what has happened in my life is strictly because of just who I am.

Coaching is a ministry because whenever you are trying to improve the lives of others, as well as yours, it is a ministry. You are letting Him use you. With our media guides, posters, and game day programs, we do not ever want one player highlighted because there is no one player that is the team. I want as many pictures as we can get and we want all segments represented — defense, offense, and special teams.

In addition, offense and defense are a given, but consistent winning comes from solid special teams play. In fact, we start each meeting and practice with special teams because, in every ball game, there are normally four to five plays that determine the outcome of the game. All of those plays are found in special teams — that's a fact! So my whole philosophy has been to not ever single out any one person, or unit. We do not ever want anybody to feel greater than thou, nor do we want anybody to be or feel they are devalued.

We included many stories and observations from all those who have helped and contributed to this program. It is not just my story and my perspective, but my wife, my family, students-athletes, and colleagues. I want my life and message to be transparent. You will hear not just from me, but my teachings through the eyes and words of others. In the business world there is something called a 360-degree evaluation. This process is very powerful because individuals not only describe their own behaviors, but their peers and colleagues also give feedback. This process has been proven to provide much deeper insights and learning. My inclusion of others in this book, I believe will also bear the same fruit.

We have created a 10-step program that is proven to work. We want to share the nuts and bolts of this program so others can benefit from what we have learned over the past forty years. There is no magic involved. It is a matter of faith, dedication, commitment, and hard work. Success is an inconvenience! It does not happen by chance. It is created by design when one is willing to put out the effort, whether he or she feels like it or not! We had a blueprint, and the blueprint is, you can't be a champion on game day unless you are trying to be a champion everyday. It starts in January. It starts with church on Sunday, classes on Monday, the weight room, and practice. Man does not decide his future, man decides his habits, and his habits decide his future!

We believe there is also a hidden message in this book— you don't throw people away! We believe "Treat a man as he is, he will be. Treat him as he can be, and he will become!" If you believe in them and expect them to achieve highly, they will. Tell them what is expected, show them how to get there — motivate, evaluate, and validate. Record the data, post for all to see and success will come!

Thank you for taking the time to read *The Making Of A Champion.*

PART I
INDIVIDUAL PREPARATION AND DEVELOPMENT

Part I discusses what it takes to prepare and develop young men so they can compete on the football field and win in life. It takes a physically strong, emotionally healthy, mentally alert, and spiritually devoted man to succeed in our program. We demand a lot of our players because that is what life demands. We do not want our players to be hurt in this very physical game. They must have a strong work ethic to prepare themselves for the battle they will experience on the field and to be successful in the classroom. Our playbook is very detailed and thorough. If our student athletes cannot master the educational material presented in the classroom, how will they ever master the material we present to them for plays and strategies? We are confident that our program prepares them and gives them the best chance to succeed in life and in sports.

This section on the individual development of our players is filled with our philosophy and many direct interviews with our former players who are now successfully contributing to society as doctors, lawyers, fathers, educators, NFL players, and college coaches. We present our blueprint for our method and provide the real life stories regarding its implementation.

Chapter 1
CONTROL THE DASH

Every now and then we hear a story or find a concept that really grabs people. Linda Ellis wrote a poem, "The Dash," that speaks to the importance of how each individual lives his or her life. This idea about "The Dash" kept coming back as a great way to communicate with our athletes. We want to impress upon them that, "How They Live Their Life," is the most important building block for success. "Who They Are," determines how they will play on Game Day. So this concept, "Control the Dash," became a perfect way to zero in on that. In fact, we made that our theme for the entire 2008 football season.

It is important to realize that many of the young men who come to us have not had a strong family background nor have they been given a solid foundation for how to successfully live life. They may lack core values, clearly defined goals, a positive self-esteem, and the understanding of how to achieve goals once they have been established. So in many ways, we are the moms and dads for these kids. We set the tone, provide direction, and maintain the discipline that is required to keep these athletes on the right path. Even those kids who came from two parent families needed guidance and direction. In most cases, this was their first experience living away from home, so we were like Dad's to them.

This chapter is filled with the actual material that we use to help guide these young men. We will share the stories, philosophy, and day-to-day behavioral principles that have been found to be successful. There is a lot of work to be done with these athletes. It is a process and a 24/7 endeavor. Everything in the book speaks to this process. Here are some of the more concrete messages and directives that we use.

THE DASH IN LIFE

Discipline: Do the Right Thing — You can't be a Champion on Saturday unless you are practicing to be a champion all week. On Sunday go to Church. Find a man's spirit, there also you will find him. Be obedient.

Attitude: Rise above nay-sayers. You are not a mistake. You are born to be successful, expect to be successful, and prepare to be successful. Flush out all negative programming.

Sacrifice: Treat a man as he is and he will be; Treat him as he can be and he will become. When young men come in as a freshman, we don't see them as they are, we see them 5 or 10 years down the road. That being the case, we design a program of hard work, discipline, and sacrifice, that when the 5 or 10 years come, they are successful men.

Habits: Man does not decide his future — Man decides his Habits, and his Habits decide his future. What you do in the Dark will come to Light.

THE DASH ON THE FIELD

Here are some more specific ideas and principles that we share to help our players control the dash, especially on the football field.

- **Trust:** If we can't trust a player to go to class, we don't trust him in a position of responsibility on the football field.

- **Character:** Your reputation is merely what others think you are. Your character is really who you are.

- **Courage:** To fix it, you must face it. Eagles fly best in the midst of a storm.

- **Communication:** Men do not decide their future, they decide their habits and their habits decide their future.

- **Commitment:** A playmaker is a combination of mental and physical skills gained from hours of practicing and living "the right way."

ARE YOU GIVING YOUR BEST?
That man is a success who has lived well,
laughed often and loved much;
Who has gained the respect of intelligent men
and the love of children;
Who has filled his niche
and accomplished his task;
Who leaves the world better than he found it,
whether by improved poppy, a perfect poem,
or a rescued soul;
Who never lacked appreciation of earth's beauty
or failed to express it.
Who looked for the best in others and <u>gave the best he had.</u>
—— Bessie Stanley

RULES OF CONDUCT
We want these young men to remember who they really are and understand what it takes on a daily basis to live a proper life. We don't want them to have any doubt about what we are asking. Here are some basic guidelines and rules that they must follow:

1.   Because you are an athlete, you are looked up to by many people particularly younger kids. Justify the pedestal they place you on.

2.   You must have PRIDE in yourself. Be selective **where you go, what you do, and what you say!**

3.   Be polite and courteous to all persons that are trying to help you and support our program, especially those persons working in the dining hall, business office, and the dormitories. Your conduct on and office campus is well observed as you are a football player. Project the image of an "Ambassador."

4.   Be well groomed, neat, and clean. This applies on and off campus.

5.   Stay away from gamblers. Be careful of strangers who inquire about injured players. You are required by the N.C.A.A. to immediately report to the coaching staff any contact with gamblers.

6. We ask you not to gamble. It is a temptation, but too often bad feelings result. At times, individuals lose money that is needed to keep them in school. The loss causes real problems.

7. Never discuss the team, the physical condition of members of the team, planned strategy, etc. with anyone. You may give information that would help our opponents and hurt our chances to win. You also may be talking with a gambler and not know it.

8. The use of profanity and swearing is the effort of a weak person to express himself forcibly.

9. Go to class, study hall, library — Get Your Degree!!!

10. Player-Coach relationship problems? Talk about it — Position Coach, Recruiting Coach, Captains, Coach Taylor or anyone. Do not let hurt feelings or misunderstandings fester.

11. Avoid use of alcohol. It will inhibit your performance. This continues to be the #1 problem on college campuses and our nation's roads. There will be no sympathy for drug users of any sort. Any discovered use will be eliminated as soon as possible.

    a. If you need an upper of any kind to get ready to play, do us a favor and quit.

    b. "There is no drug that improves the performance of an athlete." The thing that improves you is **HARD WORK.**

12. He who has a sharp tongue usually cuts his own throat.

13. If you are not big enough to stand criticism, you're too small to be praised.

So, as you can see, we are giving a philosophy of life and the guidelines on how to live effectively, especially within the context of our football program. There is a story that I like to share that fits in well on this point. The author is unknown as he sent me this story after I spoke in California but he did not want to be identified.

HOW TO MAINTAIN SUCCESS

"In the town of Content lived three men: Success, Desire and Motivation. Success was not happy in Content and moved on the find a better town to live in. Desire did not hear from Success and figured something had to be wrong. Motivation helped Desire start their quest to find Success. After a few days of travel, they met up with Exhaustion. The group was about to stop, but Motivation convinced Desire to leave Exhaustion behind. Next, the two men met Discipline. Discipline joined Motivation and Desire on their journey to find Success and kept the two men away from the town of Distraction. The group remained on the straight path until they reached the river of risk. They knew it would be hard and dangerous to pass, but the group decided to chance the consequences to find Success. After Discipline, Desire and Motivation crossed the river of Risk and they met up with another companion named Class. Class was sure-footed and confident in the knowledge that he could meet life head on and handle whatever comes his way. The three men felt comfortable with Class, due to the fact that class didn't try to build himself up by tearing others down. The group of four ran into an old wise man who strived for companionship; his name was Team Work. Each of these men needed each other and together they formed a strong camaraderie. The men came upon the town of Deception, where they thought they would find Success. Instead they ran into Quitter, Excuse, Failure, Loser, Fear, Sin and Individual. Even though Desire, Motivation, Discipline, Class, and Team Work were outnumbered, this group of men could never be whipped, because they hung together and refused to be beaten! That is how they found Success! Soon after the men were united, the group formed their own town called Champions."

Hopefully the reader can see that we create multiple ways to present the same information. The more we can creatively teach these principles, the better our players and the team will be. Here is another way approach the issue of how to "Control the Dash."

ATTITUDE — BELIEF — COMMITMENT
Remember That You Do Yourself And Your Team A Disservice If You Do Not:

1. Attend your classes. If we can't trust a player to go to class, we don't trust him in a position of responsibility on the football field.

2. Practice every day to become a superior football player.

3.   Remain focused every second you are on the football field.

4.   Play each play as if it were the determining play of the game.

5.   Believe that you can get better.

6.   Resolve that you can and must win.

7.   Attempt from the first play of the game, to destroy the will of your opponent.

8.   Always conduct yourself to reflect favorably upon your self, team, your family and program.

GUIDING PRINCIPLES

Behavior is driven by the values and principles that we hold. The more we can help these student-athletes internalize these principles, the more behavioral change we can see. We are always looking for ways to stress the importance of individual responsibility. We transform kids into men by making them strong in body, mind, and soul. We have a saying; "You must win private victories before you can win the public victories." Here are five points we address regarding individual responsibility:

Individual Responsibility

1.   Have integrity, lead by example, and maintain discipline in life.

2.   Believe in what the program is doing. Be consistent.

3.   Don't make the same mistake twice.

4.   The quality of your preparation determines the quality of your performance

5.   You were born to win. Expect to win, plan to win. Prepare to win.

Conceive and Believe to Achieve

We know that the power of the mind has great influence. We tell them, "If you can conceive and believe, then you can achieve." These ten principles are very important. We impress on them that they must:

1. Believe in Discipline/Do the Right thing on and off the field.

2. Believe in Good Decision Making/Be Smart.

3. Believe in Strong Fundamentals/Pay Attention to Detail.

4. Believe in Strong Work Ethic/Don't Be Afraid to Sweat.

5. Believe in Strong Character/Attitude Must be in Right Place.

6. Believe in High Morals/Stay Away from Pity Parties.

7. Believe in Knowledge and Awareness/Conduct Yourself like a Student-Athlete at all Times.

8. Believe in Success Now for Success Later — Who are you Becoming?

9. Believe in Life after Football — Use this Competitive Experience to Create a Lifelong Competitive Spirit.

10. Believe in Yourself, Each Other, and the Program. When a Group of Young Men Come Together as One, that's Powerful!

Make Good Choices

What a person does with "The Dash" is what defines a man. It is our choices that determine the course of our lives. We tell our players, "Choices matter! They are like elevators. They either take you up or down." Here are seven more concepts that we hope encourage them to make good choices:

1. Champions are not those who never fail, but those who never quit.

2. Character is always more important than talent.

3. Decision translates into energy.

4. Maturing comes by the acceptance of responsibility.

5. We are committed to what we confess.

6. Don't let someone else create your world for you, for when you do they will always make it too small.

7. True manhood requires courage, character, will power, and commitment.

THE GOSPEL OF THE GRIDIRON

One of the definitions of gospel is a set of beliefs. We consider the coaching profession to be like a ministry. We hold in our hands a responsibility for the lives and future of many fine young men. We know that all these players have parents who love them very much and have entrusted us with their education, on and off the field. We have our beliefs about what is important and valuable. Here is our gospel that we encourage our players to contemplate and embrace.

- Your attitude determines how high you are going to go in this life.

- You must be willing to handle your own business and stay out of other people business.

- Do what you said you would do when you said you would do it. For the only thing we have in this world is our word.

- Take the time to care. No matter how high you get you must care. No matter how low you get, you must care.

- You must discipline your soul. When you have disciplined your soul, you have set the foundation for true internal peace.

- Give energy to everything that you do.

- Take time to give enough foresight to your personal vision.

- Take the time to hear and heed the words of our ancestors.

- Build within you an institution that is able to withstand the storms of life.

- Never allow other people to steal your joy and rearrange the furniture in your life.

- Take time to know yourself, and always check yourself. Do no damage to your soul or you will find yourself alone.

- Be willing to provide leadership to and for our community.

- Meditate on life and enjoy the breath and depth it offers.

- Never allow other people to dictate your actions, or allow them to negatively influence your Decisions!

- Never Quit!

- Never fall short of your vision!

- Know that opportunity without preparation and cultivation lead to frustration.

- Remember that power has nothing to do with position or status in Life. It has more to do with the ability to define your own reality.

- Be willing to revive your soul at a moments notice. It is your greatest asset.

- Never be satisfied with less than your best.

- Strive to be on time or you will be left behind.

- If you are going to the top, take somebody with you.

- Victory will be yours as long as you remember Who you are and Whose you are.

- Always be willing to pull another behind you. Mahalia Jackson (viewed by many as the pinnacle of gospel music) said, "If I can help somebody along the way, then my living shall not be in vain."

- You are the only one standing between you and GOD's plans for your life.

CONCLUSION: COACHING IN THE DASH

Learning to "Control the Dash" is not easy. Let's be honest and realistic. It takes a lot more than handing out a lot of pages with great quotes and messages to transform these student-athletes into mature men. It takes a personal commitment and genuine concern about their growth and development. They have to know and feel that we honestly care about them for our program to be successful. Successful coaching demands a relationship with these young men. Unless we are part of their lives in a real and tangible way, we will not have any impact on them. They might hear some good information, but they will not be transformed into the mature adults for which we aspire. It is a program based on "tough love." My son, Aaron Taylor, is part of our coaching staff and has worked with me for the last eight years. He says it well.

Aaron Taylor

"We are working with 'alpha males' who have a lot of testosterone, and are extremely competitive. Sometimes their ego comes out a bit. Occasionally, it takes a lot more than just the right message to get through to these kids. A successful coach in our program has to be willing to 'be in their face,' hold them accountable, and confront their ego to get them on the right track. We do put out a lot of information, but it is in the context of a relationship that encompasses their entire life — the whole person. Without that strong, positive, loving relationship, nothing would work! They know we care about their future, not just how many football games they are going to help us win.

"The way Coach Taylor runs his programs is in the principle of tough love. Everything is not always going to be all right. If you are messing up, he is going to tell you — you have got to stand up, and you have got to do what is right — even though you might not like how he is talking to you. We tell them, 'Society is not going to care how they are talking to you!' So it was always a situation where he was challenging them to be the best that they could be. It was not a situation where he was trying to take them down. It was not a situation where he was trying to belittle someone in front of others.

It was more like a cry for help that was saying, 'You need to get it together. This society is not playing with anybody and the more you play, the more you will fall behind.' Quite honestly, some student athletes just did not understand tough love and they were gone. But for the ones that stayed, they were just much better people."

One of our players at Hampton, Corey Swinson, was a big man, 6' 6" inches, weighed 320 pounds and had five-percent body fat. He was a very talented athlete and also worked as a bodyguard for one of the Wu-Tang Clan on occasion. He was a force that few people would ever confront. Let's hear what Coach Aaron Taylor remembers about Corey's time with us and what it took to turn the corner with him.

"I remember we had this, big guy, Corey Swinson, at Hampton University. He had missed some practices that he had no business missing. Corey decided that he wanted to go to a concert that was happening on the campus. It was a popular group by the name of Wu-Tang Clan. Corey was from New York and the group was from New York, so he knew a couple of the members, plus he had been a bodyguard for one of them. He took it upon himself to go and hang out with the guys. He got home very late so he missed the next morning's workout. Coach Taylor got wind of this and decided, since he missed the practice, we will just go ahead and make it up that night. They were out there for about two hours and just looking at a 6'6" guy with 300 pounds rolling back and forth 100 yards, it really was really something to see. Coach Taylor was trying to teach him that no one is bigger than the program and he needed to be serious about it — and if he was not going to be serious about it, then there were consequences.

"Even after that incident, Corey still did not seem to get it. There was another occasion when he missed some practices that he had no business missing. Since he was a guy of huge stature, people usually talked to him in a different tone than they might with a guy much smaller than him. If you are three hundred and twenty pounds and have 5% body fat, people are going to talk to you in a monotone voice, even when they are trying to jump your case. They might be like, 'Hey guy, can you please… you know.' But if you are 5'6", 'Hey man, can you get the hell out of the way please.' I think coach was starting to see that the other coaches were starting to relate to him differently. So one day he asked Corey, 'Why did you miss the practices?' I think Corey did not really understand the answer that he gave Coach Taylor and how disrespectful it was. It was a bit of a smart talk remark. Something to the point of, 'I will get there when I do.'

"I started to see coach take his rings off and say, 'Do you want to get into a fist to cuffs with me?' When Corey saw the seriousness of my father, I saw a guy that was 6'6", 320 pounds, turn into the 5'6" guy. It was not that he was so much scared, but no one had ever challenged him in that manner. Coach Taylor was simply saying that nobody is bigger than the program. Now of course, they did not fight. But the fact that Corey saw how passionate Coach was about 'no one is bigger than the program,' — after that, there were no more issues between him and Corey. As a matter of a fact, Corey Swinson went on to become one of his top advocates and top leaders on the team because his respect for the man had skyrocketed. He went on to play in the NFL."

Sometimes we have to use different measures and some tough love to get our point across. However, our focus is always about "The Dash" — how are these young men living their lives. We want them to step up and do the best they can. Sometimes it takes a special vision to see the potential in these kids. We have to take a deeper look into their soul to predict the future. It is not easy to see past some of their behavior when they have been in trouble and created some real problems for themselves. However, with the Lord's help we have been able to see clearly and make some good decisions. My son Aaron remembers such a time.

"I remember we had this quarterback by the name of Princeton Shepherd. He was there three years from 2002 through 2005. He came straight out of high school. He had gotten himself into some very serious trouble, really bad trouble. As a matter of a fact, he was suspended from school, and the day we went to go recruit the guy, he was absent. We came back and told Coach Taylor what we thought. 'He is the greatest athlete Coach. He is 6'5", 200 pounds, runs like the wind, and can throw the ball, but we just do not know about this kid. He is not a very high character kid.' So, he said bring him on a visit and let me talk to him. Coach did talk to him and he did choose to attend the Hampton program. Coach Taylor said, 'Get your grades, and we will talk.' Well, he did not get his grades, and I thought that was going to be the end of it — that he was going to be a problem and we would never see him again. But Coach Taylor told him, 'If you come here for a year, get your grades straight and get serious about it, you are going to have one of the best careers for a college student athlete.' He left it right there because he saw something in the kid that none of us saw. I thought he was a problem kid, the offensive coordinator thought he was a problem kid, but Coach Taylor just saw something in this kid. To make a long story short, in four years the kid won three championships for us, took us to three playoff appearances, and was the quarterback with the best winning record in Hampton history. We are talking about a kid who barely got out of high school and had problems as a freshman in college. Most times if a kid does not do well as a freshman, you lose them. However, he went on to be the most successful quarterback not only in the history of Hampton University, but for Coach Taylor as well.

"Had Coach Taylor not gone with his gut, had he not gone with his expertise and his experience, that kid would not have seen the light of day. The point here is that Coach Taylor knows that this game is more than what you see on the surface. He tells all his coaches, if a kid has a problem, see what the source of that problem is. If you can help him with that problem, more than likely he is going to help you accomplish what you are trying to do as a coach. Princeton never forgot Coach Taylor being there for him. He never forgot Coach Taylor giving him a chance. I talk to him all the time on Facebook and he always writes, 'Tell your father I am just so grateful, and tell your father I love him to death.' He never forgot what he did for him."

Chapter 2

THE POWER OF THE LORD'S WORD
Reverend Jerome Barber – Team Chaplain

Our blueprint for success is designed for the body, mind and spirit of each student athlete. Each aspect of a young man's development is given attention, so the whole person is addressed. We make sure they go to class, keep in touch with the instructors, monitor their physical development in the weight room, and carefully design a comprehensive and inspiring program to awaken and uplift their spirit. I have a strong faith in our Lord and Savior Jesus Christ as I was brought up in a very religious Baptist family. My mother had a great influence on the spiritual development of all her children, myself as well as my brother and sister, Leroy and Mary. Leroy remembers those early childhood years.

"Every Saturday night we would get in one room by the heater and we would go over our Sunday school lessons. She was always quoting scripture. She would make sure that we were prepared when we got to Church for Sunday school. She was a very spiritual person and a strict disciplinarian. She instilled God in all three of us. She was the backbone of that aspect of our lives."

Leroy Taylor

I feel like my coaching career is a ministry in which I help young men become their best, in all aspects of their lives. Since the Lord has been such a big part of my life and success, I never hesitated to integrate that into our football program. I believe that when you want to be a champion, you need to surround yourself with champions. So I looked for the best man I could find to help lead the spiritual development of our team. We had many successful years of championship teams at Hampton University. I believe a good leader surrounds himself with the best people and does not try to do everything himself — having the proper attitude of humility allows great people to gather together under your direction. If your ego is too big, there is no room for anyone else to contribute. I have always believed that when you find a man's spirit, there also you find him. So I knew I needed a good man to help me develop these young men's spirit.

We were very blessed to have the Reverend Jerome Barber join our team at Hampton. He actually graduated from Hampton back in 1981 and came back to Hampton in 1991. One of my coaches was attending his Church, the Sixth Mount Zion Baptist Temple. Reverend Barber grew that church from about 100 folks who were actively attending, plus possibly another 100 or so on the rolls, to about 4,000 people. He now has multiple services on multiple campuses. His great excitement is being able to capture those young people at a very critical time in their life, and put something in them that will carry them throughout their entire life.

Over the years, I became so proud to be working with Reverend Barber and respected him so much, that I asked him to be on my weekly television show as my cohost. He would interview me and ask me questions about the week's football events. We had great discussions about philosophy of football, winning strategies, as well as analyzing the past week's team performance based upon the films we took. He helped us create a powerful program that transformed many lives. He became part of the Fellowship of Christian Athletes (FCA). The following is his description of that entire program.

THE INNER WINNER

"I was inspired to work with Coach Taylor because of his philosophy, 'When you find a man's spirit, there also you find him.' I created a program within the FCA.

We called it the Inner Winner. It helped us tap the inner motivation of these young men. It has been said that the most critical spot on the field for any play, is the space between the player's ears. So our program was designed to get into their hearts and minds and develop their character. We used scriptures like, 'I can do all things through Christ who strengthens me,' (Philippians 4:13) to let them know that there was an inner winner and we were developing that aspect within them. I loved Coach's philosophy, 'It's not Xs and Os, it's Jimmy's and Joe's. It's not just diagrams on a chalkboard, these are people who have lives, who have stories, and have histories. And, they are champions – some of them – even before they hit the field. That was the whole idea.

"In the beginning, not everyone was highly motivated to participate. However, over time, they became more interested. These young men wanted to improve and progress to their next level. Since they were in college, their next step would be the NFL. So, in an attempt to reach out to these young men and get their understanding and participation, we would bring in special guest speakers. One of our speakers asked them, 'How many of you know what the NFL stands for?' A couple of them got all excited and said, 'It stands for the National Football League.' He said, 'No it doesn't. It stands for, Not For Long!' He began to share with them the possibilities of their getting into the NFL and, then, the probability of them staying more than three years — because the average career is about three years. He then spoke about the importance of having a college education — something to fall back on.

"From that speech we developed our own NFL — our own Necessary For Life program. It became a life-coaching program primarily designed to build character. We focused on anything that would help them make good choices and good decisions. We wanted them to be proactive and take charge of their lives. We wanted them to understand that the same discipline that is required on the field is the same discipline that is required in their personal life. Coach Taylor would always reinforce it. He said, 'If you are not doing well in the classroom, then you are not going to do well on the field.' It is important to understand that the general orientation in most college football programs is, 'If I do well on the field, then it will make up for me not doing well in the classroom.' Well, we flipped that kind of thinking around to, 'If I get my character right, if I am disciplined, focused, positive, confident, and prepared, then winning is not an accident.' We wanted them to understand that winning is a result of hard work, in the classroom as well as on the field, and their efforts to develop a strong character was important to their overall life success. We wanted them to understand that there is someone bigger that can help them navigate this thing called life.

"Coach Taylor always had a choir made up of the young men in the program — it was a football ensemble. During their training camp, they would go to different churches on Sundays and participate in the services. That was all part of our character development program. Some of them were being exposed to church for the first time. They functioned and worshiped together as a team. One of the most amazing sights was to see a choir filled with offensive and defensive linemen — these big ole guys rocking in the choir stand. There were guys 6'6", 260 pounds singing in high soprano! They would go to different churches, connect with the community and share their faith— and they would be open and honest about sharing their faith. That's the confidence they gained through the Inner Winner program.

"We were always looking for ways to communicate with these young men. We came up with the 'Stay Up, Play Up' cards, which had the opponent that they were facing, their record, and our record. Then, it would have a motivational scripture for the week along with the motivational theme that Coach Taylor designed for that year."

THE USE OF SCRIPTURE

"We believe that the Bible provides wonderful guidance for every aspect of living. We chose specific scriptures that would relate and provide direction for the current themes and challenges that the team was facing. These Bible quotes provided inspiration and gave us an inroad to discuss important values and attitudes that build character. We were able to go deeper in the minds of these young men through the use of these various passages.

"In 2004 we focused a lot on the Necessary for Life (NFL) concept. Every time they heard NFL, we wanted them to think about our NFL concept as well as football. We wanted them to remember that there are important things necessary for life besides football. I did a whole series on this. One of the things I did was to discuss the character traits that people needed in order to be successful in life. We were playing against Delaware State University. It was in October of 2004: Our record was 4-0, theirs was 0-4. One of the things that Coach Taylor would always stress to the young men is that your greatest opponent is yourself. No matter who you line up against, you have to know who you are.

"So, with this game, we told them not to look at their record because it would be too easy for them to dismiss and discount the other team. After all, they were 0-4. Coach Taylor always taught that you never stoop to the level of your opponent's competition or ability. Never lower your own personal standards. Always set the bar high and just play and be consistent in how you play —be faithful to the game.

"So for this game, we used the following scripture:

And every man that striveth for the mastery is
temperate in all sayings — 1 Corinthians 9:25

"Paul, in the New Testament, speaks a lot about spirituality and athletes. There are a lot of connections and similarities there — just as you have to discipline your body to be a great athlete, you have to discipline your spirit to be a great person. So, our theme for that night was temperance — about keeping yourself under control. We spoke about being able to identify what is in your control and what is out of your control. You know, this was Coach Taylor's concept, 'Stay in the Circle.' A lot of times people waste their energy on trying to change stuff that they cannot change and they miss opportunities to change the things that are within their area of influence and are in their control.

"So, on that particular night, our NFL focus was on how to be temperate. We spoke about the importance of moderation and the need to realize that, 'My life, my words, my actions, and my deeds have to be under my control.' We tried to help them realize the importance of being temperate.

As a man thinketh in his heart, so is he.

— Proverbs 23:7

"Another thing we did was to help them understand the power of their language and their thought. The things you think about, you bring about. We showed them how you can determine a person's way of being based upon how he or she speaks. Language is powerful! If you are speaking negatively, then ultimately you will follow suit and you will become negative. It is as simple as that. The things you think about, you bring about! Your language determines your level. You need to be careful and aware about how you transfer your thoughts into words. This is what we used to teach them, 'Where you are in life is revealed by your use of words.' So, if you are negative, if you speak negative, then that is where you will stay — in a negative place and in a negative state. So our

Necessary For Life program really focused upon the importance of the process regarding how thoughts become words that then create behavior. This is really a very sophisticated and important thing to teach people. It helps motivate them to take hold of their inner life and think about how they represent themselves and how they are creating their lives. We found that these young men became more mature and responsible with this kind of teaching. They became more aware of how they used language and realized the power that was imbedded in their thoughts and words. This is great stuff for life!

So built we the wall and all the wall was joined together unto the half thereof for the people had a mind to work.
—Nehemiah 4:6

"Another year, Coach Taylor used the theme, 'Justice Prevails.' Specifically, it's the idea that if you focus on what's right and you do right, then you can expect right things to come to you. We were playing Norfolk State, which was a big rivalry. It's one of those games where you strap up and play them because they want to beat you in the worst way. They can have the worst season of all, but when Norfolk State comes to Hampton, then that's their championship. If they can beat Hampton – they can lose every other game, but if they beat Hampton – they got bragging rights in the area. So, that was always a tough game for us. We used, So built we the wall and all the wall was joined together unto the half thereof for the people had a mind to work, for that game.

"That evening we discussed what it takes to achieve real success. We were trying to help them realize that, 'You must go into life knowing that nobody is going to give you anything.' Life does not come on a silver platter. However, anything worth having is worth working for. If you have a mind to work, then things will mean something to you — you will be personally and emotionally invested. And, because you honestly care, you will work harder to get it. Once you have placed value on something, then it is worth fighting for and worth working for. Oftentimes, we would break them into smaller groups and let them share. We would ask them, 'So, what does this mean to you?' We would have the seniors stand up and respond to the questions, 'What does this game mean to you? What does your education mean to you? What does your family mean to you?' These were very powerful and moving discussions. It helped them make a deeper connection with their own life and brought the team closer together.

Be kind to one another. Tender hearted, forgiving one another even as God has forgiven you.
— Ephesians 4:32

"As part of our Necessary for Life program, we talked about brotherly kindness. We talked about how important it is to realize that the guy next to you is your brother — the importance of having brotherly kindness towards one another. Now, this may seem like a strange message for football players because in the second breath we are going to tell them look at that guy across from them, across the line of scrimmage, and now hurt him bad. But they understood we were talking about team building and how important it is to trust the guy next to you. We wanted to instill within them the attitude, 'I've got to trust that he's going to carry out his assignment. I am just one eleventh. I have to do my part, and I must believe that the other ten men will do theirs as well.' That's the real power of football — it is team sport. While you have to depend upon other folks to do their job, you must concentrate on you doing your job as well. So, as you can see, it is very important to build that team effort and a strong team atmosphere with these young men. The themes we addressed were constantly recurring: commitment, loyalty, and staying focused. We chose scriptures that allowed us to lead into those essential principles.

Iron sharpeneth iron, so a man sharpeneth accountance of his friend.
— Proverbs 27:17

"This scriptural quote from Proverbs was one of Coach Taylor's favorite. As a matter of fact, he developed it as a theme for one year. This passage is important because it talks about the process of people working together. Just as iron sharpens iron when rubbed against each other, we make each other better when we work with one another. We created a theme and message from this that, 'Every day is a great day to get better.' In addition, we wanted these young men to know and feel that, 'I am not here by accident. I am here because God put me here to be better. As I get better, I can help you get better.'

"So, in everything we did, we were trying to help these men step up to their next level. We were hoping that they will develop more personal responsibility and embrace the belief that, 'I not only have to be an Inner Winner myself, but I also have an influence over the people that are around me.' That whole philosophy that 'iron sharpenith iron' now became relevant for their everyday life. We wanted them to understand that those times when we do "rub together" in confrontation, those are opportunities to become better. I always used to tell the guys, back in the day when my mom sharpened knives, she would get two knives out and quickly rub them up against each other. It would make a lot of noise and create a lot of heat, but afterwards, both of the knives would be sharper. So, that's the same concept in life — sometimes it's in the confrontation, in the clashing of personalities that we are actually able to make each other better and sharpen each other's lives. The type of young men we are working with have a lot of excitement, energy, and motivation. You get a number of young men like this together with all that energy and you are bound to have some conflicts. The important thing to learn is that, 'You never fight against each other. You know that your conflicts are only strengthening your relationship and making you a better person.'

They that wait upon the Lord shall renew their strength. They shall mount up with wings as eagles. They shall run and not be weary. They shall walk and not faint.

— Isaiah 40:31

"Here is another passage that we used to love to share with the guys. We would use this one during the bye week, which was one of the most critical weeks during the season. It was a week when these young men needed to keep their focus and stay on the right course. Coach Taylor would have me come and talk to the young men for this very reason. He used to say, when we were at Hampton, 'If we could just keep Hampton off our schedule, we will win some games.' He was speaking to the idea that we should not be our own worst enemy. We should not be our own worst opponent.

"So our work was to help them to stay focused during the bye weeks. You can be on a roll and that one week, when you are not playing, can throw you off track. For the most part, these young men were at their best when they were on the football field. So we were always looking for ways to help them become more self-disciplined. Isaiah 40:31 helped us talk about the importance of staying focused. It was a favorite of ours.

The whole premise behind that scripture was that these were words of great comfort and it was spoken to people that were in captivity. This word gave them hope even though they might not see results immediately, if they kept their faith they would eventually see results. We related this message to the football team in the following way — by being consistent and faithful to who you are, faithful to the discipline of the football program, and faithful to the team, you will see the rewards. Your faithfulness means that you know, 'Just because I don't have a game on Saturday doesn't mean that I will go buck wild and crazy. I am going to stay true to my discipline, true to my focus, true to my team, true to myself, true to my family, and true to my aspirations.' Our conviction was, 'Your faithfulness will pay off!'"

LOOK FOR THE POTENTIAL

"I was blessed to be a part of the football program and experience his way of dealing with people. Coach Taylor had a way in which he brought out the best in folks. I believe it is the result of the positive way he looked at life. Coach would say, 'You can either use eye sight or you can use insight.' He was definitely more about insight than eyesight. Somebody said, 'Anybody can count the number of seeds in an apple. That's just simple math. But, only God knows how many apples are in one seed.' It was his ability to see potential that made him so effective. We had situations where a young man, Marcus Dixon came to us. Marcus came out of a very troubled situation but Coach was able to look beyond the obvious troubled situation and see the potential of this young man. He didn't look at him with eyesight. He looked at him with insight. Eyesight sees the obstacle — Insight sees the opportunity. Eyesight sees the struggle — Insight sees the strength. Eyesight only sees the problem — Insight sees the potential that lies there. Coach had an ability to see the potential in a seed and really function on that level of insight — not just count the seed. He could look at the same stuff everybody else was looking at, but see something deeper in a person and then go for the deeper potential. He would then watch that potential emerge.

"This is exactly what happened with Marcus. His story actually ended up on Oprah. It was a bad situation. An African American young man being raised by adoptive parents who were white, out of the Georgia area. A young lady had an intimate relationship with him. When her father heard about it, it turned from something that was consensual to something where he forced himself on her. They claimed he raped her. It was just a bad, bad, bad situation. They did eventually reverse the decision. When you actually met Marcus, it was like wow! You knew there was something here. Coach Taylor was able to see that and tap into that. He became one of the premier players that we had at Hampton and is still doing some wonderful things on a professional level.

"Had Coach Taylor just functioned with eyesight, he would have done what the other schools did —just say no. 'We just can't handle all that.' But, Coach Taylor had a different perspective about his work. He viewed it is a ministry. He told me, 'It really is a ministry. You know, this is why I was created. This is what I am here for. This is my purpose. Where others may get the folks that are already cleaned up, with no issues, no problems, and are all together, for some odd reason I am drawn to the ones that don't have it all together.'

EMBRACE ADVERSITY

"We often see people attempting to avoid adversity. However, I often observed how Coach Taylor would embrace adversity and move towards it without fear or hesitation. There was a special power about him because of the way in which he approached adversity. I would always share with the young men in the FCA how adversity serves us — it reveals the real us. I used to tell this story all the time,

'You don't know how strong a tea bag is until you put it in hot water. It may look good, but you don't know the strength of it until it's put in hot water. As a matter of fact, tea bags were made to be put in hot water. The hot water doesn't destroy the tea bag — to the contrary, it is allows the tea bag to release the flavor that's inside of it. So, your true flavor sometimes is not ever expressed until you face some of the adversities and some of your hot water situations.'

"These were the kinds of messages and training that we gave these young men. We wanted them to look adversity in the face and say, 'This is not going to get the best of me, I am going to get the best of it. The best of me will be released in this situation.'

"There are several scriptures that speak to this issue as well. We always went deeper to find a way to strengthen a man's faith in order to enhance his ability to confront adversity. When you feel God's presence in your heart, you do have more strength and courage to confront life's difficult challenges. Here are a few passages that we found helpful in this regard.

He who dwells in the shelter of the Most High will abide in the shadow of the Almighty. I will say to the LORD, "My refuge and my fortress, My God, in whom I trust!
— Psalm 91:1-2

Because he loves me, says the Lord, I will rescue him; I will protect him, for he acknowledges my name. He will call upon me, and I will answer him; I will be with him in trouble, I will deliver him and honor him.
— Psalm 91:14 -15

So do not fear, for I am with you; do not be dismayed, for I am your God. I will strengthen you and help you; I will uphold you with my righteous right hand.
— Isaiah 41:10

The Lord is my light and my salvation; whom shall I fear? The Lord is the strength of my life; of whom shall I be afraid?
— Psalm 27:1

CONCLUSION

"I am very honored to be part of this book. I have great respect for Coach Joseph Taylor and feel fortunate to have been a part of his program at Hampton University. We had so many young men that have been so success-ful — doctors, lawyers, and other professionals. He always helped them realize that the same skills they are learning which help them be successful on the football field are transferable to every aspect of their lives.

"On Wednesdays, I fly up to New York and I do a service down in the Wall Street area. I preach there on Wednesdays. It's quite an interesting trip because I fly out of Virginia right into JFK, and then I take the subway from the airport downtown. So you know it's an interesting day for me filled with lots of energy, especially the whole subway piece, because you know, you've got to put your game face on. You are in New York. You don't want them to think you are some country boy that does not know what you are doing.

"I am in the subway and, you know, you don't make eye contact with folks in the subway. You just get to your next stop. I get off of the train and right as I am walking off this big hand comes on my shoulder. I am like, 'Oh man, they going to mug me! This is it.' I already had my plea prepared. 'Take whatever you want, just don't kill me.' Right as I am getting ready to say something, I hear this deep voice saying, 'Stay up. Play up.' And, it was one of the football players. I said,

'What are you doing here?' He said,

'What are you doing here? I live here. I am from New York.'

"He works down on Wall Street and he is doing some great things. He is quite successful and had been in the program several years ago. There he was, right there on the subway saying, 'Thanks for doing that.' He was just shocked to see me up there. It just brought back to his mind some of his beginnings with the program and how the discipline helped him. It is great to know he is still living out his faith.

"I heard a story a while back where this coach was coaching on a minor league area and got a chance to move up to the next level and the next division of coaching. When he got there, he went on a tour of the campus. It was a big campus — a tremendous program. Most of the games were televised. So, he asked the folks, 'Can I see the stadium?' So, they take him down to the stadium, and he is just totally blown away. He is overwhelmed by the facilities. He is blown away by the size of the stadium. He was there with a friend and as they walked around, his friend began to feel and sense his nervousness. So, he asked,

'Man, you all right?' He said,

'I don't know if I can do this. This is more than I was anticipating.' He said,

'But coach you are successful. You've been successful at your last program and you will be successful here.' He said,

'But look at this place. Look at the stands! Look at the stadium! Look at the facilities! Look at this campus!' And, the friend looked at him and said,

'Coach, you are looking at the wrong thing. Look at the playing field because the playing field is the same size. The playing field is the same size. The facility might be bigger, but it's still 100 yards. The playing field is the same size.'

"So, as these young men come to our program, they are given character development skills — things that will carry them through life. They've been able to learn that the playing field of life is the same size. If I can be successful here, then I can do the same thing somewhere else. I can also be successful because the playing field is a level playing field and it's always the same size. So, that's been my joy —being able to help young people understand the power of that."

Kendall Langford

We have had a number of wonderful young men come through our program. The Reverend Barber did such a great job in creating a program where these men could find peace, guidance, comfort and strength. I believe it is always helpful to hear directly from the players who participated in our program.

Kendall played with us at Hampton from 2004-2008. He was an outstanding player. He was drafted into the NFL with the Miami Dolphins in 2008. He has been with the Miami organization for the last four years and is about to be a free agent. Kendall was very gracious to respond to our request to participate in this book. As we have said, our program was designed to educate the whole man: mind, body and soul. Here are some of his thoughts on his experience with us.

"His program wowed me. I came from a small school where there wasn't any structure. So to come to Hampton and see how the program was run, that was a big difference. It was a great program, from the weight room, the way we dressed, to the way we practiced. We dressed up every Wednesday and always had to go to class. Coach was big on school. After my first year, I buckled down real hard. We had study hall, we had progress reports, and we had coaches popping up. We had to give them our schedules and they would just pop up throughout the day, making sure we were in class. All the teachers knew if you played football and they would tell Coach and you weren't in class. I worked hard and I ended up on the Dean's List several times. All the little things mattered. He was real big on punctuality — be a man about whatever it is that you do.

"His program helped me a great deal. It helped me with punctuality. I was always a hard worker but he demanded the best out of his student athletes and I tried to give him my best. I was able to excel and I made it to the National Football League. So I definitely give a lot of credit to Joe Taylor's program and Hampton University. I can't say enough about the guy. I grew up in a two-parent household. I was away from home and Coach Taylor was like a father figure. If I had any problems or anything like that, I could go and talk to him. He was there for all his players and everyone appreciated him and loved the guy.

"Even though I was talented and was a scholarship guy, I definitely didn't feel there was any preferential treatment. He would treat me the same way as he would treat the next man. I think he loved all of us and he loved us hard. You knew one guy wasn't bigger than the team. We knew it was a team effort that won those championships.

"Reverend Barber was there with the FCA (Fellowship of Christian Athletes). We met on Friday nights. We had guys stand up; give a couple of testimonies, and the football choir would sing a couple of songs. I was actually in the football choir. He would come and give us a little message, give us a word of inspiration, the word of God, and then we ended it and got into game mode. He was a very funny guy. He had his ways of picking you up or telling you how it is. One time we were out there practicing, and it was actually storming outside. I believe this was my freshman year, he told us, 'If the lightening hits you, you ain't moving fast enough.'

"We used to go to the Reverend's Church, Sixth Mount Zion, and sometimes we would go to Coach Taylor's personal church. We would go as a team and sing in the choir. We represented Hampton, we represented Coach Taylor, and that was something we enjoyed doing. It wasn't every week, but the times that we did go, we had a great turnout. We all were God fearing men and we all had a strong faith in God. I do think that is another reason we were so successful when we were there. It made you remember that all things come from God and to give Him thanks —don't take things for granted. He has blessed us to be able to be athletes and go out and perform. Some of us make it to the next level, the professional level, and some of us do other things in life besides sports, that are just as big. The FCA helped me to keep God first and remember that, 'Without Him nothing is possible.' I have a scripture tattooed on my arm which is the 27th Psalm – the first verse.

The Lord is my light and my salvation – whom shall I fear? The Lord is the strength of my life, of whom shall I be afraid?"

Chapter 3

FIND A MAN'S SPIRIT — ALSO THERE YOU WILL FIND HIM

As a child, it was understood. Every Sunday, if you are in the house, you are going to get up, you are going to put on your shirt and tie, you are going to Sunday school, and you are going to church. It was not discussed — it was understood! To this day, I appreciate and thank my parents for doing that. I certainly did not know what it meant at the time. After I left and went away to college, very few of my college roommates or classmates got up to go to church, but I always found a church and went. Many college people at that time left home and stopped going to church. Not me, my values were set in stone from my mother and father.

I was roasted last May by a group of supporters. One of the guys that they invited to roast me was one of my ex-players, who is now the Head Coach at Morgan State University, Donald Hill-Eley. He said, "When Coach Taylor moves, when he gets to town, he is going to find a house and a church." So it is understood – I have that foundation. I know she had some dog days but she never showed it. No matter how bad things were, she would never expound on it. She was always on the positive side. Those developmental years, that are so vital, were very positive and very strong. I appreciate my parents for that. As a youngster, I did not understand all of it then. But so many times now, things come to me that I heard them say. They make a lot more sense now than when I was a young guy. I know the seed was planted back in those early days. My parents gave me a good solid foundation and structure. Both my parents worked. It was understood; you were going to work. They both worked. The spiritual side —that was there; that was understood. You are going to church. Those were the house rules and they were not negotiable. I think that early family life gave me the grounding in what is important and what is real.

If you are going to help bring out a man's spirit, you have to respect him. I believe if you "find a man's spirit and there you shall find him." If your expectations are low, then that is what you are going to get. Treat a man as he is, he will be. Treat him as he can be and he will become. If you treat a man like he cannot rise to the highest level, he won't. Trust, honor, respect, discipline and love for the Lord brings out the best in us. If you look for a man's spirit or soul, you can find it. "Seek and ye shall find," goes both ways. You will find the Lord within you, and you can also find the Lord in others. Honesty, integrity, value, justice, and courage arise when the Spirit is strong. Our program is about more than winning games and championships, although those are important. We are developing men of character who will succeed and contribute to society.

One of the approaches we use to help men find their Spirit is through the Fellowship of Christian Athletes. I started this back when I was teaching high school. We did not force anyone to attend. Men come if they want to, although most of them decided to be a part of this fellowship. We even have a Gospel Choir. We pray, we sing, and we share our personal testimonies. This helps to bring people closer together and creates a strong bond. It gives us strength in times of need and adversity.

In my first year coaching at Hampton, we had a very shocking and extraordinary event occur before the season even began. One of my players on that team was Jonathan Hunt. He is currently an attorney with the law firm of McKenna, Long, and Aldridge, in Atlanta Georgia and principally practices in the areas of real estate, contract law, and finance. He is a corporate lawyer. He went to law school in Cleveland at Case Western Reserve University. He is another one of our great success stories. Let's hear what happened from his perspective.

Jonathan Hunt

"I had not obviously been with him (Coach Taylor) his entire coaching career, but those two years were incredibly special. For example, we had been through our first year, we were 9-2-1 and conference champions — we were literally the last team in the conference the year before with 2-9 record. The year we were conference champions, we had gone through spring and were in summer camp. Everybody had a better sense in their mind as to what was expected of them, so excluding the new freshmen, you had a group of individuals in there ready to go. We were keyed up. There was not a lot of excess fat on this group when we came in summer camp for the fall.

"In the beginning of summer camp, we were evaluated. They did not ask us whether or not we worked out — they were going to find out. First we were enrolled, had physicals, got our classes, and then in the afternoon we did weight lift testing, squats, bench-press, and all the various weight lift exercise tests. The next morning we were out on the field by 8:00 a.m. and were evaluated for endurance. We were out on the track in shorts and T-shirts, and started at 8:00 a.m. and did not stop running until 11:00-11:30 a.m. There were breaks but this was a combination of wind sprints on the field, 400-800 distance, short distance, and agility. We did not stop moving for three hours and it was intensely exhausting. I mean physically we were broken down by the time we were finished. So the folks that were not doing what they needed to do over the summer, that would be shown. That was very clear. They do not have to say anything nor did they have to claim anything. The fact, that they were lying on the ground gasping for air, said it all.

"We had gone through all that as a team. We went to bed, got up the next day and went to church. We had a nice lunch, and in the afternoon, we had a rather long set of meetings. It was a good two to three hours. We had talks about the philosophy, the theme for the year, everything — top to bottom: team's record, how we are going to prepare, a very detailed preparation meeting, and we were all there. He finished and he brought in an inspirational speaker. The inspirational speaker came in, delivered a great message, and everybody was fired up. We were going to start camp the next morning. Coach got up to do the finish wrap and one of our players, in the front row, started to have a seizure —arms went up in the air and he was shaking. His name was Fred Siggers, and there is no easy way to put this — Fred died with his family. Fred died in the room with the team!

"Every single person that had a shot at being on the team was in that room. People who ultimately did not even make the team were in the room. He was in the front row. It was arranged in theatre style seating so they laid him down and the players ran to get an ambulance and medical attention. But he died right there. We got the pronouncement about his death the next day. It was the first day of summer camp and Coach Taylor was visibly shaken, he was visibly hurt. Fred was not a freshman, he had been there, he knew him, and he knew his family. He was close to him. In that moment of leadership he said, 'You know, team, gentlemen, we are in a new place. I have never experienced this before; none of the coaching staff has ever experienced it before. We are supposed to start practice, I am not sure that is the right thing to do, given we just lost Fred. What should we do?' He gives the floor to the captains and sits down.

"The ultimate decision — the coaches did not say a word—the ultimate decision was that we are going to practice because Fred would have wanted us to practice. We are going to grieve, but we are going to practice because Fred would have practiced. Coach is showing me in that moment, and I think he showed all of us in that moment, that sometimes leading is letting the folks you are trying to lead, guide you. It is showing that 'I' am not strong all the time, sometimes 'I' do not know. Being able to show that, in the correct time and the correct manner, resulted in the team being willing to follow him, his staff, and the program even more. It was a greater level of commitment; it is one of the best leadership lessons that I have ever had in my life. So while he had some of the best anecdotes, stories, jokes, and advice, what he did and how he conducted himself, illustrated far more and delivered far more lessons than anything he ever said. Coach's actions have proven more and taught me more than anything else."

Joe Manly

Joe Manly was another young man on the team at that time. He is currently a marketing rep for a radiology company called RadNet. It's actually the largest diagnostic imaging operation facility in America. He was present that afternoon along with many others when Fred died.

"I played for Coach Taylor at Hampton University. I was part of his first class at Hampton University. I came in 1992 and I played with him through '97, so I was part of three championship teams. I was also part of the team that switched from Division II to Division I. Fred's death was devastating. You start your season out by losing one of your brothers. I've never seen so many people hurt. It brought us together, but the day was just hard. I remember him dying and Coach Taylor rushing to the hospital, and then Antonio Poag came back, and you could just tell it was bad, because he was busting out windows and crying. Coach Taylor brought us all into the dorm downstairs, to the meeting room, and we just pretty much drew strength from it. We gathered for the whole day, really doing nothing. And then we got back to work and it pulled us all together. We won that year. I think that is the year we were undefeated, actually. That was our national championship year. I grew up at Hampton. I became a man there."

Fred's death was a first for me. My trust and faith in the Lord helped guide me and get me through that experience. I felt it was the right thing to do to be quiet and let them decide. Let the team decide. I do believe that humility will come when you try to be obedient to the Lord's will. In hindsight, I think I did the right thing. That team really came together over that. We had an undefeated season that year!

I always love to tell a good story to my team, especially when it is about success. I do not even remember the name of the guy, but he had gone over to the Olympics one year. He was a sprint guy in track and won a gold medal. Well every four years, of course he qualified for the Olympics. But in between the time when he won the Gold, and it was time to go back, he had a horrific car accident. He became paralyzed from the waist down — but he didn't give up. He trained in a wheelchair because he said, "I am not handi-capped! I am handi-capable." He went back and he won a gold medal in the wheelchair race. What a strong mind!

I am telling these guys, "Boy, here is a guy! You have got both of your legs and he did not have any. He is winning! What do you mean you cannot win?" Those are the kinds of stories I am always sharing with these guys. So many people are just so willing to have pity parties. There is another story like that in "Bouncing Back: How to Recover When Life Knocks You Down." Bob Wieland, a Viet Nam war veteran, lost both his legs to a mortar mine 1969. He only had his upper torso. He could have given up. He did not. He trained and ran marathons on his hands and eventually walked across the entire United States on his hands.

As a Head Coach, the more I can get my ego out of the way, empower the team, and inspire the young men, the better year we will have. After all, I am not the one carrying the ball, making blocks, and getting hit. Here is an-other great story that I like to share. It is actually a true one.

There was a basketball team in Iowa that went the whole year and did not win one game – not one. Well, but everybody goes to the end of the year tournament. The head coach had an opportunity to make some money as an official in another district. So he goes there but he tries to get the Assistant Coach to take the team. Well, the assistant… ah he smells a rat and says, "I'm not going down there and get embarrassed." Well, to make a long story short, they end up sending the English teacher as just a chaperone.

The amazing thing is — The guys won the tournament. They won it! They hadn't won a game all year, so when they got back to school that next week the head coach said, "Well, what the heck happened?" They said, "Coach, all year we kind of felt like it was your team, and we wanted to see you lose. For the first time, we felt like it was our team and we wanted to win." I tell every team I coach that story. "It is your team, we are just like service sta-tion attendants. We are going to give you everything you need to get to where you need to go. But it's up to you whether or not you want to get there. And so it's your team."

Another thing I try to tell my young men is that they have the power to strengthen their spirit or they can deplete it. What is in your heart makes a difference. Jesus preached forgiveness. When hatred builds in your heart, it just eats at you. That's no way to live and be successful. This is especially important for those young men who are dealing with their past circumstances. This guy, Mike Singletary, played middle linebacker for the Chicago Bears. He was a real short guy – 5'9" or 5'10" – but was very intense. Mike gave a speech at the AFCA convention and shared this story with the audience. He is from

Waco, Texas. He went to Baylor. He probably was too short to be successful. Everybody told him he was too short. "You cannot play football at Baylor. That is 1A division. Guys will just run over you." Well, most of the time we succeed because somebody told us we could not. If enough folks tell us we cannot, boy that is fuel. In addition, he was a stutterer. Baylor's Head Coach, Grant Teaff, used to make him come to his office every day with a new word. Pronounce it, spell it, and use it in a sentence. Mike went on and created a motivational company.

There is an important lesson here — you cannot move forward in life until you go back and forgive somebody for something they did that hurt you. You see, his dad left Mike and all the kids. He came out of a large family. Mike just walked around with this hatred and his resentment towards his father. It got in his way. I have been told a million times how many muscles it takes to smile versus how many muscles it takes to frown. It is so important. I do not care who it was or what it was, you have to make peace with it. With so many folks, they are still carrying stuff that happened ten or twenty years ago.

At some point in his life, he found his dad. He actually went and found him. He told him, "I did not like what you did. It has been bothering me, but I forgive you." Once he did that, he became a starter on the Baylor football team. He went on to become an all-American as a football player. Mind you now, he is a little short guy. He was not supposed to be able to do any of this, but he was drafted by the NFL and he obtained his degree at Baylor. He played in the NFL with the Chicago Bears. He went all-pro. Now he is a hall of famer. You cannot move forward until you go back and forgive someone or something from the past. When he did that, his whole life changed for the better. True story! It was great to have him on campus in Spring of 2011 for our pro day. The 49ers also drafted Curtis Holcomb in the 7th round as a cornerback. He was a great player for us at FAMU.

So when I tell that story it affords them the opportunity to find forgiveness, clean up their hearts and get rid of all that anger. I encourage them to just "flush it out." Whomever it is that seems like such a monster or just has been horrible to them — in their mind, somebody they would probably like to see dead — they can start healing. We have a tendency to think that we are getting the short end on life sometimes. We don't realize that God's plan includes suffering and sacrifice to strengthen our resolve.

THE FELLOWSHIP OF CHRISTIAN ATHLETES (FCA)

This has always been a good organization. I started a huddle group in high school at H.D. Woodson. It was so important at that high school because it was a depleted environment, everybody was feeling sorry for himself. Then I introduced this program where people would sit around a table with nine other people, everybody was asked to put their problems out on the table, and each person had the opportunity to look at all those sets of problems. By the time they finished looking at everybody else, they would pick their own stuff back up. So many times, we think, as we move through life, that we are the only one's catching hell — that we are the only one's who do not have this or that. It is God's plan. Suffering is a part of it. Once you understand that, you will stop asking, "why me?" and you will start asking, "What am I supposed to learn from this?" When you get that attitude, now you are putting yourself in position to move forward! I always tell them, look, do not ever come in here and say, "Coach, I got a problem." No, you do not. When you come in here, say, "You have a situation." Defining something as a problem already means that it is negative — "situation" means you just need to put some time into it. It is just the psychology of it.

So do not come along and tell me you have a problem. No, you have a situation. We did that with that group in high school, and I have used that throughout the years. During our first year at H.D. Woodson, we did not win anything. We could not win marbles. Then we started FCA on Friday mornings. People were reluctant at first; only two or three people would show up. About a month later, we might have had six. Long story short, we got to a point where all the teams were coming. We had to go to the auditorium. FCA was huge — and testimonies. The very next year with the same folks, that same group of high school students, we won seven city championships. Amazing! The same kids! We won baseball, football, basketball, track, and swimming — with the same kids! Why? — Because they got out of this "why me?" pity party attitude.

"Testimony" is a time when you stand up and thank the Lord for whatever you want. In the beginning, there was not anyone talking, nobody was giving testimony. It only took about two or three minutes and it was over. Eventually, we had to end the meeting because we were going anywhere from an hour to an hour and ten minutes. Everybody was standing up and sharing: "Want to thank the Lord because my grandmother just came through this" and "I had ...." They were really sharing! Look, it is feeding the soul. Now, with all we go through, they cannot wait to get to FCA. They talk about it. Because, you know, that is the cure. I tell them, "Look there is more room out side of the body. Get it out. Discuss it." Boy, does that go a long way towards healing! If you keep that stuff down in there, it just gets so… it just eats away at you and the Devil just loves it!

I am serious about this, whether we are on the road or at home, they look forward to the FCA. I know now that their attitudes are different. Now, it is not so much about "what happens to me." It is more about "what do I need to do to solve the issue." They are learning to turn things around. Rather than feeling like a victim, where life is getting on them, and they just keep feeling like they are being beaten down, they are turning that around. They are finding a new strength in the Lord and they are not afraid to confess where their strength comes from. They might start with a couple of "ugh"… but they end with "hmmm, amen." They share with each other all during the week. Boy, is that a thing of beauty! Now we can say, "we are together," "we have a brotherhood," "I love you." It sounds good, when you see tangible evidence of that — it's powerful.

A deeper bond is created when people know the truth is being told. When that starts happening, when a group of young men come together and really care about each other, then greater things are accomplished. There is power in that human bond. I like to share the story of the L.A. Lakers vs. the Detroit Pistons. Three or four years ago, the L.A. Lakers lost to the Detroit Pistons. There is no question the best talent was in L.A. But the Pistons liked each other, on and off the court. When that bond is there, that's huge! When a player feels, "I do not want to let you down, I am going to do what I have to do because it is important that I do not let you down," we see great things. But if the attitude is, "I do not care about you and you do not care about me," then I do not think you can have one of those great years. There are always going to be times when we are confronted with adversity. That is just life. But when you have that strong core, then, the human spirit is stronger, individually and as a team.

When you believe in something and "that guy is important to me," we are going to get through it together. Whether it is the last-second shot, or last-second kick, or the last-second tackle that you have to make, when the attitude is, "I am going to do everything I can to perform," then you have something. I tell my young men,

"Look, if you do not care enough about your own damn self, care about him! He does not deserve your less. He deserves your best! And when you do your best, the good Lord is going to take care of the rest."

We have a way of talking about this. We refer to it as "The Circle." We will talk more about this later, but for now let's say this. Inside the circle are the things for which you are responsible and you can control: your grades, your attitude, your work ethic, your choices, etc. Outside the circle is God's domain: the weather, other people's attitudes, playing conditions, and where you are from. He controls all of that! That is God's work.

So if you see somebody in this program attending to God's work, remind him to get back in the circle. I am talking about "my" circle. It is important to keep these young men focused and moving in the right direction. There are too many possible distractions in life! I tell them that there are consequences for their choices and actions.   Choices are like elevators — they either take you up or they take you down.

In conclusion, we are putting something out there for these young men that is vital and real. We don't try to beat Christianity or religion into anyone. We just give them options. It is a smorgasbord, you know? You decide which way you want to go. I remember a couple times at another place we had FCA and one young man said, "That's not my religion." That is all right with us. We are not going to beat it over your head to come. You decide if you want to come. He said that when he was a freshman. By the time he was a junior, he was the first one in there. I understand now he is a deacon in his church.

The truth of life is that we do not always win.   Sometimes we lose. We lose games and we lose loved ones. We can't always understand why these things happen. Fred's death was beyond all of our understanding. Yet, his passing brought that group of men together in a strong and powerful way. His death changed their lives and took them to a level that they had never known. There is often a mystery even in victory.

We do not always know the reason for defeat or victory. What is important is that we keep the faith and stay the course. Sometimes all we have is faith because our mind cannot find an explanation. Normally you say, "If we had not dropped this ball we would have won." But sometimes you have a conglomerate. You have a whole bunch of everything. Then you just have to be still. You cannot explain it all. We have had some great wins. For example, we were up in the Georgia Dome where the Atlanta Falcons played this past year. The opponent had 33 points and we had 17. We came back and won 38-33. The running back had five touchdowns. I do not want to explain that one. That was the Lord's will. We have had disappointing losses too. We lost Homecoming when we had a big lead at halftime. Everything seemed to go wrong for us. I don't try to explain it all anymore.

In these 29 years, there have been at least 21 championships. I do not know how to get any better than that. What a blessing! I know people in their whole life who cannot say they won even one championship. I always tell kids, "This year can be life changing. If we just put forth the necessary effort, commitment, and think big. Whatever happens, I know the good Lord is with us. So whether we win or lose, it is important to remember that we are being taught great lessons. The hard work, dedication, and sometimes, suffering, all have a deeper purpose.

"Through him we have also obtained access by faith into this grace in which we stand, and we rejoice in hope of the glory of God. More than that, we rejoice in our sufferings, knowing that suffering produces endurance, and endurance produces character, and character produces hope, and hope does not put us to shame, because God's love has been poured into our hearts through the Holy Spirit who has been given to us." (Romans 5:2-5)

Winning football games is part of our work. However, the deeper purpose and the way we win games, is by developing the spirit and character of our young men. The Fellowship of Christian Athletes is an important part of this program.

Chapter 4
STAY IN THE CIRCLE

Stay in the Circle is a powerful concept that I have used for years in my coaching program. It is a part of a comprehensive approach that has proven to be effective in the development and growth of these student athletes. It is simple in scope, yet far reaching in its impact on these young players. Here is the actual printout that we give to everyone.

The Circle

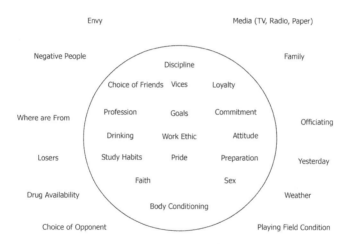

This is how it works. The things listed inside the circle you definitely have control over: your faith, your habits, your vices, your discipline, your major, and your choice of friends. Inside the circle is your domain. You can control and determine what happens with those things. We put a lot of things on the outside of the circle: the weather, public opinion of you, the referees, your family, and where you're playing. As you can see, all those things are beyond an individual's control. The point we are trying to make is:

Everything inside the circle is in your domain to control. Everything outside of the circle, that's the Lord's work. He controls that. If you devote yourself to controlling those things in the circle, God will take care of the things listed outside the circle. When you see someone in this program attending to God's business, remind him to, "Stay in the Circle."

So, this is what we are teaching:

If you want life to be manageable, if you want to have a beneficial and quality life, then you have to learn to take care of the things that are inside the circle. This is true because that's all you really can control. If you see somebody in this program trying to pay attention to things outside the circle, tell them, "That's the Lord's work. Get back in the circle!"

This is just one of the many little things or keys that we teach to help them to be successful. They probably never heard it stated in this way, but it makes sense. In fact, they mimic so much of it we know they are listening. We hear about them on the Facebook, years after they have graduated, quoting this stuff to each other.

It is no secret that we are tough, we are disciplined, and we push these young men to a much higher level of performance than they ever thought possible. We use every opportunity as a "teaching moment." We have found it is so much more powerful when the message comes in the present moment. We found that the good Lord always gave us what we needed in order to teach and train these young men.

One year when we were at Hampton, there was an enormous storm. We had our regular practice scheduled and we saw a great opportunity given to us by Mother Nature. Joe Manly was on that particular team. He played for us at Hampton University. He was part of the first class at Hampton University. He came in 1992 and played through 1997. He was part of three championship teams and also part of the team that switched from Division II to Division I. He was mentioned in the previous chapter. This is his account of what happened that afternoon.

Joe Manly

"It was honestly very tough. It was tough and extremely humbling from the very first day. It was the very first day that I actually had practice with him. It started with a thunderstorm. Then it started raining like, you know, Hampton, Virginia, it's hurricane season! And so my very first day at practice, the 'two-a-days,' it started raining really hard — you could barely see. Now I'm a freshman, and so normally at high school when it started raining like that we usually went in the gym. And so when it started raining, I'm waiting to go to the gym and he looks at everybody like, 'What are you looking at me for? I don't have nails in my palms, (holding up his palms so we can see them).' He was like, 'I can't control the elements.' The only thing we can control is how we play in it. The only way to control how we play in it is to practice in it. We learned to not let the elements affect our performance. And so my whole freshman year was an eye opening experience. I never had anybody that was so blunt, so honest, and pushed us so hard.

"I actually attribute a lot of my mental toughness to him. As a matter of fact, almost 99.9% of my mental toughness comes from playing for him. He always had a saying, 'You do or you don't!' He would say the old college try 'ain't worth a damn.' But it's more or less like, you know, you get it done. And so if you don't, you find a way to get it done. You prepare yourself to get it done and that's how your attitude goes. So that's pretty much it. I owe a lot of that to him."

Timothy Benson, M.D., was also there that year. He is now a psychiatrist and a faculty member at Harvard University. His memories of those years are worth sharing.

Timothy Benson, M.D.

"We say that we thought we knew what it took to succeed, but he basically taught us what it truly took to succeed. One of the things I always say when I am talking about my experiences with Coach Taylor is the fact that we would get up at five o'clock in the morning when it was still dark, during 'two-a-days,' and I was catching balls that I could not see and getting yelled at if I missed them! And that just gives

you an idea of the standard he held us to — it was quite the different experience.

"Coach was always pushing us. When we thought that there was nothing more that we could do, he always would help us find that next level, that other level. And that has influenced my work today. You know, always understanding that there is a next level that you can go to, even though you think that where you are is all that you can do. He really imparted that to us. And of fighting through — breaking barriers, breaking some of the mental barriers that we did not even know we had.

"There is one time where I showed up late for a practice. I was not the only one that showed up late. At the end of practice, I just remember him vividly saying, 'Alright, Coach, I want you to run them until I get tired.' He sat there and watched. And that was the way he taught. I was never late again — trust me! It was a very powerful lesson about discipline, and showing up for life. There was a level of intentionality that he helped us to realize — success was not just going to come to us. We had to do what it takes to get to it. That is when I realized that success is an inconvenience.

"I was there during that big storm and we were out at practice. And oh, gosh, it was getting crazy. It felt like a hurricane. And it was windy, and it was raining, and we were all just kind of sitting there looking at Coach. Actually, we were not sitting, we were practicing, but just looking at Coach like, 'Are you going to say something or are we all just going to die out here?' And as we were all looking at him, he said, 'What are you looking at? I'm not God. I don't control the weather.' And we were like, 'Okay, yeah, okay. So all right, this is crazy. He is crazy!' And at that moment there was a big sized lightening bolt that came down across the videographer on the tower. And then he was like, 'Okay, let's go.' We all ran in. But that was some memorable moment.

"Stay inside the circle, of course. That is something I use. You know your job is to stay inside the circle. When I lead groups I always reflect when I was playing football and Coach would tell us about staying inside the circle. He would ask, 'Who is outside the circle? The refs, the weather, and the crowd.' He said, 'These are all outside the circle. What you need to do is stay inside the circle where your attitude and your work ethic are.' So that was some of his advice. There was also one thing that he said that, and this one really struck me. I actually started some of my personal statements for medical school with this quote. 'You don't always have to be the lead dog if you have the heart to come from behind.' I think that really has encompassed my life story.

"I remember one time we were playing in the playoffs against Northern Alabama. We were on the plane and it was the worst weather. The turbulence was so bad and the plane was jumping up and down. We did not know if we were going to land —the plane was tilted! It was so bad a couple of linemen started crying. After we landed, Coach got so pissed. He was like, 'Look, if we are going to die, we are all going to die, so why are you crying?' I am not quite sure but I think he benched them. Oh, gosh, but that was just a part of that pivotal time in our lives, let me tell you."

Jonathan Hunt was another fine young man who was with us in those early days at Hampton. He is currently an attorney with the law firm of McKenna, Long, and Aldridge, in Atlanta Georgia. He principally practices in the areas of real estate, contract law, and finance. His memories of that time are worth sharing.

Jonathan Hunt

"It was during the spring practice camp and that was a very difficult time for me personally. I had lost a cousin in a tragic way. I was not on scholarship, and I was debating whether or not I should be out here, should I be focusing my time on something else, and on and on. During that spring, about half of the team happened to catch a case of strep throat to pneumonia, depending on who you were and how severe it was. Half the team was very physically ill. It was cold, it was just a nasty, a nasty time, and we had finished a long practice — full pads, the whole deal. We were sitting up there in the rain, the wind, the cold — just waiting to wrap up, thinking he was only going to say a couple of quick words. We are going to have practice tomorrow, so let's get into the showers. He chose that time to share the story about 'The Circle' and his philosophy about 'The Circle.' What you can and cannot control.

"This is what I remember, he said. 'It is raining, it is cold, it stinks right now. I do not want to be out here, I am sure you do not want to be out here after this practice, it is hard. I know you are tired, you have to study but let me tell you gentlemen, that we cannot control this and the sooner everybody realizes that there are things in your life that you can and cannot control, the more successful you will be. There are things that you can control: whether or not you go to class, whether or not you choose to study, whether or not you come to practice, whether or not you decide to sneak out and go visit that girl, whether or not you give 100% out here on the field.' He went on and listed several things. He said, 'Those are the things I want you gentlemen to focus on. Those are the things that I want you gentlemen to give your effort to — not what we cannot control, like the weather.' It is pouring down rain so that got a little chuckle. 'We cannot control the referees. We are going to get bad refs, and we are going to get good refs. It usually balances out evenly. You cannot rant and rave about a penalty call because you are just going to get another one. You can control how you react, you cannot control what plays are called, you cannot control whether or not somebody likes you. If you focus on the things that you can control, God will take care of the things you cannot control! The vast majority of the time you will see that the things that you cannot control will work out just fine because you dedicated yourself to the things that you can control, and to the extent the things that you cannot control are bad, you have prepared yourself as well as you possibly can to weather that storm. So we cannot control the weather gentlemen, and we cannot control the weather in September, October or December. But we can prepare ourselves now in case we get this weather in October, November, or December.'

"It was another one of those moments where it was a window, although it was in my youth, it was a window where I saw some clarity. I said this man, this coach, and the coaches he has around him are doing something different. This is something different that I have never experienced before in my football career."

Coach George Small came over to be on our staff back in January of '08. He had been the Head Coach at North Carolina A&T State University. He is our Assistant Head Coach at Florida A&M. He makes a great contribution to our staff. We are very grateful to have him here. This is his perspective on the circle.

Coach George Small

"That circle consists of the things that you can control. That is the circle. The things that you cannot control are outside the circle, and those are the type of things you do not worry about. That is part of staying in your lane. Coach Taylor he always says, he taught Driver's Education, and he learned very quickly how to stay in his lane.

"We play the game in an environment where we are outside; and it is not always going to be sunny and bright. You know what I am saying? You are going to have elements of the weather that you cannot control, and you have to play in those conditions. So I know when we first got here, it was similar to that time at Hampton. The wind was coming up and it was dark. I mean, it was just like a monsoon as far as the weather. And the guys are like,

'I am getting ready to take off.' Coach was like,

'Where are y'all going?' And they said,

'Well, we always go in when it starts raining.' And then he was like,

'Well, those days are over. No, you do not play football indoors. You do not run to the gym when we are in the stadium. People are not

coming inside to watch a football game. We play outside in the weather like this, so this is how we are going to practice. So get used to it.'

"All of them looked like Benson. They were shocked! And he has not changed. No, and so we practice in the monsoon weather, wet and everything. It teaches you how to be able to play the game in those types of elements, to be under control, and to persevere through it. And so when that type of situation does occur on a Saturday, when we are playing, it is nothing new to us. And sure enough, over the years, since we have been here, those types of conditions do not bother these guys now. If it starts raining, the wind starts blowing, it gets real cold or whatever, those are distractions; and we do not let that bother us because that is something that we cannot control. But we can control how we perform in those types of situations. That is staying in the circle!"

So, in conclusion, The Circle is one important part of our larger program, which we will discuss in great detail. But for now, it is important to see how powerful this concept is for each individual. It works to teach these young men to focus upon what is important, to "stay in their own lane," to "stay in their own tree." When the mind and focus is in the right place, then we have the best chance to succeed in life. That is what we want. We want to give these young men the best chance to be successful in our program and in life. The facts speak for themselves: many conference championships and a very high graduation rate. This program works and we are very proud of what we are able to accomplish with the Lord's help.

The staying in the circle model helps us to manage our lives more effectively. Time management is very important for success in life. Success is about maximizing our time. If we can find out how not to waste time, we can focus on the things that are most important. The "Staying in the Circle" model helps us to manage our lives more effectively.

Chapter 5

HARD WORK DOES NOT
GO UNNOTICED

O ur football program is built strong, just like Chevy trucks. It is "Built to Last!" Just for the record, this is not an endorsement for Chevy trucks. I own a couple of cars of other brands but I do like their motto. We are building young men for a lifetime, not just a four-year college football experience. I always tell them, "You are student-athletes." You are not an "athlete-students." Your education comes first. Colleges are primarily built for teaching, learning, and research — not for athletics. Once you get that part straight, now you might be successful in other things — but first, let's get that part straight. Athletic programs are part of a bigger picture for the total education of individuals.

Sometimes we hear, "I'm going to college to play football." "No, no, no, no we don't major in football." It is important that we develop a reputation that we are about educating the whole person: body, mind and spirit. We have a 9:00 a.m. meeting every morning with my staff. Nobody around that table is without a degree. Most have two degrees because you cannot tell somebody to go to class if you did not.

The goal is to march down the graduation isle because I think it's a sin for a young man to come, go out there and beat his brains out for four or five years, and leave without a degree — that's a sin! The athletic department supports the University's need for financial support. People do come and buy tickets and we raise money for the University. The question is, "What are you going to get out of it?" Get that degree then everything else is gravy. Like I said, I don't like to hear my recruits saying,

"Well I'm just going to play football."

"No, no, you're not going to college just for the football. I believe that minimizes you because the good Lord didn't put you here just to be a uniform rack! There's more to you than that, so let's use this experience and, hopefully, it can finance your degree, but make sure you are putting something between your ears."

We want people to understand, from kindergarten through doctoral programs, that was your educational experience. From pee wee to the NFL, that was your athletic participation. If you maximize those two experiences, both your formal education, and your participation in sports, now you have the foundation to create a quality life. The average life expectancy of a male is anywhere from 76 to 80 years. The playing expectancy in football is around thirty years. So, when you have finished, are you going to do? We want to make sure that the rest of your life has quality. We are trying to prepare you for that, when the itineraries are no longer there, you have to make your own. Are you still going to be organized? Are you still going to be disciplined? I do not know why we should expect you to be that way once you have left us if we do not seek to show you how to accomplish that. Your life should have quality long after you leave your playing days.

We are about building character. Our program is tough, but it works. We believe, "You Can't Win Public Victories Before Winning Private Battles." It goes back to the idea, "It is what you do when people are not looking that really determines who you are." We want people to graduate and have a solid foundation that is embedded in their core self. We are not going to be around watching you every step of your life. These values and behaviors must be internalized if you are to be successful.

Coach Darrell Mudra was one of my mentors. And we have maintained a very close relationship over the years. I played for him in college at Western Illinois. He was known as Dr. Victory. That was his nickname because he repeatedly did the same thing wherever he went — he won games. He hired me when he got the job at Eastern Illinois to coach the offensive line. Eastern had a horrible football record — not a winning season in about 15 years. We won the national championship our very first year. I was always impressed with Coach Mudra because he had that ability to create self worth in an individual. That's the whole key. If you have that self worth, if you realize that you are not a mistake, that you were put here for a purpose, then you have a tendency to pursue that purpose.

Sometimes we get guys who have been told for their entire life "what they couldn't do." "In your neighborhood, nobody ever did anything. Nobody in your family ever did anything." So, they start believing it.

Our job is to help them reach down inside, grab that handle, and flush out all of that negative programming. Then we can start them on a new track where they believe, "Well maybe I am somebody. Maybe I can get it done. That the Lord put me here for a purpose." We have been using our blueprint for the last thirty years and a lot of young men have been listening. As a result, we have had a great career. But more importantly, a lot of young men have gone on and reached heights that, at one point in their life, they did not believe possible. That has been a real gratifying thing about this profession.

I'm a firm believer if you are going to perform on the field, who you are away from the field, is the same guy you are going to be on the field. So if you're not disciplined off the field, you are not going to be disciplined on the field. There is no light switch. You cannot just be a champion on game day when you've been a butt hole all week — they just don't go together. So we want them to buy into being a champion every day. I know it's tough. I know it's not easy. In fact, it is probably tougher these days than it was when I was coming along — The advent of social networks and social media, everything is out there. Everybody knows what the hell everybody else is doing! And then the young ladies are so much more aggressive than they were, at least the one's I knew weren't as aggressive as these young ladies today. Today they do not mind expressing what their needs are or what their desires are.

There were times that some players did not get to play during a season. They were very good but they didn't go to class. Maybe some places they look out for them and overlook their grades, but I don't want to be that crutch. When you get out there and you're not prepared, I do not want you to blame me for creating a crutch for you. I would be to blame if I allowed that to happen. The bottom line is that you have to get it done. This whole program, any program I've ever been involved with, is designed to prepare these young men for life after football.

We put together this program in order to help a young man who might have a tendency to sway, get off track, be undisciplined, or not get out of bed in the morning. It is difficult for someone like that to give in to those bad behaviors with us. In some of my meetings, we have the players stand up and shake each other's hand and tell each other, "You can depend on me." This is peer pressure, but the right kind of peer pressure. It is positive. It internalizes the feeling that, "Sometime I might not want to do what's right, but if I'm committed, if I just told you that you can depend on me, then I will put out that extra effort and not let you down." They begin to feel that they cannot just get away with missing class. Now there is a whole team involved. We are teaching them to care about others as well as themselves.

Our theme, "Success is an Inconvenience," evolved out of this way of thinking. Every year we have a theme, and this is a good one. We used it last year and now as the subtitle for this book. "Look, you do not want to get up, I understand. But to be successful, that's one of the inconveniences that we talk about." We want them to have a theme that they can cling to. "Coach, I made it today, but boy was it an inconvenience." Now it is becoming part of their way of thinking.

It takes more than one player to win a game. In fact I always tell them, "One eleventh, there's eleven guys on the field, you're one eleventh, but it takes all one eleven to make the play work. Do not ever be that guy where the play did not work because of you." I do not care how talented you are. Unless you have a sense of team and are team oriented, I am not interested. I am more concerned with what is inside of you. I have seen guys who are 6'8" and 300 pounds but they were not assets. We need to look beyond the Xs and Os and see what is underneath the helmet. The most important area on the field is that space between the ears.

We want to share some of the personal experiences from our past students. These stories show the power and purpose behind our program.

Coach Don Hill-Eley

"I'm the head football coach at Morgan State. My staff are guys who have played for Coach Taylor: Coach Alonzo Lee is my Defensive Coordinator, Coach Herbert Parhan is my recruiting coach co-coordinator, and my tackle coach We all played ball together for Coach. We have all stuck together. The reason I hired those guys is that we share the same philosophy. Coach Taylor trained us all and we understand that we are there for the student first — we are there for that young man to get him to better places. We work well together because we all were taught to lead in the same way.

"Coach used to give us T-shirts with our Grade Point Average (GPA) on them. Most coaches gave you T-shirts with your bench press weight class. He would give us a T-shirt that showed our grades. We had a 2.5, 3.0 or 3.5 club. We wanted to shoot for one of the clubs and he always talked about that. Our education was important to him.

"I use a lot of the interactions that I had with Coach to help me through my days. He would say, 'Well, it was lonely out front.' I was an assistant coach and Coach always talked in parables. Sometimes, at the time, I did not really understand what he was saying. He always said, 'It's lonely out front.' Once I got out front as the leader, I understood exactly what he meant. A leader wakes up every day knowing that he can't look to his side, either side for strength. He can't look in front of him for strength because he's the one out front. And, he dare not even look behind him because those are the ones that he's leading, and to look behind would show a sign of weakness that you should not be up front. As the Head Coach, you're responsible for the path that these kids take and you are also responsible for making sure that they do not run into any danger ahead. I learned a lot from my time with Coach.

"During that time, we didn't have two buses where the coaches had their own bus. We had one bus with two coaches on it. Coach had a '88 Oldsmobile and, me being a young coach, I would drive Coach Taylor and the two coordinators to and from the game. I was able to hear a bunch of men talking about life and talking about football as we went back and forth to the games. I had a great opportunity to get real personal with him and his wife. By spending so much time with him, I became known as son. They took a lot of responsibility for me. I didn't have money coming from home. Coach Taylor bought clothes and shoes for me. He took it outside the realms of football when I started working with him. I became his responsibility outside of football. He took care of me. When I needed to be corrected, he and his wife would pull me aside and say something to me. I became a part of the family.

"There were things he used to say that we still use today. We call them 'Joe-tellisms.' We still use them twenty years later. A couple of these saying that really stuck with us are: 'Find a man's spirit and there you shall find him.' 'Treat a man as he is, he will be. Treat him as he can be and he will become.'

"With regards to the first one, 'Find a man's spirit and there you shall find him,' that really meant that if you saw a man that had no spirit, you really didn't see a man. Without that self-knowledge a man really would not know himself. So it was important to have some type of spirituality for a couple of reasons. First, it gives a man a real sense of self and, secondly, when a man has that realization of spirit, other people will see it. Other people will respond positively to that presence of spirit.

"He also said, 'Treat a man as he is, he will be. Treat him as he can be and he will become.' Many of us would have succumbed to all the baggage that we brought to him as players if he had treated us as if we should not be in college. I know I brought a lot of baggage with me. If he had treated me like I should be mediocre, then I would have stayed that way. But because he treated me like I should be a college graduate, like I should be a success, I became that! Those are the things that he left with me.

"My mom was in prison, maybe two miles away from the school, when I arrived at Virginia Union. The highest education in my house, out of the sixteen people, was a ninth grade education. So as stats would have it, I was not supposed to be in college. I believe with all my heart that if I hadn't met a person who did not pity me, who didn't embrace me and say, 'Well, because you don't have this, man, you should just feel good that you're here.' He didn't embrace me that way. He basically embraced me by saying, 'Look, did you come here to be what you were or did you come here to be better than what you are? Nobody cares how your life starts out. It only matters how you finish. You can't control your birthday nor can you control your death. The only thing you can control is the dash in the middle.' Sometimes he may have seemed hard. But he was not looking to have a pity party with anyone. He wanted people to focus on their goals and where they were going, not where they have been.

"Those clichés and little parables may not mean much to a lot of people but it took a poor boy that had no guidance and put him out in front of the pack, leading other people. If I had not met Coach Taylor, I do not think I could have ever gotten to where I am today. I don't think I could be the type of leader that I am. I still give God the glory for where I am. I believe everybody gets the opportunity. What you do with it is the result of who you encounter. Some leaders lead the wrong way because they were taught wrong. I try to lead the right way because I was taught to do right by people. I was taught not to measure a man on how he came, but measure him for where he is going. That came from Coach.

"I would see guys come and they would try to take over the conversation about why they 'shouldn't' and then he would always say, 'Well, tell me why you 'should' because I know we didn't get together to have a pity party.' His approach would change the whole conversation. It wasn't that he didn't care what you were going through. But if you cared about succeeding, and you cared about your big goals, he would not let you bring in your issues, get lost in them, and end up with them as your goals. He was focused and kept us on track. He would not let us wallow in our problems.

"Another thing he would always say is, 'You have to be better than your neighbor.' At first I would think, 'Why do I want to compete with my neighbor?' But he didn't mean that. He meant, 'You have to be better than the neighbor you dislike because he was showing you some bad stuff. You have to set an example for those to follow.' He had his way of letting you know that life was not supposed to be easy. He would say, 'There's no genie in the bottle. There are no three wishes.' He had his different little phrases. He would help us stay grounded and down to earth. With regards to value and money, he might say, 'Now you have this money in your pocket or, do you want to eat caviar and steak. If I follow you home, I hope there will be neck bones on the front porch.' What he meant was, 'Don't get outside your box.' He would say, 'Don't come out of your tree now, don't come out of your tree.' He was telling us to 'stay in our lane,' stay within our means — don't spend money that we don't have.

"There was a little story he liked to share when he was talking about intelligence. This farmer had a little boy and he got hold of daddy's Swiss watch. The watch fell into the hay. The little boy was going all crazy trying to find the watch, but he couldn't find it. The daddy came in and asked,

'What are you looking for?'

'Well, Dad, I lost your watch in the hay and I can't find it.' The dad then said,

'Well, just be quiet and listen for the tick.'

That was Coach's little cliché about having common sense. If you drop a watch and it's ticking in the hay, why the hell look for it when all you have to do is just listen for the tick. Most of us are throwing hay all over the place — just pause and listen for the tick.

"Here is another good story that he liked to tell. It's about this little boy that wanted to have muscles so he asked the lumberjack,

'How did you get your muscles this way?' And, the lumberjack said,

'Let me think about it. While I'm thinking about it, you cut these trees down for me. Take this ax and start cutting.'

So the little boy's was so anxious to get the answer he kept cutting the trees. This went on for about two weeks and the lumberjack kept saying,

'You cut the tree, and I will think about it.' One day the little boy finally said,

'I'm so tired of coming out here doing your job and you haven't thought of anything to tell me yet. I asked you to help me get muscles and you got me cutting these trees down and cutting up this wood, and while you lay back over there and watch.' And, then the lumbar jack walked over to the little boy and felt his little arms.

'It looks like they are coming along just fine.'

And, that parable meant that most of the time you really don't know that what you are going through is leading you to what you really want. That was often the case with all of us.

"There are a lot of guys that Coach has helped. If you looked at their beginning and where they are now, you would never project it. It took someone who cared first and then corrected. Coach used to make us wear a shirt and tie, and none of us even had a shirt and tie. The only time we put a shirt and tie on was to go to court. I didn't even know how to tie it, but he took the time to teach us. He told us, 'You have to be comfortable in your own skin. This is a part of what it takes in the real world — this is part of America.' He would make us wear a shirt and tie so that became part of our identity as a man and we were comfortable. The truth is we shared clothes when we went on interviews. He assembled a lot of guys from across the country and many of us didn't have a whole lot. But, together we had much more, and we shared clothes if guys had to go on an interview. I don't even remember locking our doors in the dorm because we trusted each other so much. We knew that we were all there to become better. 'If I have something that can help you to become better, then just take it.' That was our attitude.

"Coach Taylor would often say, 'There's two institutions raising men in this town. You have Virginia Union and you have 500 Spring Street.' When I first arrived I am thinking, 'Where in the hell is 500 Spring

Street?' Everybody kept asking, 'Where is 500 Spring Street?' 500 Spring Street was the penitentiary that was maybe two miles away. Coach was telling us, 'You have a choice. There are two institutions. You don't have to be here. You can go two miles up the road and do whatever you want. But you won't do that here.' He was a strong disciplinarian.

"Every moment was a teachable moment for him. That was the way he led. He would always say, 'Life is ten percent what happens to you, but it's ninety percent on how you respond.' I remember when we drove to play Savannah State in Charlotte; hurricane Hugo was going through the State. We were driving so we never got the information that the town had been hit by a hurricane. We arrived and it was dark, it was rainy, and people were out on their grills cooking. We were wondering, 'What the hell is wrong with these people down here.' So we were looking around at the trees and stuff blowing around. The power was gone in the town, and we got to the hotel. The hotel manager said, 'I'll let you all stay here, but there's no light and we don't want you turning around on the road.' The only place we could get something to eat was McDonalds. By that time the guys were hungry because we hadn't fed them since early that morning. Coach told me to buy so many hamburgers, cheeseburgers, etc. We were just buying everything up.

"I got back on the bus and started passing it out to the guys. There was no order now because everybody was trying to get some food. They were grabbing the sandwiches and stuff, and Coach said, 'Hold up, hold up, give me the box, give me the box.' I took the box back and Coach said gentlemen, 'I promise you. I will give you cheeseburger, no burger, and I will give you ice water, no ice, and salad with no dressing. Grab something else and then see what happens!' When he got mad he let you know it. This was another moment for teaching. We were in the midst of hurricane Hugo and trying to get some food, but he was still holding a high standard.

"Coach won a lot of championships. However, there is much more to the man than his championships, than the rings on his finger, or his two hundred victories. There is a secret to success in that man. He knows how to create success. Unlike baking a cake where you have to have the right ingredients to make a great cake, he can take the ingredients that you have and make a cake out of anything. If you accept what he's bringing to you — what he's giving you through spirituality, through leadership, through hard work, and through direction, the finished product will be success. If you absorb what he brings to you, in the end, you will find success. I've seen that from all different walks of life. Not just kids like me who didn't have a mom or a dad. I've seen kids with two parent families and single parents, they all played with me. In the end, we are all better because we all said okay, 'I'm going to allow – I'm going to try it his way.' It saved us a lot of steps. Regardless what you bring to him, he can create success if you allow him to teach you. If you allow for his instruction, in the end you will find success. As I look back, I realize that the time I would have spent wondering why 'I can't,' he took the time and showed me how 'I can.' I am very grateful for what he did for me."

Jonathan Hunt

Jonathan is another student I am very proud of. He is an attorney with the law firm of McKenna, Long, and Aldridge, in Atlanta Georgia and practices in the areas of real estate, contract law, and finance. He was there with me in the early days at Hampton University. Here are some of his reflections.

"The first thing he said that I distinctly remember was, 'We are constantly evaluating everyone and nobody has a scholarship, nobody in the room has a scholarship!' Now obviously there were scholarship players and people who had been recruited to the school, but he was saying that nobody was guaranteed a scholarship for the following year. Needless to say that sent shock waves to the room and that commanded everyone's attention. He said the people who perform during the training session would potentially earn a scholarship. I knew right then that this man, who I did not know at the time, operated from a pure perform and you will be rewarded policy. If everybody performs, we will all be rewarded, and that proved to be true. It is a day that I will never, ever forget.

"I was a walk-on at Hampton University. I had not gotten a scholarship, but at the time Coach Taylor said, 'As long as you perform, I will offer you the opportunity to earn a scholarship on a fair playing field.' By the end of the spring, he interviewed everybody in a normal interview fashion — you had to come in shirt and tie, the whole deal. I had earned a scholarship. So the very first lesson that he imparted to me was his character. He showed me that he was not only a man of his word, but if you do what is asked of you, and perform your very best all the time, you will be rewarded. He never asked for more than 100%, he did not believe in that, 'Oh, give 110%.' It is impossible; you can only give 100%. However, as a walk-on, to have that opportunity to show my skills in football, that was tremendous — it was tremendous.

"When I was a sophomore in college, nobody could have told me that by the time I was a senior, I would be very close to playing for a national championship. I would not have believed that we would be ranked as one of the top five programs in the country. I would not have believed you when you told me, 'You are going to have less time, less spare time to do the things that you need to get done, less time for homework, college romance, all that stuff, but you are going to be more successful at it during those times.' I would have never believed you. So instead of asking us to believe that, he showed us.

"He had a very interesting way in which he coached. He was very much a teacher, with a lot of psychology behind it. I saw him do things that made us far and away better than our competition. I have seen him do those sorts of things hundreds and hundreds of times. I did not realize that is what I was seeing when I was younger. At the time, I did not realize that those challenges, those little needles, the gentle needles were prodding me to go faster or study harder or do whatever it took to be successful. He used his position as the head football coach to show me another way, that success and failure are not just on the field; he was dogmatic about that.

"He really made use of the group psychology that was around us. We were usually together in some form of group and, at that age, everybody wants to fit in. He would say, oh, Tim, Jonathan, Malcolm, or whomever,

'I heard about that A. I guess you are going to go home and study.' They would just say,

'Yes Coach," and quickly leave.

Sometimes they laughed and he would say,

'Well what are you going to go do? Watch TV?'

'I am going to go to the Café.' He made a point,

'Enjoy, have a good time or be in by ten but relax.'

"At the time, I did not know what he was conveying other than you need to study harder and you do not have to be in my face. What he was really conveying was, if you study, if you get good grades, if you dedicate yourself — that will afford you choices and options. Because you have chosen not to study, not to get good grades and focus, you do not have the option of going back to your room. He made a point to single out those folks, in a non-confrontational manner, in front of other folks who were not doing quite as well academically. He wanted to show them that this person has a choice. He never ever said it that way, but that is exactly what he was saying. You know youth is wasted on the young. I was too young to understand the lessons that were being imparted. But as I got older, I gained a great appreciation for it.

"He gave me an opportunity to see a new way, but it took some self-sacrifice and some determination for me to achieve it. He used all the time allotted under the NCAA rules, but it took additional sacrifice to get me to that next level. He supported me, but I really had to want it. I did earn a partial scholarship at the end of the semester. It was half or three quarters. He wanted those players who needed academic help to receive tutoring. He suggested me as the tutor. It turned out that not only did I get an opportunity to tutor the program; I served as the program's first student director. He offered me an opportunity, all be it earned, this was not a 'work an hour and you are done job.' He offered me the opportunity to be a leader, and thankfully, I jumped at it.

"One of the most important things he imparted to us was that faith without work is dead. He taught us that we are not going to become a good football player, a good team, or a great team without work. Nothing in our life is going to come to us without some level of work and commitment. But if we approach it in the right way, with a sincerity and enthusiasm, if we focus on the things that we can do and can control, and give everything of ourselves, the rest will fall in place. This is what he used to mean by, 'Stay in the Circle.' Nine times out of ten – we shocked ourselves by how well or how much we've exceeded our own expectations.

"There is something very important that I learned from my time with Coach Taylor. It is that work is one of the few things in life that provides an opportunity to challenge our creativity and measure our accomplishments. Without work, life can become soul-less, so the least we can do is approach it with sincerity and enthusiasm. I think about this every day and is something I try to convey to my son. I want my son to approach anything that he does, whether it be school work, sports, his future job and profession, life, or his wife with this attitude."

Timothy Frazier, M.D.

I am very proud of so many of the fine young men who played for me over the years. Dr. Frazier is another man I was blessed to coach. He is currently a Navy physician serving with the Marines in Palm Desert. He is a primary care doc out there, but does have the role of a sports medicine guy because of his orthopedic background. He recently returned from a tour of duty in Afghanistan. Here are some of his thoughts.

"I would say the biggest thing that I learned from my time at Hampton was being able to deal with and persevere through difficult times. I learned that life is not supposed to be easy. You know, college football is not supposed to be easy and he never made it easy. But he always made sure we knew that it was doable; that it was something that we could accomplish even though it was not going to be easy. I took those lessons with me all through med school. Whenever things got tough, I thought back to the winter runs when people were throwing up and he was yelling at us, 'Go ahead and quit if you are weak.' I made it through that, so I knew I could make it through this night of studying or even out there when I was employed to Afghanistan — out there hiking in the field with a pack. I was like, 'All right, I only got five more miles to go, shoot that is nothing compared to spring practice or two-a-days.' That is probably the biggest thing.

"I would also say that he taught me how to be a leader. A lot of the things I do now with my staff are things that he did — demanding accountability and integrity. You know, if you let things slide, people will get into a habit — a habit of half-assing things. I do not let my staff slide and I think that they appreciate that. For example, today I did a procedure on a guy in one of the rooms and my guy was kind of lollygagging in bringing me one of the needles that I needed. Afterwards, I pulled him aside and let him know the consequences of possibly waiting and having someone on a table even seconds longer than they are supposed to be there. Just do it right — that is what Coach Taylor would always do. He would not wait around. If you were messing something up, he would tell you right then. I definitely pulled that from him.

"My fondest memory was not in a game. It was either in my junior or senior year. I was taking Organic Chemistry during the football season. It was a very tough class. I think it had seventy percent failure rate at Hampton. It was the 'weed out class' for pre-med. I went in and talked to Coach Taylor about it. I told him that I would have to miss Thursday's practices because my lab was on Thursdays. It was a freaking four-hour lab in the afternoon and I just knew that it was going to be an issue. I had seen it before when coaches had a problem with that. I did not get any pushback at all. 'Tim, I am totally 100 percent behind you. Make sure you get to your labs.' That had a big impact on me. Coach always was able to push us hard on the field, but he also remembered who each one of us was off the field as well. I ended up getting an A in Organic Chemistry and I think that had a big part in where I am now.

"I would say he was an influence in my life. I always know that he is somebody I can call. Even now, almost ten years later, he is somebody that I can call and ask for advice, or ask for a favor. He is always open for that. He was a father figure for me while I was away for the first time in my life. I still see him that way. I think, other than my real father, he is probably the only other person I still see that way."

Joe Manly

This last individual we want to share with you comes with an interesting story. It has been said that our training program leaves a positive stamp on our kids. It is like when you have been in the marines, you can spot another marine just by the way he carries himself. My sister, Mary Johnson, is a school administrator. She found Joe for us. He is currently a marketing rep for a radiology company called RadNet. It's actually the largest diagnostic imaging operation facility in America. Let's hear from Joe on how he got rediscovered for our book.

"I went to enroll my twins into a daycare program and the lady there said,

'I don't know if I know you, but are you from Washington, D.C.?' I said,

'No, I'm not from Washington, D.C.' She responded,

'Well, did you go to college here?' I'm like,

'No.' She continued,

'You know what, there is something about you that I'm familiar with. I don't know if it's your dress or somehow you, I just know, I feel like I know you. Did you play college football in D.C.?' I responded,

'No. I said I played down in Virginia.'

'Where did you play at?'

'I played for Hampton University.' And she said,

'I knew it! You look like one of my brother's kids.' I was like,

'Who is your brother?'

'Joe Taylor.'

'No way, no way! But there is no way you could have known that.' She's told me,

'There's something about his kids that I could always kind of tell. You know, I don't know if it's your dress or how you conduct yourself, but I

can always pick out his kids.' And it happened really just like that.

This is what my sister Mary had to say about that meeting.

"The young man told me, 'Coach Taylor, he made me who I am today because he made me get up. You know he had to get up every day.' They had to go through what you call off-season training. He had to get up for what they call two-a-days. They got up at four or five o'clock in the morning. And now he still has that mentality. Joe used to preach. 'You know you have got to sacrifice. If you want to be successful, you have got to sacrifice.' This is what the young man said because Joe made him sacrifice his sleep and sacrifice his meals to get out there to practice. He still does the same thing now. Even before he told me that, he exuded a professional quality as he came in to register his child. You know? I could see it."

Let's go back to Joe's thoughts on his time at Hampton.

"I actually attribute a lot of my mental toughness to Coach. As a matter of fact, almost like 99.9% of my mental toughness comes from playing for him. He always had a saying, 'You do or you don't. The old college try ain't worth a damn.' Excuse my French, but it's more or less, 'you get it done or you don't!' And if you don't, you find a way to get it done. You prepare yourself to get it done and that's how your attitude goes. So that's pretty much it. I owe a lot of that to him.

"Here is a good example of what I am talking about. It was in the spring. We used to always have what was called cardiovascular and plyometrics in the morning, at six in the morning. And one time, the power had gone out, because we had a hurricane warning or something. The power went out and almost 80% of the team was late, we were all late. We all got there at 6:30 am. We figured we were going to get out early because everybody had class, plus you know, we couldn't do so much, it wasn't our fault. Well, we did our normal conditioning and then he ran us to death. In fact, it was almost like we were punished. At the end, we were all confused. We were thinking, 'It's not our fault, you know, it's not our fault.' I know he probably doesn't remember this but he said,

'You know, the challenge of having a baby is that a newborn needs to eat. They're not going to care about your problems about what happened or whether you lost your job, or whether the power's out. The baby's still going to cry because it's hungry.'

"So basically just like the baby needs its food, I need my work. This is what I took out of that. I don't really have to feel sorry for myself when things that are out of my control go out of whack. I just have to get it done.

"You know what? About four years into my career, I was laid off from Black & Decker while my wife was having twins. And, of course, I was super stressed. But I actually thought about these things during that time. I thought about it and the way I looked at it was, I don't really have time to feel sorry for myself. Even though things are out of my control, I still had to feed my kids. I still had to get money to support my family. I pulled strength from that experience. That's a real true story!

"I was probably laid off for about a month and a half to two months. I was just pounding the pavement. And then luck came my way and I got with this company. A lot of the training materials I use are stuffed with Joe Taylor quotes. I talk a lot about Coach Taylor and my experiences with him. Everybody thinks I'm this genius. I know I am just pulling from my Joe Taylor experiences. If you were to ever get all his past players in the same room, you would hear the same stories."

In closing, I have always believed that the harder you work, the harder it is to fail. You can develop a mentality of never taking "no" for the answer. Reverend Barber defined the word PUSH for us – Pray Until Something Happens.

Chapter 6
THE MIND OF A CHAMPION

Great champions are seldom born — they are developed. It takes a lot of hard work and a well-designed program to prepare a young man to receive the information that will transform his life. We have learned that you cannot force new information and demand new ways of being from these young men. We must get them ready to receive the knowledge that we have. We might have great game plans, however, if our players are not ready to hear what we have to offer, then we are wasting our breath. Our job is to prepare them to be champions. This chapter will show you how we turned the FAMU program around in one year. We work with the mind and soul along with the body. Young men need direction. We give them something to focus upon and work for so everyday they can move closer to becoming what they want to accomplish. It is a process. As we have said, "Treat a man as he is – he will be; treat a man as he can be – he will become."

THE ATTITUDE OF A CHAMPION

The foundation for success it built upon the proper attitude. A champion, whether it is an individual or a team, must have the proper attitude, belief and perspective. Attitude is the way you think. Your attitude is something other people can actually see. They can hear it in your voice, see it in the way you move, and feel it when they are with you. Your attitude expresses itself in everything you do, all the time, wherever you are. Positive attitudes always invite positive results. Negative attitudes always invite negative results. Attitude makes a difference in everything you do for your entire life, every hour of every day. What you get out of each thing you do will equal the attitude you have when you do it.

Anything that you do with a positive attitude will work <u>for</u> you. Anything you do with a negative attitude will work <u>against</u> you. If you have a positive attitude, you will look for ways to solve the problems within your world of influence, and you will let go of the things over which you have no control. You can develop a positive attitude by emphasizing the good, by being tough-minded, and by refusing defeat.

Greatness is not created in an instant. It is a process that is nurtured as one matures as a man, and gains the wisdom and understanding to live a victorious life. Life and the road to success is not easy, it is an inconvenience. Winners are not those who never fail, they are those who never quit! We go to great lengths to help our players develop the attitude and ability to be tough minded and never quit or accept defeat. Booker T. Washington said it best, "The measure of a man's success is not by what he has accomplished, but rather by what he had to overcome to accomplish it." Great accomplishments take extreme effort. Lazy people do not accomplish great things. Vince Lombardi, a great football coach in his own right, was once asked to sum up the difference between good and great football teams. He didn't hesitate and summed it up in three words — **"And Then Some."**

1. Top teams loved and respected each other- **and then some**.

2. Top teams did what was expected in the film room- **and then some**.

3. Top teams did what was expected in the weight room- **and then some**.

4. Top teams did what was expected in practice- **and then some**.

5. Top teams did what was expected on game day- **and then some**.

6. Top teams are trustworthy, dependable, and responsible, to themselves and teammates- **and then some**.

7. Top teams give their all- **and then some**.

A champion is prepared to go the distance. He does not give up. He does not whine and complain about the hard work and sacrifice that is required. He steps up to the plate and does whatever it takes to come out on top. This winning attitude strengthens a man and builds character. We tell these young men:

"Going the distance means chasing your dream.
Going the distance means doing the things necessary
to nurture your self-esteem.
And when you replace fear with faith, you will have the strength to go the
distance — to go the length.
Going the distance
No matter how far
If you're truly determined to be successful
You already are."

We want to turn these kids into men. We ask them, "How are you playing the Game?" We push them to think about who they are.

The LOSER is always part of the problem.
The WINNER is always part of the answer,

The LOSER says, "That's not my concern".
The WINNER says, "Let me do it for the team",

The LOSER sees a problem for every answer.
The WINNER sees an answer for every problem,

The LOSER sees only one thing on the TEAM- 'I'.
The WINNER understands that there is no 'I' in Team,

The LOSER says, "It may be possible, but it's too difficult."
The WINNER says, "It may be difficult, but it's possible."

Are you thinking and acting like a winner or a loser?" We only want winners on our team!

Maturity brings the realization that everyone faces disappointment at one time or another. The winners are the ones who refuse to let one disappointment become a series of disappointments. Success isn't a matter of being the best. Success is a matter of handling the worst. It is being able to deal constructively with life's disappointments. Who are the winners? Who are these people who refuse to be done in, who refuse to be defeated by their disappointments? How do they take their losses and turn them into gains?

WINNING ATTITUDE
We believe that there are five important facets to a winning attitude:
1. Keep the faith.
2. Continue to work.
3. Be gracious.
4. Have class.
5. Stay committed to a cause.

1. Keep The Faith
Our program draws upon the strength of our Lord and Savior Jesus Christ. We always have a Pastor who provides spiritual guidance and inspiration to our young men. We will share in much greater detail what and how we integrate Faith into our program in a separate chapter, but for now let us just

say that a player's faith in himself and the Lord provide an inner strength and bond of fellowship that cannot be broken. Our men will go the distance for each other, "and then some," because they do feel united at a spiritual level. We pray together, we sing together and we go to Church together. We teach them to never give up on themselves and never give up on what the Lord can do for them when they are willing to work hard. And most importantly, we do not give up on them! We have faith in their ability to succeed. History has validated our faith. We have so many success stories, a few of which are presented here in this book.

I look to You
When All My Strength Is Gone
In You I can Be Strong.
— Whitney Houston

GOD KNOWS
For every pain that we must bear,
For every burden, every care,
There's a reason.
For every grief that bows the head,
For every tear drop that is shed,
There's a reason.
For every hurt, for every plight,
For every lonely, pain-racked night,
There's a reason.
But if we trust in God as we should,
All must work out for our good.
He knows the reason.
— Author Unknown

2. Continue To Work

Success is not measured by what you have accomplished in life, but rather by what you had to overcome while succeeding. Nobody achieves success without hard work. We demand a strong work ethic in all areas of our players' lives. In their academic life, they have to maintain good grades or they just don't play. It is as simple as that. There are no excuses and no exceptions. We don't care how physically gifted a player may be. If he does not make his grades, he is not on our team! We will do whatever it takes to help them academically. We have study hall and a tutor program. We want them to graduate.

We expect our men to work on their physical conditioning. Football is a physical game. If a player in not in top shape, he cannot help us and go the distance. Individuals who are not defeated by life's disappointments keep working to achieve their goals. They do not quite because of setbacks. Champions never give up and they keep bouncing back from adversity. We test a man's resolve in our physical demands.

We also expect our men to keep growing emotionally. Emotional intelligence is important in order to make good life decisions. People who overcome adversity learn from their mistakes and keep striving for personal development and improvement. Too many fine young athletes are taken off course when their emotions get control over their lives. It is important to know who is running the ship. Wisdom is not born from impulsivity and reactivity. We teach our men to be emotionally clear, calm and focused.

3. Be Gracious

Winners are gracious because they also know how to win and lose. They live with self-respect and respect others. They don't gloat with victory nor do they caste blame in defeat. They maintain an attitude of appreciation for their personal gifts, victories and all that is given. A deeper sense of Faith allows a man to be gracious because he knows the source of his strength. He does not gloat nor inflate his ego. He knows if it were not for the Grace of God, little could be accomplished. He also realizes that we are tested and defeat and obstacles sometimes provide great opportunities to learn and grow. He is not bitter with defeat, but uses life's setbacks as opportunities to grow and gain deeper acceptance for God's Plan. He does not throw childish temper tantrums or emotional fits when life gets tough. He digs deeper into his soul for strength and the wisdom to go the distance and carry on.

4. Have Class

Class is an important quality that is instantly recognizable. It shows in a person's presence, ever before he acts or speaks. It is based on respect for others. It is a deep and genuine respect for every human being, regardless of his status in life.

Class is having manners. It is always saying "thank you" and "please". It is complimenting people for any and every task that was done well. Class is treating every other person in the same manner that you would want to be treated.

Class never makes excuses for one's own shortcomings, but it always helps the other person to bounce back from their mistakes. Class never brags or boasts about one's own accomplishments, and never tears down or diminishes the achievements of another person. Class does not depend on money, status, success, or ancestry. The wealthy aristocrat may not even know the meaning of the word, yet the poorest man in town may radiate class in everything he does.

If you have class, everyone will know it and you will have self-respect. If you are without class — good luck, because no matter what you accomplish, it will never have meaning.

5. Stay Committed To A Cause

A commitment to a cause creates a sense of meaning that is greater than just you. It is too easy to fall into a downward spiral of self-absorption — a proven formula for failure and despair. A cause, which is based upon serving and helping others, uplifts the soul and inspires you to act and help make your world a better place. Your world may be your team, your family, your work, or your country — whatever it is, you want the highest good for all. A cause gives you a reason to get out of bed when life is difficult. It gives you a reason to work harder and longer because you care. Winners stay committed because they do not give up. Martin Luther King had a cause. He gave his life for it. He never gave up, even to the very end. His commitment changed this country and uplifted millions of people to a higher level. Commitment keeps you going when the going gets rough.

A PLEDGE TO MYSELF

We want our young men to step up to the challenge of our program and commit themselves to the process. We want all our players to feel they can trust each other in the best and worst of times. We often have each player look at the man next to him and say, "You can count one me." This is a pledge we ask each young man to make — to commit to a cause and commit to himself.

Today I pledge to be
The best possible me
No matter how good I am
I know that I can become better.

Today I pledge to build
On the work of yesterday
Which will lead me
Into the rewards of tomorrow.

Today I pledge to feed
My mind with knowledge
My body with strength, and
My spirit with faith.

Today I pledge to reach
New goals
New challenges, and
New horizons.

Today I pledge my loyalty
To this program and my teammates
Who lead me onward
In search of my dreams.

Today I pledge to believe in me!!!

ON BELIEF

A champion has a strong belief in his ability to overcome adversity, persevere and be successful. No one wishes to be a second-class person with second-rate accomplishments. But there is a difference between wishing and believing. Many wish for success, but believe they will fail. They simply don't have the faith to climb the ladder of success. They get a rung or two off the ground and doubt will not permit them to go any higher.

Belief is related to faith. There is "blind faith," and "true faith." Blind faith is based upon a hope that something can or will happen. It may be the result of stories heard or people known. Blind faith can be very strong if one has deep convictions. True faith is based upon direct personal experience. If you have felt the presence of God, seen real tangible example of miracles in your life or in the life of others, or overcome great personal adversity, then your faith is true because you have first hand knowledge and know in your heart and cells what is possible. True faith is unshakable.

Our goal is to give our athletes a real tangible experience of winning, success, achievement, and breakthrough so they know in their bones they are capable of achieving great things. They may ask them to begin their college experience with blind faith because we tell them what is possible, but they leave with true faith after having accomplished what they thought was impossible.

Doubt is a negative power. It cripples initiative and cramps energy. It makes failures of us even before we start. When the mind begins to doubt, then it begins to marshal in reasons to support its disbelief. It has been said the "environment is stronger than willpower." This is why it is so important to surround yourself with positive people and positive influences. Champions must make difficult choices to protect themselves from all obstacles to success. They must maintain a strong, positive mental focus to be physically healthy and mentally strong.

"Our doubts are traitors,
And make us lose the good we oft might win,
By fearing to attempt."
— Shakespeare

PREPARATION
THE FOUNDATION OF SELF CONFIDENCE

The greatest pep talk in the history of locker room coaching won't help an athlete who has cheated on his preparation. Athletes are either ready or they're not. If they are not, it's because they haven't worked hard enough — that is, they haven't prepared. Preparation enables you to perform to the best of your abilities. It also gives you the freedom to perform without the fear of failure holding you back. Preparation is a combination of mental and physical skills gained from hours of practicing "the right way." You must develop the mental confidence, which allows you to push yourself physically – that's the winning edge. Together, mental and physical preparation gives you the edge. It's impossible to "think like a winner," unless you can prove to yourself that you have the capability to be a winner. That's why preparation and practice are so important. You can't just wake up one day and think you're good — you have to become good.

A coach can't tell a player to have confidence – although many do. Others criticize their players for lacking confidence. What they should do is point out that if a player hasn't prepared to win, then he or she hasn't worked hard enough. It's not a lack of confidence as much as a lack of preparation. When an athlete has totally committed himself to hard work, sacrifice and practice, it's easy to get him fired up. He's earned the right to be fired up; he knows he's ready. All you have to do is remind him of the price he has paid. Coaches will take a well-prepared football team over a highly talented one any day. When an athlete has totally prepared himself through hard work and film study, he knows he is ready. He is ready to receive his just rewards.

Jim Brown, considered to be one of the greatest football players of all time, played for the Cleveland Browns. His thoughts about preparation and self-confidence appear in *Bouncing Back: How to Recover When Life Knocks You Down*. Here is another great champion talking about the need to prepare.

Jim Brown

"You need repetition and hard work. Now, there are two things that hard work gives you. One is, it familiarizes you with everything, it gets you in great condition, it prepares you, mentally and physically to approach your profession. The other thing that it really gives you is confidence, which is about the mind. If you know you haven't worked hard enough and prepared yourself properly—now you're going on what you have naturally. But a lot of times, if things don't go right, psychologically you lose ground because you know you haven't prepared the way you should.

"If you know you're in total shape and you've prepared in every way and something goes wrong, you can bounce back from it much easier. You don't necessarily lose confidence; you can just stick in there because you know you have prepared yourself, and you can max it. That's very important. It's hard to get around.

"A great talent that cheats on hard work and preparation is never going to be a strong psychological force. You just can't do it, because you tell yourself the truth. You can bullshit your opponent. You can deal with a facade, but it's a very hollow facade, because you know that you have not properly prepared."

ON WINNING AND LOSING
He Who Has Never Failed Somewhere,
That Man Cannot Be Great

There are times when we cannot explain the adversities that come to us both on and off the field. If we feel sorry for ourselves, we will only prolong the situation. We act as cowards if we blame others, but to press on gives us a strength and direction to rise above. When we rise above, we reach new heights and horizons. We must work to a bigger scheme, and the most important thing today is how we pull together as a team.

Anyone can stand tall on the high peaks. It is the people who survive in the valleys between the peaks who will emerge the strongest. Those survivors will be the leaders – the ones who are <u>mentally tough</u> and have the perseverance to keep going. The ones who have the nerves to think big, act big, play big — for the battle is lost or won by the spirit of the team. Set your mind and set your will on the goals that's just in view; it's helping your teammate – it's forgetting self till the game is over and fighting for the team. If you are not afraid to lose, then you can win.

HOW ARE YOU PLAYING THE GAME?

"Life is a game with a glorious prize if you only play it right.
It gives and takes bends and breaks and often ends in a fight.
But he surely wins who honestly tries regardless of wealth or fame.
He can never despair who plays it fair, how are you playing the game?

Do you wilt and whine when you fail to win in a matter which you think
you're due, or do you snare at the man in case that he can and does do better
than you?
Or do you take your rebuffs with a knowing grin and
laugh though you pull up lame?
Does your faith hold true when your whole world is blue,
how are you playing the game?
Get in the thick of it friend, whatever your cherish goal.
Brace up your will till your pulses thrill and you dare your very soul.
Do something more than make a noise,
let your purpose burst into flames.
As you plunge with a cry, I shall do or die!
Then you're playing the game."

— Anonymous

CHAMPIONS' GUIDING PRINCIPLES

We are always trying to guide and inspire our young men to great
heights. We find that it is very helpful to provide concrete goals so they know
where they are going. It is very hard to get somewhere if you do not know
where you are supposed to go. We do not want our program to be a guessing
game. We want it to be simple and clear. We pass out a lot of paper over the
year. One page we give to each student is titled, "Self Evaluate/Re-Commit."
We want them to clearly think about where they stand with regards to the
"mind and actions" of a champion. We want them all moving in the right direction. Here are the ten principles we share regarding champions:

1. Champions Are Positive Thinkers; They Believe In
   Themselves, And Teammates.

2. Champions Visualize Their Successes, Long Before
   Game Day.

3. Champions Surround Themselves With Positive People
   And Avoid Negative Influences Or Vices.

4. Champions Are Goal Setters, And Goal Driven.

5. Champions Have A Burning Desire To Win On Every Play.

6. Champions Are Disciplined And Consistent In Their Lifting, Practicing, Film Study, And Decision Making.

7. Champions Have Incredible Powers Of Focus And Concentration. They Are Playmakers.

8. Champions Have A Deep Love And Boundless Enthusiasm For Their Sport And Competition In General.

9. Champions Strive For Constant And Never Ending Improvement, On And Off The Field.

10. Champions Are Hard Workers; They Are Willing To Go The Extra Mile — They Are In It To Win It.

LEARN TO HANDLE SUCCESS

We do so much to prepare our student athletes so they can be successful, it is a shame to see them break down and lose ground when they have achieved an important goal. It is one thing to get to the top; it is another thing to be able to stay there.

Michael Bailey, the current Athletic Director and Head Football Coach at Virginia Union University in Richmond, Virginia, played for me at Virginia Union in 1985 and 1986. He was a fine man and I knew he would continue on for a productive and successful life.

As is often the case, sometimes these young men learned their lessons the hard way. When they screwed up, I was there to help them, and get them back on the right path. Learning how to stay successful is so important, because it takes so much work to get to the top and one bad decision can quickly bring you way down. We don't want our players to lose after they have won. Michael shares his experience about that learning process.

Michael Bailey

"My last year in '86, we went 10-0. He had a major impact on us from the beginning. I remember him preaching to us on a lot more than football. He talked to us about managing our time. I was in the middle of coming out of my sophomore year and going into my junior year and never in my life had anyone ever talked to me about managing my time. It was really a crossroads for me because I began to manage my time. Since then I've had a lot of success, prior to meeting Joe,

I was just doing things as they came, he put us on a time managers schedule and I'm still on it today. Everyday was laid out and we graded

ourselves. His message was, 'A good day will lead to a good week. A good week will lead to a good month. A good month will lead to a good semester. And a good semester will lead to a good year. So, every day counts.'

"When we went 10-0, we won the CIAA championship. We were at a team meeting and he was going to give us our rings. But prior to that meeting, we got in some kind of trouble that week. I think we had gotten into a fight or it was just something that didn't go well. I can't remember specifically. But it got to the point where he was called in and somebody had to tell him something about his team. He didn't like that. I'm never going to forget that meeting. I just felt like we really disappointed him.

"I guess we didn't know how to handle success. All season he talked to us about every thing's bigger than football —decorum, behavior and character. Character! He was so mad at us I thought he was going to throw the rings at us. They were in a box or something. So we were kind of scared there, but we felt very bad because we disappointed our coach. And at the same time, we understood the lesson immediately.

"He was so mad because he felt like, although we won the championship, he didn't get his message across to us. His desire was to develop character, to help us be a contributor in the community, to position ourselves, and give ourselves an opportunity to be successful. He was trying to teach us how to win in life! It's not just on the football field. You have to win in the cafeteria, in the classroom, in the library, and with your look. He also told us that nobody's going to help us if we don't position ourselves to be helped, because nobody's going to waste time with us. If we at least position ourselves to receive the help, we will get it.

"I am never going to forget being in that meeting, because he taught us that you don't just reach a goal, win, and then act like you haven't been there. You can't position yourself where you can't handle success. It felt like we disappointed him. We had won the championship and it was going to be a celebratory event. I never saw him that mad before. So although we won, it was like we took a step back. It taught me a lesson about how to handle success — when you reach a goal, you make a new goal, or you still position yourself for oncoming success. You don't put a black eye on something you worked so hard to attain. I'm never going to forget that. Although we won, we disappointed our coach. We all learned a valuable lesson and the ring symbolized the lesson that we learned that day, more so than the championships. I never disappointed him again after that."

Chapter 7
THE ROAD MAP FOR SUCCESS

We continue to speak about the reality that it takes a lot of dedication and hard work, along with God given talent, to be successful. This entire book is filled with the details and stories about what it takes to be a winner. Over these past thirty years, we have developed a program that is philosophically sound, spiritually uplifting, and grounded in down-to-earth values and behaviors that lead to success. It is a road map that has been proven to work. Through our football program, we develop leaders, fathers, professionals, educators, and businessmen who contribute to society and lead productive, creative lives. In this chapter, we will share with you more about the details regarding our blueprint for success. It is grounded in a strong faith, discipline, hard work and integrity. We believe that, "The Lord does not call those who are equipped — He equips those who are called." Those young men who hear our call and join us, do get equipped with everything they need to succeed.

Vince Lombardi shares his wisdom regarding, "What it Takes to be Number 1."

"Winning is not a sometime thing; it's an all-the-time thing. You don't win once in a while, you can't do things right once in a while, you do them right all the time. Winning is a habit.

"Every time a football player goes out to ply his trade, he's got to play from the ground up — from the soles of his feet up to his head. Every inch of him has to play. Some guys play with their heads. That's O.K. You've got to be smart to be number one in any business. But, more importantly, you've got to play with your heart — with every fiber of your body. If you're lucky enough to find a guy with a lot of head and a lot of heart, he's never going to come off the field second.

"It's a reality of life that men are competitive and the most competitive games draw the most competitive men. That's why they're there — to compete. They know the rules and the objectives when they get in the game. The objective is to win — fairly, squarely, decently, by the rules, but to win.

"And in truth, I've never known a man worth his salt who in the long run, deep down in his heart, didn't appreciate the grind, the discipline. There is something in good men that really yearns for discipline and the harsh reality of head-to-head combat.

"I don't say these things because I believe in the 'brute' nature of men or that men must be brutalized to be combative. I believe in God, and I believe in human decency. But I firmly believe that any man's finest hour — his greatest fulfillment to all he holds dear — is that moment when he has worked his heart out in a good cause and lies exhausted on the field of battle — victorious."

ON COMMITMENT

Our goal is to develop young men who will be number one in every aspect of their lives. Our vision goes far beyond the National Championships; it is a vision for a lifetime of success. Our program requires commitment from our players. Without their one hundred percept commitment, there is no hope for success. With it, they will succeed in life. We are very direct with our players. We speak the truth to prepare them for what it takes to succeed. Sometimes, we may seem blunt, but we are honest. We find no value in sugarcoating the facts about the sacrifices needed for success. Throughout our program we constantly remind these men that, "It's not about how you feel — It's about a process. We have not invited you to a 'pity party,' but to an opportunity to step up and become a man." We frankly tell them that when it comes to commitment, there are really only four types of people:

1. **Cop-outs**: People who have no goals and do not commit.
2. **Hold-outs**: People who don't know if they can reach their goals, so they're afraid to commit.
3. **Drop-outs**: People who start toward a goal but quit when the going gets tough.
4. **All-outs**: People who set goals, commit to them, and pay the price to reach them.

They have to make a choice and decide at the very beginning who they are. There is a price to pay for success, and the rewards are great! There is no question — this is not a convenient path. It is not easy to get up for a team workout at 5:00 a.m. when it is dark and cold. Personally, I do not want to get up that early either. But that is what it takes to find out who is committed, who will show up consistently, and who is able to do what it takes to work together, create a team, and be trusted. If a man decides to go "All Out," then he came to the right place. Quite frankly, if he does not go "all out," he will eventually "get out." People do not stay in our program if they are not fully committed. I don't have to cut them. They will walk away.

We have found that sometimes men speak of desiring something but they do nothing to realize that desire. They say, "Above all things, I desire to become a great athlete." But they do not train, they do not practice, nor do they make the total commitment for excellence. The harsh truth is that they do not, in fact, desire to be great athletes — they only <u>wish</u> to be so. To be good is a "w" word, but it is <u>work</u> not <u>wish</u>.

This is what we tell them. "You have to do whatever it takes to succeed. You cannot let anything deter you or this team from success on and off the field. Each one of you must commit to doing the right thing to be a <u>playmaker</u>. <u>Plays</u> don't make <u>Players</u> — <u>Players</u> make <u>Plays</u>. Either you <u>DID</u> or you <u>DIDN'T</u> — Nothing else Matters!" I will "try" to get it done does not cut it. There is no trying. We need men who will "Do." This theme permeates our culture, but not everyone hears it or understands what it means. Nike says — "Just Do It." That is the bottom line of success. Whining and excuses will not take you across the goal line, will not feed your child, nor keep you committed when times are tough and your resolve is tested.

We do offer inspiration along with the hard facts of life. We do not have the time and luxury to pretend that this is not hard work. It may be the hardest work they will ever do in their lifetime. We are direct and flatly tell them,

"Face it, nobody owes you a living! Whatever you do or fail to do in your lifetime is directly related to what you do to succeed or fail to do. It is totally up to you! It is as simple as that.

"No one chooses his parents or childhood. But you can choose your own directions. Everyone has problems or obstacles to overcome — but that too is relative to each individual. You can change anything in your life if you want to badly enough — excuses are for losers! Those who take responsibility are the real winners in life.

"Winners meet challenges head on with the knowledge that there are no guarantees. They give everything they have — one hundred percent — and never think it is too late or too early to begin. Time plays no favorites and will pass whether you act or not, and it will pass faster than you can imagine. Take control of your life now. Dare to dream and take risks.

"If you are not willing to work for your goal, don't expect others to do it for you. Believe in yourself, live your life and compete!"

MENTAL TOUGHNESS

You must realize by this point that we believe that it takes a lot of mental toughness to succeed in our program and be successful in life.

We need to discover if a potential player has the ability to perform well under pressure, to stay positive in the face of adversity, and maintain the willingness to fight and be confident. If they do, then they are mentally tough. We need to know this, not only in order to win, but also to protect these young men and prepare them for the battle on game day as well as life. Football is rough, physical and has extreme contact. If a player in not mentally tough, he can be seriously hurt. Without a high degree of mental toughness, he will not train sufficiently, prepare adequately, and maintain the needed focus to compete successfully.

It is our observation that every person who wins in any undertaking must be willing to cut all sources of retreat. Only by doing so, can he be sure of maintaining that state of mind known as a "burning desire to win," which is essential for success.

We do have a method and strategy to develop this tough state of mind. This is what we tell our players. You must impose a strict code of acting and thinking under pressure.

- Never show weakness on the outside.
- Never talk negatively.
- Never whine or complain.
- Think positively.
- Look energetic and confident at all times.
- Follow a precise way of thinking and acting after making mistakes.

We do believe that mental toughness allows you to control fear. Fear is a natural part of combat and football is very physical if you want to win. Unless you are tough enough, both physically and mentally, you will never make it.

Toughening does not occur without exposure to stress. That is why our training is so demanding. It is just like steel. It is the fire that makes the steel strong. One of our previous players at Hampton University, Timothy Frazier, M.D., who is now a Navy surgeon attached to the Marines, told us that his training with us was more demanding than the U.S. Marines. Our training greatly helped him when he was deployed to Afghanistan. We know that the mental toughness achieved by our players enables them, under extreme pressure, to remain calm, which allows them to think clearly, non-defensively, and constructively, resulting in positive and realistic decisions and choices.

The reality is that sometimes you have to perform at your best when you are feeling your worst. The moment demands that you mentally block the hurt, block the pain, and block the sickness that you may feel for the short time you must perform. You have to shape up and get it together because excuses don't count. This may seem hard, but nobody cares if you are sick or hurt — you either do the job or you don't. You must force yourself to work harder even when you are sick, hurt, sad or troubled. That is mental toughness!

THE PROCESS OF SUCCESS

We say it over and over again, "It's not about how you feel — It's about a process." No matter how you feel, you have to keep on striving for excellence. Here are the building blocks that we have found for creating success. It is a formula that works over and over again.

Discipline

Do the Right Thing – Deep down inside, a true student athlete yearns for the grind of early rising – pain of physical training – that burning feeling that comes from exhaustive running and sweat covering the entire body, from resistive work outs in the weight room.

We work our men hard and expect that they maintain the discipline to do the right thing in all aspects of their lives. The choices they make determine how successful they will be. Do they continue to study, go to class, workout in the off season, refrain from alcohol and drugs, avoid bad company, act socially responsible, and maintain their faith in the Lord? This is a lot to ask, but this is what it takes. Did we say, "Success in an Inconvenience?" Is there any question about that? One of my players, Tim Benson, asked to come out and jog with me in the morning. I didn't think it would last too long but he actually came out for practically a year. He wanted to ask questions about my success story as a coach. In the end, he was convinced that to be successful was an inconvenience. I shared the many sacrifices that I had made, the many late nights of study or phone calls. The early morning workouts, the long road trips recruiting, the many hours of planning and counseling I experienced. To be successful, there are a lot of things you must do that you don't feel like doing but success is not about how you feel – it's about a process. Success is about a body of work.

Priority

Some things are more important than others. Map out a course that involves a step-by-step process of paying attention to what brings value to your life. Man does not decide his future – Man decides his habits and his habits decide his future.

We have to prioritize our life based upon our values, goals, and objectives. We have to introspect to know what is important to us, and then we need the discipline to follow the plan we have developed. We must put "first-things-first." Sometimes that requires making tough decisions that other's may not like. But in the end, we are alone with our choices and the results of our actions. Our habits are formed by day-to-day decisions and actions. The more we are doing something, the more it becomes a habit. Each action — moment to moment — determines the future. Make the right choice in the moment, and the future will take care of itself. We must develop habits that lead us to our goals.

Persistence

Any degree of success comes with a price tag. Abraham Lincoln had a failed business, lost several senatorial races, lost several congressional races, endured the death of a sweetheart, but became the President of the United States at age fifty-two.

Persistence is the key to success. Ask any successful person and you will hear, "I never gave up." Thomas Edison had hundreds of failed attempts before he finally invented the light bulb. Each failure provides an opportunity to learn something, correct, and move on.

There was a man who worked for IBM and made a terrible decision, which cost the company two million dollars. He was certain he would be fired. The CEO called him in for a meeting. The man's first question was,

"Are you going to fire me?" The CEO responded,

"No, of course not. We just invested two million dollars in your education. Why would we throw all that away?"

This is one of the great keys to success — never give up! But do learn from your mistakes. Don't just keep making the wrong decisions over and over again.

Sacrifice

Success demands a tremendous focus on your goal. You must see it before you can reach it. However, once again, you have to make difficult choices in order to stay on track. When others may be out partying, you may need to be home studying. When others are sleeping, you may need to be out in the dark and cold working out and practicing. When others are out late at night, you may need to be in bed sleeping to be ready for the early morning rise.

You must get up each day and chisel towards your vision. Sacrifice requires that you honor your bigger and higher goals and do not give in to your little desires and temporary pleasures. If you are willing to give up the false promise of satisfaction from temporary pleasures, you will experience the lasting rewards that result from hard work and success. It is easier to sacrifice when you feel inspired about your goal. When you are filled with the presence of Spirit, which walks with you along the way, it is easier to stay on track.

Work Ethic

The formula for success is 5% inspiration, 5% motivation and 90% perspiration. The cleaning formula 409 got its name from many failed outcomes. The first 408 attempts to create this product were unsuccessful. However, the inventors never gave up or stopped working — 409 was the magic number. Success is the result of what you **can** do — not what you **can't**.

So what does it take to maintain such a strong work ethic? Look above at our principles. Once the goal has been set, you must maintain the **discipline** to keep working and showing up to finish the job. If you are going to work hard, you can't be side tracked by diversions and passing fancies. You have to keep your **priorities** in line. Four hundred and eight attempts take a lot of **persistence**. If you never give up, you are still working hard. Finally, a strong work ethic does require **sacrifice**. When the little self and ego are put aside, it is possible to "keep on keeping on."

You can see this formula contains building blocks of success. They all fit together to make a strong man who will bring honor to his life and community. We will share several stories of fine young men who have progressed through our program and are now successfully contributing to their families and communities. As you read their stories you will see all these principles at work. To their credit, they all had the inner strength and sense of self to rise to the challenge. They all worked harder than they expected and accomplished more than they ever thought possible. Together we made this work!

WEEKLY MOTIVATIONAL DIRECTIVES

We use every opportunity to help prepare our men to receive the game plan for the week. The fact is, the losing team is the one that made the most mistakes. We want our players to be mentally ready to play their best, to fully understand and execute our game plans.

Every week we pass out motivation material to keep each player on track and focused on the goal. We create material based on their previous week's performance. We want to share with you the nuts and bolts of what we are doing to create so many successful seasons. Here are several of the actual handouts that we created. This first one has the theme of "Play 60 Minutes!" This was designed after a loss earlier in my career that should have been won. It appeared that the team lost focus and did not keep their heads in the game for the entire sixty minutes — hence the theme — "play 60 minutes."

CHOICES STILL MATTER
They are Like Elevators–They either Take You Up or Down–2010
Vision-Goals-Accountability-Commitment-Adversity
<u>Play 60 Minutes!!!</u>

1. Play as close to perfect, understanding no one is perfect. Use discipline to perfect your technique.

2. Special Team, Defense, Offense must support each other to win (2 of 3 must play well to win).

3. A defensive player's value to his team can be measured by his distance from the ball at the end of the play.

4. Don't ever give up the ball without a kick (Avoid the turnover) Control the ball, stop the run to win. A prerequisite to winning is being PHYSICAL

5. Coaches/players must study opponents, we must defeat on our schedule (Research teams to eliminate surprises) Remember: Alignment, Assignment, and Execution.

6. In your assignment/responsibility, move with urgency and a sense of purpose.

7. Never try quitting, never quit trying (If you believe in yourself and have dedication and pride, and never quit, you'll be a winner.) The price of victory is high, but so are the rewards.

"SUCCESS IS AN INCONVENIENCE"- 2011
It's Not About How You Feel – It's About A Process
The Seven (7) Steps To Success

1. Make up your mind what you want out of life.
2. Declare war on wasting time/doing things you know are wrong.
3. If you slip or stumble, admit it, get up – stay in the race.
4. Must be willing to take calculated risks for the good.
5. Must want to be better and deny losers your company.
6. Got to expect to be attacked by losers.
7. Keep your eyes on Jesus Christ daily.

ALIGNMENT – ASSIGNMENT–EXECUTION

TO GET <u>TO</u> — YOU MUST GO <u>THROUGH</u>"! — 2009
Academics–Attitude–Faith–Work Ethic–Accountability
Must Be Consistently Good Before You Become Great
<u>DON'T BEAT YOURSELF</u>

The Seven Commandments

1. No breakdown in kicking game. (Often the determiner of outcome)

2. No missed assignments. (Study playbooks/Practice hard)

3. Play great goal line offense/defense. (Be Physical)

4. No foolish penalties. (Play Smart)

5. Allow no long touchdowns. (Pursuit/Tackling)

6. Must hold fumbles, interceptions to a minimum. (Protect the football)

7. Enthusiasm and persistence – mind, body, soul in a spirit of never giving up. (Commitment to the cause)

Discipline — Assignment Football

Winning teams win because they master the basics. Blocking and tackling are the single most important factors in deciding the outcome of a ball game. Know your <u>alignment</u>, <u>assignment</u>, be disciplined in your responsibilities, and <u>execute</u> each play to the best of your ability – *Sixty Minutes*

ALIGNMENT — ASSIGNMENT— EXECUTION

"SUCCESS IS AN INCONVENIENCE" — 2011
It's Not About How You Feel – It's About A Process
"Blueprint For Success"
Must Win Private Victories Before You Can Win the Public Victories

1. Academic, WTS/Conditioning, Discipline in Social Life, Living Quarters.

2. Believe in What the Program is Doing – Be Loyal – Have Integrity.

3. Don't Make the Same Mistake Twice – If you do, you don't care.

4. Don't Worry About the Past or Future – Respond to Now

5. (Win–<u>W</u>hat's <u>I</u>mportant <u>N</u>ow) – Have Balance in your Life.

6. Men Do Not Decide Their Future – They Decide their Habits and their Habits Decide their Future – Evaluate your Habits.

7. The Quality of Your Preparation Determines the Quality of Your Performance – You Get out of it what you put into it.

8. You were Born to Win, Expect to Win, Plan to Win and Prepare to Win. You are not a Mistake.

QUITTERS NEVER WIN
WINNERS NEVER QUIT

"SUCCESS IS AN INCONVENIENCE" — 2011
It's Not About How You Feel – It's About A Process
Live Each Day To Its Fullest

1. To handle yourself, use your head. To handle others, use your heart.

2. Learn from the mistakes of others. You can't live long enough to make them all yourself.

3. The tongue weighs practically nothing, but so few people can hold it.

4. Anger is only one letter short of danger.

5. Great minds discuss ideas; average minds discuss events; small minds discuss people!

6. He who loses money, loses much. He who loses a friend, loses more. He who loses faith, loses all.

7. Beautiful young people are Acts of Nature; but beautiful old people are Acts of Wisdom.

MAXIMIZE EACH MOMENT
TRUE GREATNESS IS TYPICALLY MEASURED BY THE ABILITY TO RESPOND TO ADVERSITY – KEEP FIGHTING!

"SUCCESS IS AN INCONVENIENCE" — 2011
It's Not About How You Feel – It's About A Process

Performance

Take nothing for granted   If you aren't "up" everyday, something or somebody, will knock you down.

Take pride in what you do   The things you do well are the things you enjoy doing.

Take setbacks in stride   Don't brood over adversities; learn from them.

Take calculated chances   To win something, you must risk something.

Take work home   To get ahead, plan ahead.

Take the extra lap   Condition yourself for the long run. The tested can always take it.

Don't take "no" for an answer   You can do what you believe you can do!!!

    The single most important factor which will determine how far you go in life –is your attitude. Your attitude will compel you to work hard, dispel your fear of losing, and inspire you to encourage others.

As you can see, we keep finding ways to work with the mental approach to life with our players. The more we can help them mature, stay responsible, make good decisions, care about others, and keep God in their life, the greater success they will have. We continue to design our message based upon their needs. Every year is different and every week allows for new opportunities to learn and grow. We just try to stay on top of what is happening and unfolding, to keep them on track, so they do what they need to do every day and every week. We know when they are focused and moving in the right direction, success will follow — not only on the football field, but for the rest of their lives.

We often hear coaches give advice that a player should be doing this or that. However, unless we give them a way to accomplish that goal, we are not doing our job. It is not enough to tell someone to do something. It is our job to show them how to accomplish it.

Football coaches love to talk "technique". We are always looking for an edge in the area of footwork, ball security, blocking, tackling, and all the other important ingredients to winning football. But, by far the most important technique is that which affects the attitude of the people in our program. Here are the six steps that we teach to develop the proper attitude.

SIX STEPS FOR PROPER ATTITUDE

1. Make a Commitment

This is where goal-setting from realistic perspective begins, and causes each person, unit, and team to focus on exactly what is desired now and later in life. Are you truly committed (every fiber?) – Your every action or thought must show it – academics, weight room, conditioning, discipline in social life.

2. Set a Target Date

How many times have we all said we are intending to do something and that we will get around to it sooner or later? The setting of a target date to achieve each commitment is basic, forcing each of us to move in the right direction — procrastination is an illness. So a man thinketh in his heart, so is he — you get what you expect — If you expect to make plays in the Fall, you cannot blow a rep in weight room, fail to attend class, or miss workouts.

3. Assemble the Ingredients

Each project involves knowledge, people, resources, and other items necessary for success. You must study, and utilize the ingredients of this program for your growth and development. Take advantage of each other's knowledge, the faculty, study hall, human resources, coaches, and the program.

4. Give of Yourself

This is the most difficult and the least understood of the six steps. Sacrificial giving is fundamental to the success of any unit of people, and is required in the Attitude Technique. Don't be selfish. The more you give – the more you will receive. True joy is found in serving others. Don't worry about the past or future — respond to NOW.

Mother Teresa has a great story about the power of giving. She was taking bags of rice to the very poor. She gave a bag that would feed a family for a day to a woman and watched her carefully divide the bag in half and take half to her neighbor. Mother Teresa said she could have easily given that woman more rice for her neighbor, but she did not want to deprive her of the joy she would feel when she gave that rice away. Mother Teresa went back the next day and gave the woman another bag of rice.

5. Visualize Yourself Successful

Time must actually be set aside to sit quietly and see with your imagination exactly what you want to happen. This technique becomes more powerful as you are able to deepen your concentration and quiet your mind. This technique has been proven repeatedly to be crucial to great success in sports performance and life in general. When you consciously have focused thought and create a visual image through the use of imagination, then the body responds. Mental preparation through imagination is actually a way to rehearse and prepare for a given action. This is why it is so useful in sports. Modern physics has discovered that everything is energy, even thought. Energy follows thought — How you think helps to create what you become. What you think and imagine has a powerful effect at many levels. Champions maintain a positive attitude and view themselves as winners.

6. Believe That What You Are Doing Will Succeed

When Christ healed, he very often asked them what they thought about it. The response was, "I believe you can heal me." Only then did he tell the cripple to stand up and walk, and his statement was, "Your belief has made you well." You must have faith, positive self-image, and motivation. Repeat steps 1-6 daily.

YOU WERE BORN TO WIN, EXPECT TO WIN, PLAN TO WIN, PREPARE TO WIN

Chapter 8

THOSE WHO ARE CHOSEN
WILL CHOOSE THEMSELVES

We have provided a lot of information and stories about the demands of our program and how we prepare and support our student athletes to succeed in the classroom, the football field and life. The truth is not everyone stays. Some young men walk away from the demands of our program. Corey Swinson has been mentioned a couple of times in this book. He could have walked away, and I did come close to telling him to leave and go home. His story is more dramatic and more powerful than almost any other, perhaps with the exception of Marcus Dixon. While Marcus had a much more difficult time prior to coming to Hampton, once he got there, he integrated into our program, accepted our philosophy and excelled both in the classroom and on the field. He was a Dean's Scholar, drafted into the NFL, and currently plays for the New York Jets. Corey, on the other hand, demanded more discipline and attention. He was also a good student, drafted into the NFL by the Miami Dolphins, and played one year for the St. Louis Rams. However, his road had more bumps and obstacles. We believe his personal story and perspective is worth sharing because it gives an insight into the personal demands, choices, and issues that are part of this developmental process. As the saying goes, "You can lead a horse to water but you can't make him drink." I guess when you get thirsty enough, you decide to take a drink. Corey was recommended to me by a former player, playing for the New York Jets –Michael Brim. We believe it is instructive to understand the dynamics around his inner turmoil and his decision to stay with us.

Corey is currently the director of security at the Bay Shore School District in Suffolk County in Long Island. This school district is about 8.2 square miles, seven building, 6,000 students and maybe 3,000 faculty and staff.

COREY SWINSON

"There were some people that resented Coach Taylor's tactics and resented the way that he did things. But they were young, they were immature, they had never been through any adversity. Some were spoiled and some were soft. There is a parable in the Bible (Matthew 22:14) that says many will come but only few will be chosen and those who are chosen will choose themselves. A lot of people came to Hampton University with the intention of being a student athlete, but they forgot how much discomfort was involved, and how much pain was involved in being a student athlete — especially one of Joe

Taylor's student athletes. The strong will survive and the ones who were left standing, they certainly chose themselves, they played with a purpose, and they played for something. I chose to attend Hampton and I chose to stay in the football program. This is my story."

"I graduated from high school in 1988 at a school in Long Island and I went to University of Hawaii on a basketball scholarship. I did not have much interest in football at the time other than just watching it on television. My father passed away in 1988 and I transitioned from one school to the next, trying to find my way, trying to figure out what my purpose was. I knew that athletics were in my life, but I was not sure to what capacity or exactly what was going to happen. After going from university to university my brothers told me that it was time for me to really rethink my path. They told me, 'Man, the heck with basketball. You are too big, you are too strong, you are too athletic and you are not Charles Barkley. You are not going to the NBA.' They said, 'You need to look for a school that will take you based on your athleticism, somebody that is going to give you a shot.' At that point I ended up calling around to several universities. I spoke with Coach Taylor. I told him that I was 6' 6", 315 pounds and I was a basketball player that had the football gene. My brothers Mark and Matthew are twins. Matthew was a tight end at the University of Maine. My brother Mark was a defensive tackle at Syracuse. It was in me to transition to football, even though I never played in high school, never played a down in high school. Coach Taylor trusted Michael Brim who played for him at Virginia Union University. I guess just by him taking his word on my size and my athleticism, he made a commitment to me. He never saw me before in my life.

"When I first arrived at Hampton I went into the football office and said hey, Coach, I am Corey Swinson. He looked at me and said, 'Well I will be damned. Wow! Usually when they are on the phone and they tell me how big they are, they are four inches shorter and 50 pounds fatter. I will tell you what, you certainly did not lie son. You are one big son of a gun. I will also tell you something. If you do what I tell you to do, buy into my philosophy and what I am trying to do here,' he said, 'We are going to win some championships together. And if you work hard, you might even get yourself a shot at the NFL.'

"After my dad passed away, I will not say I was a wild child, but I had lost some focus. My dad was a superman. He might as well have worn a cape. My father could fly as far as I was concerned and my brothers and sisters will attest to that as well. I never thought or felt that there would be a man that would ever have that type of influence or effect on me in my life, that I would think could actually sprout wings or a cape and fly. But Joe Taylor certainly was — he certainly came the closest. He was certainly in the same mold as my father, and he was the first man other than my father, outside of my immediate family, or some male elders, that I grew up under and actually respected.

"Coach Taylor was a tough love kind of man but he was nurturing and I understood his message. It took me a minute or two to buy in. I would call home, and I was a little frustrated at times, as I was not used to someone talking to me in a particular manner that I was spoken to. Sometimes I was frustrated and I would tell my brothers, Mark and Matthew specifically, the ones closest in age to me, the two football players, I would tell them, 'Man, I am not used to this. I want to say something.' And my brothers would tell me, 'Keep your mouth shut. Keep your mouth shut and do not say anything. He is harder on you than anybody else for a reason. It is because he sees something more in you. He sees something greater in you.' Mark and Matthew said to me, 'You need to worry when he starts to ignore you. That is when you have a problem. He is on your behind because: A, he cares, and B, he sees something greater in you.' I immediately bought in. That was when the light bulb went off that he was a special man. I mean, I was not too trusting, but after the counseling session from my brothers, I understood that he was in my life for a reason. I was no angel. There were some bumps along the road. I broke some rules and I pushed the envelope.

"There were times I remember going on road trips with Coach and curfew was big for him. It was not necessarily that he was worried about his boys getting into some trouble. It was about a gauge and a barometer in discipline. I remember going to play Morris Brown in '94 in Atlanta, Georgia, another historically black college. After the game, my uncle came to the hotel and he was all excited to see me. He lived in New York and he had moved back to the South. We won and my uncle came to pick me up. I introduced him to the coach and everybody. Coach Taylor gave me that look like, 'Do not blow curfew, son.' So we went out and I made the choice to ignore curfew. He saw me coming in right around the time that we needed to pack up and get on the bus to get to the airport. He said, 'Son, you are going to pay. Not only are you going to pay but your teammates are going to pay.' We got back to Hampton University and he said go in the locker room and put on your clothes. He made us run the equivalent of what most college teams would run in four months. He ran us until we were blue in the face and our tongues were wagging like a dog on the Iditarod. He was upset with me and he was disappointed because again, here I am making knucklehead mistakes. I made a knucklehead choice. I do not believe in the word mistake. I made a choice to go against what he was teaching us. It was not so much about the curfew. It was about following directions and listening. I chose not to follow and there are consequences that come along with that — Again, a lesson learned. Coach Taylor was big on discipline. He was big on respect.

"There was always a reminder that there are consequences for breaking rules. It could have been a morning fun run, which was anything but fun. I found myself on many morning fun runs with him and his wife and the dog around Armstrong Field. One time he ran me so bad that his wife said, 'Joe, that is enough. Joe, you are going to kill that poor boy!' As I am running the track, he is doing his slow jog and every time I passed him he would say, under his breath, 'I hope you die.' But I knew he did not want me to die. I knew better than that. It was the total opposite. He wanted me to live forever but there was a lesson. There was a lesson, and the lesson was — 'You did this to yourself. I am just the reminder of what you did. And let this pain and discomfort you are going through, be a reminder of the choice, not the mistake, but the choice you made, and how it is counterproductive to what I am teaching. Your father taught you something, he left, and you got off track a little bit. Well, you know what? Not with me. I am going to get you back on track. I am not going to let you get off the beaten path. We are going to continue what your dad taught you. We are going to continue along those lines.' Without him ever even knowing my father or what his philosophy was. He detected that I came from something that had a lot more good in it than anything else.

"There were episodes where I broke curfew before. And there were reminders or consequences that we had to stay in line. Sometimes he did stop talking to me and that is when I panicked. But he would always send someone to me. I did not know at the time but he would send Coach Parham who is an amazing mentor. He is now the assistant head coach at Morgan State. He was a graduate assistant at the time, but he and I, we hit it off. He was a tough love type of guy but I think that he saw and understood my potential. He also saw what I could do and that I was not a bad guy, I was just a little bit of a knuck-lehead and my maturation process was a little slower than maybe they would have liked it to be.

"I remember there was a rap artist that came down to Hampton University. He was a good friend of mine, a famous rap artist, and I decided to miss a practice. Now this is really pushing the envelope. I missed a practice to hang out with my buddies, these rap artists, and I mean world famous rap artists. So I went to hang out with the Wu Tang. I tried to use the excuse that my knee was messed up, a little swollen, but certainly I should have still been in practice, even if I did not practice. I should have still been there to continue to support my team. Well I decided to go hang out with the rap group and we had some fun. It was a great time, but I paid for it — I paid for it. That is when I thought I really messed up — I thought this is it. He is ready to let go. I never saw him that mad in my life. I did not think that a human could be that mad. I tried to avoid him. Coach Parham came to my dorm room and told me, 'Swinson, Coach Taylor is furious.' I thought, 'Oh man, whatever.'

"A couple of my buddies who knew Coach knew his psychology. We knew when he was mad and he was trying to send a message or trying to scare you or when he was just absolutely fed up with you. I had never seen the 'I am fed up with you' Joe Taylor. Well I saw it this time because I kept getting calls, and kept getting calls, and kept getting calls. I am like, 'Oh crap, I screwed up.' Finally I had to go pay the piper. Finally he called me in my dorm — he never called a player in his own room. He said, 'Son, meet me at the stadium now. Now!' And he used some colorful language.

"I went into Holland Hall. I am telling you, there was smoke com-ing out of his ears and his eyes must have rolled back in his head. He was the Exorcist that day. I am 6' 6" so I am quite a bit taller than him. He put his head in my chest. He said, 'You want to fight me? You want to go?' And he poked me in my chest. I thought he was poking me with a metal rod. I was like, 'holy shit, this hurts.' And I took it – I knew I screwed up. He said, 'Son, you want to go? I will kick your behind, son!' I was like 'Oh, crap, this is bad.' He said, 'Get your clothes on or go home, and I am not f...... playing with you!' He said, 'Get your clothes on and meet me outside or go home! I was like, 'Man, Coach Parham cannot even save me now.' Coach Parham looked at me like this is bigger than me son. So we get outside and my knee was bad, I just had a cortisone shot and it was still swollen. But that was still no excuse for not being at practice. I said, Coach, I cannot run. He said, 'Then roll!' So he made me log roll the equivalent of one mile. A mile is 5,280 feet. Do you know how long that is? That is 1,760 yards. He made me log roll a mile! I threw up, I had no balance — I had no sense of even where I was. He was merciless and relentless. However, I never 'cussed' him. I said to myself, 'You are an asshole and you deserve this, and he should have sent you home. You did this. He is just the reminder of you screwing up.' I understood what self-reflection was. I never made an excuse — I did it. It woke me up. And it scared me to death because the last thing I wanted was for him to turn his back on me. I understood how important he was and I understood the message and the messenger. I knew it was greater than him and it was greater than me.

"There is a quote in the Bible that says "And a servant who knew his Lord's will and prepared not himself, neither did according to his will, shall be beaten with many stripes." (Saint Luke 12-47) This refers to the individual that knows better but chooses not to do better. Well, I knew better and chose not to do better, so I was beaten with many stripes. That was one big life lesson. A lot of times we talked about the subtitle of the book, Success is an Inconvenience. It certainly is, but again, it is all relative. Many will come, but only few will be chosen, and those who are chosen will choose themselves. We say that, to say this day — that inconvenience — some people say I do not want to deal with this structure. I do not want any part of this. The ones who choose themselves, they supersede that inconvenience, and that is when they have success, when you supersede the inconvenience — what appears to be an obstacle.

"When I was hanging out with those rap artists that day, that is when I thought one of two things. I was either going to get into a fight with my head coach, and he was going to kill me, because I did not have the rage that he had. I saw it in his eyes and I thought I am dead, or I am gone. I guess that was the first time he scared me. There was such uncertainty and I was off balance. I did not know what he was going to do, but I knew he was poking me in my chest like there were two metal rods. His fingers were metal rods. It was like, 'All right, that is it with screwing up. That is it. I am done.'

"I was probably disciplined more than most at Hampton. I guess I needed it more than most and maybe sometimes it was just to test me too — just to test me to see if I was going to be able to supersede that adversity. I superseded a lot, and I have to give a lot of credit for that, a great deal of credit for anything that I was able to overcome, to Coach Taylor's philosophy that he instilled in me. He is living proof of his philosophy. You are what you teach and he is going to live forever in us. You would be a fool not to pass this down or pass it forward. How do you not share this with somebody, what he gave us? You just cannot let it go. You have got to give it to somebody else, whether it be coaching youth football or baseball or anything else. It is all relative to life.

"My crowning moment, and one of the ways I share what I learned, is with my son. I have the opportunity to raise my son as a single father. I am a single man and my son spends a significant amount of time with me. His mom is equally involved in his life as well. He is eleven and he thinks he knows Coach Taylor. He heard me talking to him the other night on the phone. He was excited like he knew him, like they had spent time together because he hears me talk so much about him.

"Sometimes I think I messed up just to spend more time with him, in a very sick way. I was okay with the perceived abuse because it was not abuse. It was just like I can get closer to this man. I can really suck up some more of his wisdom. He was not Paul Bear Bryant, or Joe Paterno, or Bobbie Bowden in the sense that you can go in his office and strike up a conversation about anything. You did not need an appointment, you can go in there and sit down and just talk. He would always have something to say. I remember him talking about Bullet Bob Hayes. I guess he was a sprinter and Bob Hayes also played with the Dallas Cowboys. I do not know if the story goes he was in college or he was in the NFL at the time, but Bob Hayes caught a pass and he was running down the sidelines, and everybody was just like 'Go, Bob, Go' — the gentleman was fast. The guy that was covering him was fast, just as fast as Bob Hayes, equally as fast. He was running down the sidelines and he was gaining on Bob Hayes, and as the story goes, Coach Taylor said that Bob Hayes is just blazing down the sidelines and the man is gaining on him. He is gaining and everybody is yelling 'Go, Bob, Go.' He said that all of a sudden the guy that was chasing him, was right there ready to tackle him, and he stopped. He is like what the heck, why did you stop? You almost had him, you were right there. You were ready to make the tackle. And he said, 'Man, do you know who that is? That is Bob Hayes, I cannot catch him.' So he never believed that he could catch him, so his failure was already implanted in him. There was never any success that was going to manifest itself from his God-given talent because he never believed that he could catch him. So he quit. He had a self-defeatist attitude and said, 'I cannot catch Bob Hayes.' He was defeated by his mind.

"Coach Taylor used to talk about pain, discomfort and injury and how different they all were, how they all had their own life, and how neither was related to the other. Sometimes you wake up in the morning and you feel a degree of discomfort. But that should not stop you from getting out of bed and going to work. Sometimes you might stub your toe in the morning and feel some discomfort — that is pain, and that might slow you up, but it does not stop you from getting out of the bed, going to work in the morning, and setting an example for your kids. You might not only stub your toe, you might even slip and fall and break your leg. Then you are injured. Some people would just wrap it up and still go to work. This might seem extreme and unrealistic. But look at Tiger Woods. He won the US Open on a broken leg! Success is an inconvenience. What does it take to be number one in the world?

"There used to be a big sign over the locker room door, with a bunch of acronyms, but I remember this one specifically — NEAT, No Excuses Accepted Today. I know that in order to be successful you have to be NEAT. You cannot accept any excuses. I was raised being self-reflective and introspective. I knew I was the one responsible for whatever I did, or chose not to do. I had to own it. I could not make any excuses. So, I made no excuses for my behavior and choices. When I missed practice, I knew that I had done it, so I took the punishment — No Excuses Accepted Today. No excuses accepted any day. Death is not even an excuse. It might slow you up but it cannot be an excuse.

"He used to tell us, 'I won't accept any excuses because if I do, I will be justifying your failure. This program is not designed to justify failure.' Coach Taylor taught us, instilled in us, and fortified in us, there is no ceiling. I tell my son all the time. The bar is high, son, the bar is high. Do not tell me what you cannot do. There is going to be some difficulty along the way. There is going to be some pain, there is going to be some discomfort. There might be some injury along the way, but still there are no excuses accepted today or any day. That is what I remember and that is what I take with me — just one of many, many philosophical aspects of what Coach Taylor instilled in all of us.

"The year prior to my attending Hampton University they did not have a good season. They were 2-9 as I remember. We were 9-2-1. He turned that program around in one year! I remember that we were always prepared and he always used to say things like, 'You have to be cerebral, son. If you are out there, you call yourself student athletes. We are students first, and if you are the type of football player that does not go to class, sleeps in, goes to class late, and is not prepared, then how can you be a good football player? We have a playbook as thick as a New York City phone book. I need the best students on my football team because those are the best thinkers. We are training you to think the proper way. How are we going to trust that you are going to execute the plays we are teaching you, if you are not training your mind to be the best student you can be? If you are missing class, I cannot trust you and put you out there. I do not care how big and how strong you are. You can have a body like Tarzan, but your brain could just be mush, and that is not the athlete I want. I want to go out there with a cerebral athlete. I want to go out there with the most prepared cerebral athlete. I want to go out there with a man that is committed from the top of his head to the bottom of his feet, mind, body and soul.

Those are the young men that I want to bring out there with me to win games. Those are the ones that I am preparing, not the ones that have an excuse for not going to class. Not the ones that have an excuse for not suiting up, getting their ankles taped, or getting treatment instead of being on the football field. It starts in the classroom. I want cerebral athletes. I want thinkers, people that are going to know what to do in critical situations.'

"He was not just about Xs and Os and winning football games. He was about winning in life and he understood that it went far beyond the football field. It went far beyond Hampton University. This was just another stepping stone as young men, as parents, as athletes, as citizens, as people in our community, as young black men. And certainly there were not just young black kids on the football team, everybody, whether they were pink, white, black, or pink with purple polka dots.

"I wish that experience could have lasted forever, but it was time for us to go ahead. 'You got enough between what your mama and daddy gave you and what I gave you — now go ahead. I gave you enough. Now go ahead and be men. You are going to be all right.' And most of us were. Most of us are. There are some doctors, and there are some lawyers, and there are some potential senators in the works that played for him.

Chapter 9

A WINNING PHILOSOPHY:
BE BETTER THAN THE GUY NEXT DOOR

We have created a very successful program. Over the past thirty years we have won many championships and seen many, many players graduate and move on to lead very productive lives. They further their education, obtain professional degrees, contribute to society, get married, and create strong families. We are often asked how we accomplish all this?

We believe that the foundation of our success lies in our commitment to the young men in our programs. We are not just about the Xs and Os. While is it important to win games, it is not our highest priority. We do not want our players only to be champions on game day. We want them to be champions every day.

ACCOUNTABILITY

Our program is based upon accountability. A man has to trust that you are going to do your job so he can do his. If you miss your block, I am not going to make my play and I might get hit really hard. We know that these men are ready to bleed for each other. They do that because they trust each other and know that everyone is putting out one hundred percent.

Well, accountability starts with us. We are hired to teach these young men and help them develop. So the buck stops with us, the coaching staff. We have to be an example. We have to model the type of attitude and behavior that we want to see in our players. I tell my coaches that they are hired to solve problems, not to create them. They have to have their "head on straight," and have the right attitude. I tell them that we have to be better than the people next door where they live. What I mean by this is that back home in the local community, you often hear the neighbors screaming, yelling and getting upset. We have to be better than that. Our players have to be better than that. We need to be centered, focused, and emotionally mature. Everything was probably confrontational and loud where some of these young men grew up. You know, that is the norm in a lot of the neighborhoods and that's how they learn to handle situations. You get irate. You get loud. So, we have to be better than those people next door back home. I don't believe in getting excited. My dad told me a long time ago, "Son, die any death, but don't ever get excited to death." And all he was simply saying is, "Always be in a thinking mode." All right?

Because whatever happens, good, bad, or indifferent, it's for that moment. All right, get all you can out of it. But don't stay there. I know that when we are looking at the bigger picture it is our responsibility to inspire these young men, then that changes how we respond to them, especially during adversity. I let the coaches know. We hire you to solve problems, not to create them. So, it's important that they understand the bigger picture —it's all about developing young people and developing future leader. Our goal is that once they leave here, they're in a position to be productive people who positively impact people in their communities.

THE HUMAN ELEMENT

It is important to realize that we are building on the human element and enriching the human spirit. We organize our program around discipline, education, structure, focus, personal development, responsibility, consistency, trust, and a deep love of God. We are about developing leaders! Of course we teach football plays and strategies. We have lots of meetings, discussions and practice around the Xs & Os. But it is important to realize that a total focus on plays and an obsession with winning does not yield the results we have achieved. Of course, you can win some championships with that limited ap-proach, but we are looking at the big picture. We are about total success in every aspect of life. We define success as a good education, a good career, and caring about others. We strive to develop men who have an open heart, love others, and maintain a strong spiritual self with values based upon honesty, integrity, service to others, compassion, and forgiveness.

I think it's a sin to go to a ballgame and just wish that you will win. Do what you need to do all week, be a champion all week, then, when you get to the game, you already are a champion. So many coaches put so much em-phasis on Xs and Os that they forget that it's a human being that's got to do it. It is the human being that has to take all of that bright scientific diagnosis and scribbling that you put on that board and apply it on the field.

You do not get to be a champion by sitting around and wishing you could be great. Some people say, "Boy I wish I could have done that." I wish – it's a "w" word, but it's not the right one. There is a correct "w" word. It's called WORK! I remember one time taking a group of Upward Bound kids to a concert. There was a young lady playing the piano — she was really great. Afterwards we were allowed to go behind the curtains and speak with her. We introduced ourselves and spoke for a while. A lot of the kids were saying, "I wish I was as good as you." They kept saying, "I wish" so many times she finally went into a rage. She got up and showed us her hands, "See how raw my fingers are? Don't ever tell anybody you wish to be good. You work to be good!" There are no shortcuts. If you want to be an All American, go find out what it takes.

Everything that you want to be, somebody already is. Go and read or talk to people who have accomplished what you want to accomplish. Find out what they did to get there. If you want it bad enough, do it! Don't wish for it —work for it! If you want a great result, then put something great in. Whatever you put in, you're going to get out.

So you have to develop the people in your organization, not just always be talking about plays. We work hard to keep our kids focused on What's Important Now (WIN). If you do what's important now, by the time you get to the season, you are ready. You can't circumvent what's important now. You can't jump over basic steps. It's a body of work. Those guys who make All American, who are winning the bowl games, it did not start that day. When you go and watch a great movie by Steven Spielberg, it did not just start when the curtain went up. Hell, you know a lot of hours went into that.

Jonathan Hunt, one of my players from the early days at Hampton shared a very interesting story that relates here. I never knew about this until we did this book.

"We were having a great season we just had a big victory the night before and I was out celebrating into the early morning hours. It was nothing wild, but I was out having a good time much later than I should have been. Well as I came back, I was walking across campus and I was passing the stadium, it was approximately 5:00 am. I saw somebody on the track. I found that a little unusual because it was still really dark outside. I get a little closer. Coach Taylor is very fit and he has a very distinctive profile. You have to imagine this as 20 years ago — he really worked out, slim waist, barrel chest, and very authoritative. I looked across the tracks, I saw this man jogging in a sweat suit, one of those rubber sweat suits to keep you warm, and it was the Coach. I sat and watched him for about ten or fifteen minutes go about his normal workout and early morning routine. Maybe it was a time for him to mentally take a break and get away, but I found it exceedingly impressive that he was up, and out, doing what he needed to do before anybody else even thought about being up and out. Now that is quite commonplace but his level of dedication — he had a family at that time. He had a wife and two young kids. I knew how much time that I put in, and I knew how much time that it required for us to win in the fashion that we were winning. So, to see him doing even more than that hit me in my heart. It was a real gut check. "Am I doing all that I can do to get to the next level, to get the team to the next level, to win things that I really want to win?"

"I have never told him this. But after I saw him that morning, and it was relatively early in the fall, from that day forward I changed the way in which I practiced. You probably wonder how does somebody change the way they practice. Did you try harder? No because you have to go back to the earlier statement that you cannot give more than 100%. So I still gave 100%, mentally and physically. This is what I did. I changed the dynamic within which I practiced and it elevated my game.

"Every football team, every position has its elite player and the weak link. Nobody wants to be the weak link, but everybody usually knows who that elite player is. One thing I did differently was this. From that day forward, when we scrimmaged against each other, which we did constantly, I demanded that I practice against the best on our team. Whoever he was, I chose the best. So we were having a running drill, the best was on the other side. If we had a pass drill, the best was on the other side. If were went against the defensive line, I demanded the best. Every single day, and the individuals that I practiced against, both of them were drafted in the NFL. One went to the Jacksonville Jaguars; one went to the New York Giants, every single day to improve my game. I would never practice against freshmen. I would never lineup and do any kind of individual practice or individual drills with anybody that was below me in years or below what I thought was the elite. Because I knew, the person on the other side arguably was better than me and arguably could beat me at any given moment.

"As a result, I had to practice consistently at a higher level. As a result, by the time I got to a game, when I am playing opposite a sophomore or a freshman or somebody who is not that good, or even somebody who was good, I never played against anybody who was better than the individual that I practiced against in the way we would practice. It is a cliché, people say, "Oh, the games are not easy but the practices are going through the motions." The manner in which we practiced was arguably harder than the way a game was conducted. There were fewer rest breaks, there was more confusion injected, and there were more physical and mental challenges placed upon us as a team. The result was that when we played the game, it appeared rote. It appeared easy! This all happened because I was inspired by Coach Taylor running around that track so early in the morning."

FAITH

I am a very spiritual person with a deep personal relationship with our Lord and Savior Jesus Christ. That is how we stay calm. We do draw strength and comfort from the Lord. If we do have a tough loss, I talk to the Lord. I say, "I know you have blessed me. But, today, this one wasn't for us, you know." This helps keep me in the right attitude, the right frame of mind. When you look at the overall record, it's somewhere around 230 wins out of 317 games, which is 75 percent. That is still good. You have to remember the big picture. I think a lot of coaches sometime get out of their tree, lose their composure, because they really don't understand the big picture. They get too caught up in just winning games.

I do believe that my faith in the good Lord certainly helps me to be a better leader with a clear head. I trust the Lord to guide my life and take me to where I need to be. I look to the Lord to protect me. I need to constantly pressure everyone around me— coaches and players alike, but I do not want to create too much anxiety and tension in them. In competition, anxiety is always present but it must be manageable in order to be successful.

We present that perspective to our players, but we do not shove it down their throats. We create a spiritual community in which Obedience and the Love for God is present. If our players want to embrace these ideas, values and practices, it is here for them. It is totally up to them. Most of them do. We started a Gospel choir composed only of student-athletes.

I have been in games I won that I probably shouldn't have. I remember back in the '80s, playing a game against a team in Charlotte, N.C. We were down and there is no way that we should have won that game. The other team kept throwing the football. You know, every time you throw the ball, if you don't complete it, the clock stops. Well, every time the clock stopped, that was working in our favor. So, they gave us enough time to go back out there and get into field goal range and we kicked the field goal to win the game.

We got back that Saturday night real late. And I told the people at Church the next morning, "Boy the Lord was with us on that one." I was the first one at the Church that next morning. I was there so early they thought I was opening up the Church! I didn't think we should have won that one.

EMPHASIZE THE POSITIVE

If you are putting good things into your players' minds, you will get positive results from them. Darrell Mudra was one of my coaches and mentors. He had a real innate ability to create a sense of worth in people. He helped people realize that they were not a mistake — that the good Lord put them here for a reason. They had a true purpose in life. You saw them go about their daily routine with so much more zest and zeal. They started getting excited about life. When you put an individual in a situation to have little successes, he looks forward to bigger successes. I always tell my coaches, "Find something everyday for which you can praise him. I don't care what it is — it can be any little thing."

If it has to be something small like, "You look really good today with your pants pressed and neat," praise him. But if he brings you a test paper and he got an A, don't just share it with you and him. Take that paper and show it to the team. Get on the phone and call his mother or father. And say, boy this guy is awesome. Everybody feels good with a pat on the back.

Here is a memory from Dr. Timothy Benson who also played at Hampton during those early years.

Dr. Timothy Benson

"I remember when we would be coming home from a trip and the only light on the bus that was on would be mine, because I was doing my homework. And Coach would say, 'Awe, folks, if it wasn't for Benson, the whole team would have a 2.0 GPA.' He would try to highlight what he thought were good behaviors. He acknowledged people and that was something you appreciated."

So, we try to find ways to create moments where we can praise people. The more you praise them, the more they're going to want to be praised. And when they get it, they're going to remember what they got the praise for. This year (2012) I gathered all my seniors and spoke with them. I said, "I am really proud of you all. Many of you never thought you would make it this far. You have accomplished a lot by getting here and making it to your senior year. Now, I want you to do more. I want you to be a mentor for our younger players. Help them do their best." I am so moved by what I am seeing. This group of young men has taken our team to another level. They are showing up early for practice and working with the younger players. They are stepping up as leaders to inspire others. This is really a wonderful thing to see.

We are here to lift up these young men, not to tear them down. We care about every aspect of their lives, especially the academic part. We want them to attend class and graduate. We believe that in the long run if they think, "I can," then they will accomplish great things. However, if they are full of doubt and have been treated negatively, we don't see how that can help them. We are always telling them, "When you go back home, you can't be like that guy next door. If you still look the same as the guy next door who didn't go to college, and nobody can tell the difference between you and him, then, you are wasting your time and ours. The program is bigger than anybody, including all of us coaches. So, we don't allow things that are considered demeaning. We hold a high standard. We tell our athletes, "Don't embarrass yourself, the school, your parents, or this program."

Of course, sometimes they're going to do some things that they shouldn't do. But you don't embarrass them in front of everybody. We bring them into our office, sit them down privately, and let them know what we think about their behavior.

The important thing to emphasize is that we do not ever brow beat these kids — that happens too much as they grow up. We are always trying to help them get rid of all the negative programing that they may have. We emphasize how they have to reach inside and flush all that negative programming out of their system. We try to stay away from all that negativity. Our message, right from the very start is, "You are somebody and you can be successful!" Like I said, we are always looking for ways to motivate them. If you believe in them and help them to believe in themselves, and give them a chance to perform at the highest level, you don't know what they can achieve.

The word "fan" is a root word for fanatic. And the more you understand human nature, the more you understand how to deal with it in a way in which it doesn't cause you to lose your cool. Because the louder you get, the louder the audience is going to be. Whether it's the players, the media, parents or the administration. This year I thought we had a solid year (2011 at FAMU). We were seven and four. We were up 21 to 0 at Homecoming and we ended up losing the game. It was a beautiful day, a great crowd, and a great atmosphere. It was awesome. There were two minutes left in the third quarter. And it was 21 to nothing. We lost 28-27. So, they scored 28 points basically in fifteen minutes!

Well, to say the least, I was disappointed. Well, rather than to go off and start yelling at everybody for blowing the game, I just said, "I lost that game." At that time, everybody was looking for somebody to take the blame. So, all we did was just take the air out of all of that negativism — all of it. It was a tough situation. I did not want to make it worse by pointing fingers. So rather than saying, "Well, if he hadn't fumbled that ball, or the refs weren't any good, or one of the coaches called a bad play," I just put it on me. Now that kind of tempers everything out. Even though I might not have felt that way. We fumbled six times and had ten penalties. Well that's a pretty good prescription for losing. But, it was important to move forward. You have to get past where you are. And the only way to get past such a difficult moment is to bring resolution — to bring closure. So, to bring resolution, I went ahead and took the blame so that everybody else could feel better about himself. I could have blown up and said to the defense, "Look, I don't care if the offense didn't do anything. We didn't give up 21 points in a whole game. Now we're giving up 28 points in 15 minutes? You guys missed tackles; the same guy that you covered all day and he didn't get one catch, and now he's catching the ball!" No, that would have only made things worse. So, those are the kind of games you look at and say, "As many opportunities as we had to win, that was one of those days that the good Lord had touched us on the shoulder and said, 'This is not going to be your day.'

As a team, you have to be able to move forward. And the only way to move forward is by bringing closure! I never said, I didn't fumble those five times. I didn't drop those six balls. I didn't create those ten penalties. I said, "I didn't have you all prepared to play 60 minutes." For the rest of the year, that became our theme — to play 60 minutes. I did that because the players evidently thought the game was over. Mentally they were out of it. They felt the game was over because they had such a big lead. They were already looking at where they were going after the game.

So, you take a negative and turn it into a positive. I've been coaching 29 years, but that was probably the worst I've ever felt after a game. I've lost some before. But didn't feel anywhere as bad as that because, in everybody's mind, including mine, that's the one we should have won. After homecoming, we won four straight games. And one of those teams we beat was a team, which we had not beaten in ten years. Maybe that loss gave us the focus and determination to go on and win all those other games. Who knows? I just had to give it to the good Lord for allowing us to move forward from the homecoming loss.

So, if you're in this game long enough you are going to see a lot of great moments. And there are going to be some teachable moments. But, the important thing is that you have to get over whatever happened. In fact, we have a 24-hour rule. I don't care what happened, win, lose, or draw, after 24 hours we're into the next game.

When your back's against the wall, that's when the real substance of a man comes out. I don't believe that adversity develops character. I think it reveals character — if you do have character, you will get through tough times. It may be bitter, it may be painful, but you get through it! You have got to learn and move on. If you don't, it becomes catastrophic.

Here is another good example of what I am talking about. If a kid screwed up, he knows he's screwed up. Everybody in the stand lets him know he screwed up. Then when he comes to the sideline, he's waiting for you to tell him how not to screw up again. He does not need you in his face being confrontational and irate. Because if you do, as bad as he's feeling, now he is going to feel worse after you finish yelling at him. You see, in my mind that assistant coach, is the last line of refuge or salvation. We do not want to destroy a man's spirit.

Jonathan Hunt has some memories that relate to different approaches to coaching.

Jonathan Hunt

"In high school, the coach was a local guy, an ex NFL player, a real hard-nosed, hard charger. We lost a game to his alma mater in another town, not badly but we lost. He made us walk home. This was a different era; this was in the 80s so things that are an affront now were no big deal then. He made us walk home.

"In college, before Joe Taylor, the offensive coordinator at our school, if you made a mistake, missed the block, dropped a pass that you clearly should have caught, ran the wrong route, or made mental errors, he often took that opportunity to berate you. Not in the typical like, "Come on, what are you doing, focus!" Not in that normal way, but personal attacks about you, your family, etc. It was the worst coaching that I had ever seen in my life.

"Coincidentally, under any other coach that I had, we never really won. Now with good coaching, better teaching and mentoring, and the drive and dedication to better myself on the field and off the field, my grades got better, I was physically stronger, and faster and the team was phenomenally better. The second year that he was there, we attained the best season in Hampton University history. We went thirteen and one, and only lost to the National Champion. That does not happen by accident, the time and effort that he put into us was extraordinary. Now he demanded a lot of you. What he expected was far and above the norm and anything we were used to."

ON DISCIPLINE

We are dealing with a lot of young men from all aspects of life. We believe that, you cannot take people somewhere if they don't know where they are going. So every week we create a mission statement. Every week we make it crystal clear as to what is expected, because it's been proven, if you do this, you're going to give yourself a chance to win.

I cannot understand when coaches do not cover certain things, and when a kid does not perform well, they are jumping all over him. When players are messing up on the field, I look to the coach. I believe, "You have either taught it or you're allowing it. There's no difference." And that's a big reason why I don't jump up and down, and start ranting and raving at players messing up on the field. I just look to the coach.

We believe that structure, discipline and clearly stated rules yield success. These young men need discipline along with love and support. They will test you and you have to be ready to respond with love and strength.

Joseph Manly, my former player at Hampton, who is now a Marketing Rep for a large diagnostic imaging company, remembers at time when I was pretty tough with the team. He shared this with us.

Joseph Manly

"We were playing Virginia State, which was an away game, and everybody, with the exception of myself and my roommate, everybody took the towels from the hotel. Coach Taylor came out as we are about to leave to go home. We had dinner and were looking forward to going home. He walks in and said, 'If you all are leaving with something that you didn't come here with, go get it now and return it.' Nobody moves. And so we go outside to the bus. So now he said, 'Everybody get your bags, come out and empty your contents on the ground.' You know those towels are starting to line up almost two layers deep. And so then he's embarrassed. We even see trainers pulling out clocks and towels. I guess nobody really thinks about taking hotel towels. But he sees all the stuff coming out. We used to have what was a fun run on Sunday, the day after the game. You would try to run out the scar tissue or whatever was created from the previous day. It was usually like a mile. He's standing there with his hands crossed and his glasses, and his thick mustache. He's just looking. He's not saying a word, but the hotel manager's is next to him. He, after the towels piled up, he was like, 'Look, bring your track shoes. It ain't gonna be no fun run. You ain't never going to forget this day!' We did like twenty-six 200s the next day. People were cramping, I mean, it was crazy. He ran us to death, ran us to death. I mean, he was thoroughly embarrassed, so he definitely ran us to death."

It is important to realize that in our society rules are not put in place to harm people. Rules are put in place to protect those who want to do what's right. So we have rules and we have to be consistent with them. Once we have defined our rules, we are going to make sure that we are doing the right thing and enforcing them. For example, we can't put a guy out there who misses practices and misses classes with a guy that does everything right. We want them to trust each other and trust the program. We cannot accomplish that by being inconsistent. Once again, we don't punish a man by sending him away. We are protecting those that want to do the right thing.

For example, there is this one guy who went to his grandmother's funeral this past Friday. Here's a kid who's a pre-med biology major, on the Dean's list. He is the strongest guy on the team — he benches over 500 pounds. He's an ordained minister and we never had any social problems with him. I cannot line him up with a guy that does not have any of those qualities. Because if I do, I'm confusing the guy that is doing what is right. I do not want the guy who is doing the right things to be thinking, "If am doing everything right, and this guy is not, and we are getting the same treatment, then something's wrong." So, as coaches, we must be cognizant of that.

Our expectations are not a mystery. We make everything very clear and simple. We test everyone so we know how he is doing. We look at the film and grade every play. It is in black and white. Sometime a coach can get so excited about a guy. "You know Coach Taylor, he didn't do it right in practice, but, Coach he's going to get it right at game time." How do you know that?

Look at the film. If he can't execute in practice, what makes you think he will in the game under pressure? If he did it right, that means yes, he is going to get it right. But don't get so caught up in "he's from such and such neighborhood, or he's somebody's son." His father may have been great, but that does not mean he is. Now, if you put him in a situation and he performs, then you can believe the film. We grade practices. We grade games. Each player who can win seven out of ten plays has a chance to start.

In addition, we cannot play someone because we like his mama, or we like his family. We have to really be fair and being fair means having rules. The rules have to be clear. Our job is to keep telling them to make sure they understand what we are doing. Education is this: when you really think they got it tell them again. That is what it takes. Let them know what's expected. Teach them what's expected.

KEEPING IT SIMPLE

We do not want anybody in this program, not even for one day, trying to figure out, "What do I do? What do we do next?" Sometimes they say we kill too many trees because we put it all on paper. It's there and it's visual. This is important because some people learn more from a visual mode. We do not want anybody saying, "I just didn't know." We want you to know. We're going to make sure you know. If you don't know, you didn't want to because we make sure that you know. We don't want to be coming out here with a cap that has three brims. You know, like you don't know which way to go. This is not a random free for all! We have a method and a process. If it's boring, that's good. That's good because again we want to keep it simple. And we want everybody locked in and understanding what we are doing and where we are going. Winning usually comes down to the team that made the fewest mistakes. So we are a stickler for keeping it simple. And that's why when we talk to them, we look for the best way to simplify things.

We are different that many of the teachers you find on college campuses. Sometimes teachers think that if everyone fails my test, I am tough and a good teacher. Well, we want everybody to pass and get an A. We want our kids to know exactly what we're doing. We want them to know everything in this program. We do give tests every Thursday during the season on our game plan. If you don't pass, you don't play. So, I'm not like those professors up there who sit back and get excited if everybody passes the test and worry that it was too easy. We want our test to be easy because we want everybody to know what's going on. The bottom line is on Saturday if you are evenly matched physically and talent wise, you lose because of mistakes.

So, in conclusion, rules have to be a part of any organization. The country needs laws. Each state needs laws. Cities need laws, each town, each community, and each organization. And, they have to be clear. It has to be understood that nobody's exempt. That is the way to create a strong organization.

RESPECT BRINGS OUT THE BEST

I have had a lot of young men transfer to my program that did not do well at other places. There was this one young man whose household was very loose growing up. Different men were in and out and he did not really know which one was his dad. So, when a coach got in his face, he could not handle it because he did not have respect for men — at least men who were confrontational. So when he transferred to our program, he couldn't get along with his coaches. His mom and his guardian told us, "The coaches were coaching too hard." We got to know him and he began to trust us. He ultimately had a great career. He ended up getting his degree. He was a great player. He just needed the right approach.

Marcus Dixon was another interesting story. He plays for the New York Jets. Marcus was incarcerated for fifteen months. He was accused of rape but the charges were eventually reversed. After Oprah Winfrey got involved, I received a bunch of calls from clergy, lawyers, and judges when he got out of jail. Marcus had a full ride to Vanderbilt, but after that incident they dropped him. They called me because they knew about our program at Hampton. I went to my President and we discussed it. He said, "Well, coach, I trust your gut. If you feel good about it I'm OK with it, I trust you." I did a little research and the first thing I saw was his transcripts with all A's and one B.

I saw all those A's and a B and I was thinking, "He is not a bad decision maker. He's pretty disciplined." So that sold me. However, when he first came to Hampton he didn't trust much because he went through a pretty bad ordeal. He only saw daylight for one hour a day for a period of time while he was incarcerated! So, quite naturally it is going to take him awhile to learn how to trust again.

But, as I have said, we were like clockwork. We were consistent. We didn't change. We could see him each day getting more and more comfortable. Well, to make a long story short, this guy becomes the captain of the football team. In addition, he's on the Dean's list the whole time he's there! He was a free agent with the Dallas Cowboys and now plays with the New York Jets as a Defensive End. Well, he just wanted discipline, a place that he could trust, and he wanted to be successful. He worked hard and earned it. We had a program in place that supported him. What a great story, you know, that's true!

In fact, The New York Times called me just before Thanksgiving — 2011. They did a story on him. They called me and asked, "Why did you take a chance on him?" Well, I told them, "You know, when I saw that transcript plus the people who called me, I trusted them as well." The judges were some real prominent people in Atlanta who were aware of the case and one of the judges knew Marcus. Here is his perspective on our program.

Marcus Dixon

"When I first met him it was just like open arms. I was ten hours away from my hometown and when I got there, as soon as I walked into the building, as soon as I walked into his office, he didn't have to say anything. But when he looked and brought me in, he was telling me, 'You're here. We got you. Everything's going to be okay.' That was the feeling I got as soon as I met him.

"You know how they always say you earn respect. I respected him as soon as I got around him. There's just something about him that made you respect him and listen to everything and hold onto everything he said. That's just the type of coach, the type of man he was. He's a guy that I respected as a father that wasn't my father, but I respected him like that.

"The program was definitely tough. I mean you go through Coach Taylor's program you can make it anywhere. You've had to buy into the program and humble yourself. In high school everybody was 'the man.' The same thing in college — everybody was 'the man.' If you're in the NFL, you were pretty much 'the man' at your school. If you were in a college, had a college scholarship, you were probably 'the man' in high school. With Joe T, if you didn't humble yourself you were constantly going to bump heads with him. A lot of people came and tried to do their own thing. They couldn't buy in — they couldn't handle that. Joe T. was a tough coach. He was a lovable guy, but he's a tough guy and he's not going to let you do just what you want if he knew it was not the best for you. A lot of people couldn't handle that so they would just leave. They would give up. I guarantee they regret that choice.

"I bought into the program. I guess because I was already humbled from what I went through. So when I went to college, I already had the mind-set, 'I can't take anything for granted.' I'm coming in, and given this opportunity of a scholarship after what happened, I'm going to buy into it and I'm going to see what happens. Everyday I kept buying into it. I just kept becoming a better individual, better as a player and better as a student, too.

"Our program was so strict with regards to being on time, working out and, being on top of your schoolwork, I think it prepared me for the NFL. When we have meetings, I'm on time for the meetings. It doesn't matter what times it is. In college, I got up on Tuesday mornings at 6 o'clock doing scholar reports. And did not have a class until 8 o'clock. When I got to the league it was easy. Our whole program was set at such a high standard, now that I'm in the league I don't get it twisted. The NFL has a high standard too. But I feel like coming out of the program with Joe T, I am ready for it.

"The guy was smart and he always had ways of getting to you both mentally and physically, through the whole program for all those four years. It transformed you from that high school kid and football player to a man and a great human being. That's what you got out of Coach Taylor's program. It's like he just took scraps. He took scraps and put them together and just molded this great individual. He prepared you for life outside of college, outside of everything and just had you ready for everything in life.

"I just want everybody to know how he was. He wasn't just a football coach. He was a mentor and a father figure to most. I mean he had guys coming to college who probably didn't have that father figure and he was their father figure. Do you know what I'm saying? He was all that and above. And was he tough? Yeah, he was tough, but at the same time, you bought into it and kept going through it. I'm truly blessed that he gave me a scholarship that allowed me to come play for him. There should be a statue of Joe T at the Hampton University campus."

It does not always work out that way. I received a call from an NFL team Chaplain about a retired player. He spent four years in a university before being drafted in the western part of the country. He finished the pros and this minister called and asked if I would take him into our program as a graduate assistant and help him get into coaching.

I knew that he had a very shady background so; I had to decline that request because of what I knew. So over the years I got this reputation for being a real disciplined person. I like to think that I can save everybody, but I need to feel that they are willing to do their part.

When coaches learn to avoid putting the cart before the horse, they will began to focus on what is really important. When players began to value themselves and see themselves as a tabernacle created by God to do great things, only then can he be coached. I have always been more concerned about who is inside of that uniform more so than how the uniform looks on his body.

Chapter 10

THE CORE VALUES OF A SUCCESSFUL COACH

In a previous chapter we spoke about the need for a good organization and the components that need to be in place in order to provide the proper environment to create a successful experience for our athletes and the university. It is important to remember that any organization is composed of people. Machines, rules or paper are not living entities. Our program is designed to change lives and that can only happen if we have quality people in our coaching positions. In order to help these young men become their best, we have to be our best. Let's now take a look at our coaching philosophy.

A coach is somebody who can take you where you cannot go by yourself. There has to be trust for that to occur. When everyone can trust each other, and know that each person is doing his best, then we can all move forward together. It takes good people to create a good environment. I always say "you get what you inspect, not what you expect." You can't expect to be great if you do not know what it takes to be great. So let's take a closer look beyond the Xs and Os, and inspect what is required to be a great coach in a winning organization.

- **Develop Relationship Skills Based On Authenticity And Genuine Concern**

- **Communicate Effectively**

- **Be Positive**

- **Lead By Example**

- **Be Compassionate**

- **Be Consistent And Disciplined**

- **Be A Visionary**

- **Be Faithful**

- **Volunteer And Contribute To Society**

DEVELOP RELATIONSHIP SKILLS BASED ON AUTHENTICITY AND GENUINE CONCERN

Something I picked up years ago has stayed with me — It's about real manhood. There is a myth about manhood. Most people think that manhood is about three "B's," ball field, bedroom, and billfold. If you are good in all of those three, then you are a man! Nonsense, there is more to being a man than that. Manhood is about relationships, caring about others, and others caring about you. Real men have a purpose. They don't complain about where they are. They contribute and make their life and the lives of others better because they are a part of it. That's what real men do.

A successful coach must have exceptional relationship skills. Coaching is a people business — you must have the ability to communicate, interact, encourage and motivate. What is needed to successfully possess all these skills? A genuine love and concern for humanity. People feel authenticity. If you are acting like you care, but deep in your heart you do not, they will know it. A great coach cannot be in this profession just for the money. The demands are too great. Monetary gain is not enough to sustain the dedication and desire to keep working day after day, year after year, 24/7. It has to be a calling from a real love of people and a desire to help them grow and develop. So, most importantly, you have to be sincere and genuinely care about people.

I have a saying that I use a lot. "We don't care how much you know, until we know how much you care." My college coach, Darrell Mudra, told me, "When you become a coach, if the young men really appreciate what's happening to them, if they are having a good experience, they will show you on game day — because they're going to go out and give you their best effort." If you care about the young men in your program, they will perform.

A successful coach is able to get the players ready for game day and get their mind in the right place. Everybody's attitude must be in the right place. This reminds me of the story we already told about the high school basketball team that lost all their games because they did not feel their coach really cared about them. When an English teacher took over the team, who knew nothing about the game, they won because they felt they were playing for each other, not the coach.

One of the secrets to our success is that we care about our players as people, long before we care about how well they play football. We believe the Good Lord didn't put them here to be a uniform rack. There's a lot more to them than that. We believe that we must use this experience to help these young men discover and realize their real purpose. That is the deeper value in life and our work.

It is always great to hear someone talk about these values, but it may also be helpful to get an outside perspective on this issue. One of my dear friends, Dr. Dennis Thomas has known me for many years. In fact, he was the one responsible for getting me to Hampton University as the Head Coach. Here is what he has to share.

Dr. Dennis Thomas
Commissioner, Mideastern Athletic Conference

"I have known Coach Taylor for quite a few years. When I was the Head Football Coach at South Carolina State, Coach Taylor was Head Football Coach of Virginian Union. We played each other twice, and he beat me both times. When I later became the Director of Athletics at Hampton University, and we were looking for a Head

Football Coach, I recommended that we hire Coach Taylor. It was a great decision.

"A lot of people don't understand or recognize that Coach is a spiritual man. He is a man of sustenance, which encompasses uncompromising integrity, character, and compassion to help people in general — young people specifically. He has a unique ability to motivate young people to be better people and perform to the best of their capability.

"I think a major part of his success derives from the fact that he cares about them, and young people see and feel that by the way he interacts with them. Sometimes his actions are tough love. But the key element is you can get young people to respond much better if they know you care. He has a passion for coaching and having impact on young people, especially influencing the lives of young African-American males.

"A lot of people do not understand, minimize and underestimate the intellectual capacity of young people. They are very perceptive and they know veracity, probity, and sincerity. Once they categorize you in those categories, then that is a conduit to whether or not they are going to connect with you in a real manner. So once young people decide who you are, they are going to make a determination about whether or not they are going to buy into what you are selling. That is why Coach Taylor has had so much success and longevity, because of those values – his rock solid values.

"Coach Taylor is not a person of conveniences. You know, some people will demonstrate character and integrity only when it is convenient. Just like the subtitle of this book, *Success Is An Inconvenience*, character and integrity are not always convenient to maintain. Coach has always demonstrated character and integrity during tough times, and he is unwavering in his belief that young people are here to be educated and become productive citizens for our society. Joe never wavered from that even when he had to be a disciplinarian. It did not make any difference if you were a starter, an All-American, or, as Tim Benson was, an All-American academic — he was the same way. He expected everybody to conduct themselves in a mature manner that would make their family proud and then make the football team proud. Coach Taylor is an authentic man. He is not trying to be somebody he is not. He is Joe Taylor.

"It is very popular now — everybody wants to be committed. The word 'commitment' is spread around a lot and that is all well and good. People may say that they are committed, but the execution part of a commitment comes with courage, and a lot of people do not have the courage to execute on their commitment. At the first sign of adversity, their commitment wanes. Courage has nothing to do with what is going to happen with you politically or publicly. Courage means that no matter what, you are going to execute what you believe in, and let the consequences fall where they may. A lot of people base their commitment on the degree of adversity they face and that should not be a component.

"I firmly believe that successful people share a common denominator — they are grounded with a moral, ethical and spiritual compass. I believe that all successful persons across disciplines are grounded in these qualities. Now you do have successful people who lack these values and when they look in the mirror, they do not see their reflection. They just see the mirror. Their motivations are for the material things in life. Therefore, they will virtually do anything and feel badly about nothing.

"Coach Taylor is just the opposite of that. When he looks in the mirror, he sees a reflection of Joe Taylor and intrinsically it matters what that reflection has done over life's work. People can see and feel that by the way he carries himself and lives his life. He could have been a successful lawyer, a successful doctor, or a successful businessperson, but his passion is coaching."

COMMUNICATE EFFECTIVELY

Communication is really important for a couple of reasons. The media is going to come and they are going to put a microphone in your face. You have to be able to talk, and you have to be able to say the same thing; everybody must be on the same page and say the same thing. Some coaches don't want their assistant coaches talking. I want everybody talking, because that is also growth. You have to communicate with the faculty. They need to know that you are concerned about education. And everywhere I have gone, they know that. The administration is not really aware of what you do. So you have to let them know what you are doing. They want to win, so you have to tell them how and what you need to win. The community, if you want them to come and buy tickets, you have to go out into the community and do community service. Your staff, they have to be aware of what is going on. In addition, your players and your family —you have to be able to relay the program's philosophy and mission to all constituents. It has to be clearly stated, and it has to be unwavering. Again, you are not some separate entity that's on the other side of campus. You are ambassadors. You must take a strong message out to those areas and get them involved with you. They can help you have a successful program, or you can have a bad one if they don't understand what you're trying to do. So you have to communicate with those different areas.

This is so important that you have to do it even when you don't feel like it. I do a lot of speaking in the community and across Florida and Georgia.

The media is always around. If you are one of those guys that would rather not do all this and make the sacrifice, you probably should be in another profession. This is what has to be done —we do not always like it, but we do not have a choice.

The ability to effectively communicate is especially important with the players.

I used to go down the hall and see one of our athletes, Joe Manly, in coach Jerry Holmes' office. They would be sitting there, one-on-one, just going back and forth watching films. Coach Holmes would be explaining to him what had to happen, how it needs to happen, and when it should happen. You could just hear Joe say, "Oh, okay. I have you. I understand now." From those one-on-one sessions, he was able to go out on the field and actually perform, because he understood what his coach was asking him to do. That was an example of a great coach, because he was a great teacher. He could get across to his players what had to happen. Joe went on to have a great career, and, of course, Coach Holmes played and coached in the NFL after a great college career at West Virginia. He was one of the great coaches that has been on my staff of assistants.

So it is the responsibility of a great coach to explain what he wants in a manner that the student understands. How well does he understand what he is supposed to do? That is always more important to me than what the coach knows. So it is important to have effective communication skills and keep things simple. If we get too complicated, we create paralysis by analysis. We need to just keep it simple. The reality is that games are won by what the players know, not by what the coaches know. It is the players who have to execute the play. Just because a coach may have a great conceptual understanding of the game and have some sophisticated plays, it is not worth much if the players cannot understand what he wants them to accomplish and how to put it into action on game day. A lot of coaches get on the board. They're very smart. They have a good delivery. But do your players understand what it is that you're trying to get them to do? I'm not impressed with a coach that has a good gift of gab or a great knowledge of the game, but can't get his players to understand what he wants to accomplish.

BE POSITIVE

Coaches must have character and be positive role models. We are ambassadors. We are the front porches of the University. We are always being observed. People are looking at us, not just on the football field, but when we're downtown, in the grocery stores, wherever we go. It's important that we are positive because we are role models for our players. This is the fourth year that I have been here at Florida A&M University and we have not had any negative publicity, thank God. Neither the players nor the coaches have made any bad social decisions. We need people to respect us so they will want to come to the games and buy tickets.

It is also important to have a positive attitude to be the most effective coach. Always pointing out what's wrong is not the best approach. We want to look for the positive and look for an individual's strengths and build on that. We do not see situations as problems, we seen them as something that needs to be addressed. Reverend Barber will speak about this in the next chapter. It's so obvious that when you think negatively, negative things will happen. However your attitude going into a situation, however you are thinking, creates the outcome. That inner mind is really who you are. If you think a certain way long enough, that's what you are going to become. Good coaching is all about encouraging and empowering others to be their best. We know we have some obstacles against us, but let's not be against ourselves.

I think it is very important to praise each other — it is how we empower people. It's always important to be recognized for doing the right things. I know some coaches like to tear down players and use that authoritative approach. It is my way or the highway. But, I have always believed in praising people and being complimentary. Coaches need to do that with other coaches as well. Coaches have to do that with players, players need to do that with other players, and players should express their appreciation to their coach when they are successful. Since the coach is teaching them to be successful, I think we should give credit where credit is due. It is a way to empower each other. The more confident the organization, the more powerful it becomes.

LEAD BY EXAMPLE

A coach is many things — a mentor, a father figure, an educator, and a disciplinarian. People learn more from how and what you do, than from what you say. You have to "walk the talk" to have any lasting credibility. Young men will naturally follow your direction when they see you living a life of value, integrity and purpose. You will uplift them by your presence and impact in the world. You will have a strong, unspoken, magnetic influence on those around you. You will be surprised to find that people give testimony to the fact that their life was changed because of your influence. It was like the time Jonathan Hunt saw me jogging around the track with my wife at 5:00 am. He was inspired to take his life to the next level. I never said a word. I did not even know he was there.

Because football is such a physical game and proper conditioning is critical to the health, safety and success of each player, I think coaches should work out. They should run, lift, have some kind of regiment where they can lead by example and model the behavior. Do not ask players to do something that you are not doing, because when they see you doing it, then they believe in it more. Personally, I do not want anybody calling in sick — they cannot make it in today because they have an upset stomach or something. Work out and you'll be healthy and you will be here! We don't have sick leave. Your vacation is your sick leave. If you are positive, think positive, act positive, and live positive, you will be healthy. We do not like pity parties. There is enough doldrums and people wanting to go to pity parties. That is not the mind of a champion!

In addition, I think coaches should continue their education in some manner. They need to keep learning and growing. That is what we want to teach our athletes — they are students first and foremost and their education is important. All of our coaches have degrees, many of them have two degrees. Live the life that you want these young men to emulate. I always say to my coaches, "My job is to hire you, but it is your job to keep it." If you lead by example, you will always have a job.

You do not have to reinvent the wheel. Others have reached the level of success that you desire to achieve. Learn from their example as well. You are asking people to learn from you, demonstrate that you are willing to learn from others. Read up on what they did to reach their level of success. I have always told people that Eddie Robinson and Jake Gaither were my idols. I thought they were awesome. Eddie passed about four or five years ago. I definitely went to his funeral because I felt here was a guy that really had it right. He was over 75 years old and he would be at AFCA the National Coaches Convention — sitting up front. He was still eager to learn. He won over 400 games!

I tell people there is a philosophy; I call it the "apple philosophy." If you are ripe you are rotten, if you are green you are growing. That is the way it is with an apple. Here is a guy over 75 years old still trying to grow. He had that green philosophy. Some people think they know it all and you cannot tell them anything. They do not last very long in this profession!

We played each other and I was never supposed to beat any of Coach Robinson's teams at Grambling. They had the biggest, the fastest, and the most talented athletes. We played each other 10 times and he never won. I never wanted to disappoint him. I wanted to let him know, because of him I was trying to get things done the right way. I wanted him to know that I was trying to be as good as he was — to emulate him. He said, "Look I am impressed, now stop whooping me!" I was just so impressed with him that I wanted him to be impressed with what I was doing. I brought him to Hampton one year to talk in my annual clinics. He was a great role model for me, and I wanted to state that publicly.

BE COMPASSIONATE

We have a saying in our football program, "Treat everyone like they are hurting." It is our way of simply saying, "Always be positive towards each other and treat people with compassion." If you knew someone was hurting, you would not jump all over him for being hurt or injured. You would want to find out the source of the problem and the reason they were hurting. I request this of all my coaches: if a young man misses practice, don't automatically jump on him and think that he is careless. Talk to him because maybe he just received a call from home and his mom and dad just broke up, or he just lost a girlfriend, or his grandparents just passed. Look before you jump all over him for missing practice. Let's find out why he has missed practice. This is so important because now we are showing compassion. Especially when this guy has been a real asset to the program and he's normally doing the right thing, if it is not his character to miss, and all of a sudden he is not doing the right thing, find out why. Do not just automatically say, "Well, you didn't make practice, so you're not going to play." Before you fly off the handle and be negative to a guy, find out what's going on — sit down and discuss it with the young man. Sometimes he might just need a shoulder to lean on. He might just need somebody to talk with and listen.

I believe that coaching is like mining. When miners go out digging, they are digging for gold. They aren't digging for anything else. So, in relationships, when you start digging into people's lives, you should look for the best in them — not the worst. Always look for the gold — for the positives. Always try to expound on what the kids are doing right. So, whether they're hurting or not, you always want to be a pleasant person for them. You always want to have a smile. You always want to have a hug. You want to approach them with a positive attitude. This is very important.

BE CONSISTENT AND DISCIPLINED

In order to have a successful coaching career, you have to be consistent in your approach with your athletes, which will result in a consistent winning record. It takes a lot of discipline to hold steadfast to one's values and principles. It is very important to treat everyone the same. We know of course that the outcome sometimes is not going to be the same. But you have to treat everybody the same way. If you favor someone because he can run faster, is a little bit stronger, might catch a little bit better, or throw a little bit more accurately, you will create an environment filled with jealousy and envy. You want to create a team with high morale; a team that values everyone and everyone supports each other. You can speak with some of our best players that have progressed onto the NFL: Marcus Dixon, Corey Swinson, or Kendall Langford. They will tell you we did not give them special treatment because they were outstanding football players.

More importantly, if you want to encourage everyone to play their best, maintain high expectations for everyone. I have always thought that you are going to get what you expect. There have been research studies in schools that have shown that a teacher's expectations can determine the student's performance. Even if a guy's not doing very well, I don't keep telling him he can't play better, or he can't perform higher. He can. A lot of times, if you tell a kid enough times that he is not good, then he's not going to try and get better. He will start believing, "I'm just not good enough." It is important to be consistent and say, "Listen, son, you have great potential. If you just change this little detail here I think it will really help you." Be a coach and help them to be their best! Create that environment where he can reach his full potential. Always have high expectations for everybody and treat everybody as if they are going to get better — that they are equipped to get it done. In fact, in the Bible, it says, "God does not call the equipped. He equips the called." We take that same approach. Just keep consistently telling each player what we are looking for. We let them know what we expect. At some point, he's going to get there because he's going to keep working at it on a regular basis.

The football program is a business and therefore it cannot be personal. We have to be honest with the young men. We have to be fair in our evaluations and play the best players. This also applies to other coaches. If a coach is not getting the job done, then he can no longer be a part of the organization. As I have said, "My job is to hire you. But it's your job to keep it." Our job is to be successful and that means both players and coaches have to be an asset — they are doing things that help the organization move forward.

If a young man feels that he should be a starter, but as we look at the film and see that he's making certain errors, he's making mistakes, then, he cannot start. Players must understand that we have to go with the guy that's performing at the highest level. That is the business part of it. It is not that we dislike you. If we hope to be consistent in our success, we have to put the best players on the field.

It is also imperative that a good coach is consistent and well disciplined in their approach to teaching athletes. When you evaluate the film and if you see something that you like, that means that you taught it well. Now, if you see something that you do not particularly like, well, that means that you did not teach it well or correct it. So, if a player is not executing well, either you taught it or you allowed it. For me, there is no difference. Technique is the result of good teaching. When it is good, that means you taught it well. If it is not very good, that means you did not teach it well. You were not detailed enough, or were not in a correction mode when you evaluated that kid's fundamentals.

You were not self-disciplined enough to be in the moment and take advantage of a teaching opportunity. So no matter if it is good or if it is bad, you have to take the credit.

I often tell my coaches this true story. An NFL team was scouting some players at a local university. They were interested in a young wide receiver. His performance level was just really outstanding and the NFL scouts were really impressed. They were so impressed with the performance of this receiver, they kept asking, "Where is the coach that coached this guy?" Not only did they draft the player, but they also hired the coach. So I tell my coaches, "Your segment performance is a reflection of you." Good performance and hard work does not go unnoticed. People are going to see you and they are going to evaluate you based on the performance level of your players. You don't have to be looking for a new job. If you are doing a good job where you are, people will find you.

I have been elected to three Halls of Fame: Western Illinois University, Virginia Union University, and The Central Intercollegiate Athletic Association Conference. I did not campaign for these honors. They were given as a result of my success at the various universities. I believe this merely documents what we have been saying about doing a good job and the rewards will follow.

BE A VISIONARY

I believe there is a difference between a dream and a vision. Dreams are things you do while you sleep. A vision will not let you sleep until it comes to pass. A dream develops from a desire, a wish to have or accomplish something. A vision is driven by inspiration. It comes from deep within your heart. An inspired vision is stronger — it is more intense. It almost burns. It sets you on fire and really motivates you to take action.

It is almost like you cannot do without it. Visions are embedded within you. It becomes a yearning — I'm going to get this done even though it will demand great sacrifice.

Dreams, on the other hand, may be a passing thought. They do not drive and motivate you in the same way. If you are motivated by a dream and are confronted by challenges and obstacles, you may turn away and decide, "I really did not want that anyway."

Visions are different. You know it is going to be a lot of pain and hardship, but you are still committed to doing it. It is something that you feel has to happen and you know it is going to be good. You decide to put in the necessary time to accomplish whatever it is you are working on. I am always looking for people to be around my table who have a vision, not just a dream. I want that intensity. I want that determination. I want that "don't give up attitude." Be a visionary, not a dreamer.

BE FAITHFUL

I believe a strong faith in the Lord is important. I am a Baptist and believe in my Lord and Savior Jesus Christ. I am not trying to convert anyone to my belief, but I think you have to believe in something that is bigger than yourself. Life is too hard, too complicated, too demanding to do it all on your own. The Lord provides strength, wisdom and guidance for every part of my life. My job as a coach is to prepare young men for life. That is a big job and we need all the help we can get. My greatest source of strength and wisdom comes from my spiritual life. God's inspiration has guided me and helped me create an environment, through college football, to educate and uplift thousands of fine young men. We have been able to keep many from going down the wrong path that would only lead to destruction and pain. We have brought kids out of the darkness into the Light to lead proud and productive lives. The Fellowship of Christian Athletes (FCA) has always been an essential part of our program.

We have a firm belief that everybody is put here for a reason. Nobody is a mistake. He put you in this program at this time for a reason. So now, let us make sure that our coaching staff creates the best environment for you to succeed. Coaching is a ministry and my life purpose. We are all here for a reason and have a purpose. This is mine. My spiritual life makes me a better coach and gives me the strength to keep moving forward when adversity strikes, and it will. That is part of life. The important thing is because I follow Him, I do not let folks get in the way. Some people do not understand what we are doing and that is all right. I am following Him, not them.

Dr. Jimmy Franklin has been a close personal friend for many years. He was at Eastern Illinois from 1970 through 1986 as a History Professor, for ten years served as the NCAA representative, and Chairman of the Athletic Board. He received his Ph.D. in American history at the University of Oklahoma. He was kind enough to share some thoughts on his perspective during our years together.

> "Joe and Bev have adhered to Christian values many, many years and that is one thing that I like about the two of them. Now having said that, Joe does not peddle religion to his players or the people around him, that is a prescription of his. And that is not always true for coaches. We had one guy at Eastern Illinois who was the opposite. I mean if you were not Christian, he would begin to look at you cross-eyed. But I have always valued the kind of faith they brought to their lives and you see it, they live it out. They do not have to articulate it."

VOLUNTEER AND CONTRIBUTE TO SOCIETY

I believe it is important at a personal and professional level to give back to one's community. Contributing to society is a virtue and is one way to express gratitude for all that is given. Volunteering can be an act of charity to help others in need. We encourage all our players and coaches to volunteer and contribute to society in one form or another.

On a professional level, being involved in local and national organizations is an important way to help others and further one's career. This may be one of the best ways to market yourself and enhance your career as well as contributing to your own personal growth. I always tell my coaches and my players, "An informed mind is a better mind." This is one way you can get it, by going to the organizations and serving in them. Somewhere on your resume, there needs to be some mention that you volunteer — That you are a person who believes in giving back and cares about others.

I have told coaches, if you want to get a better job, find the closest high school clinic, call the coach or whoever is organizing that clinic, and tell them that you want to be a part of the program. Tell them you do not want any money. This is the deal. If you want to sell yourself, how are you going to sell yourself if you do not let anybody know who you are? Go talk and give a presentation. Do not always demand payment. I have hired several coaches because I was so impressed when I heard them speak. In fact, there is a young man at the University of Illinois, Chris Beatty. He used to be one of the great high school coaches in the area. Every year, I would invite him to come and speak. He would tell us what he intended to do that year and then went back and actually did it. I invited him back again and finally got smart. I said, "Look I need to hire you." We were successful in getting him. Since that time he went on to West Virginia University, Northern Illinois University, Vanderbilt University, and now he is at University of Illinois. All this happened because he was at clinics speaking.

My advice to all coaches is, if you are interested in building your brand and getting your name out there, volunteer and be generous with your time and knowledge. In fact, I tell folks all the time that when you get hired, you are actually hired long before you signed the contract. People are always talking about you. You are directly responsible for what they say. So, go out and contribute as a way to let people know who you are.

I have been involved in the American Football Coaches Association, which is the biggest athletic group in America, for many years. I have served voluntarily on about twenty-one different committees within that organization, been the President, and serve on the Board of Trustees. In 1994, Grant Teaff had just been appointed the Executive Director. He asked me to be on the Board of Trustees. I was floored to be invited on the Board. I felt it was a great honor. I still feel that way. When I was asked to come and join the Board of Trustees, I was amazed that this little old country boy from Sussex County, Virginia, had risen to a Board of Trustees position at the biggest athletic organization in America. We have members who are in the NFL. It is such a great honor to be a part of this organization. I am currently the Chairman of the Minorities Issues Committee, which makes me an ex-officio member of the Board. I have been on that Board now since 1994.

You do not get on that Board unless you are doing things the right way. Being on the Board is an inspiration to work hard and keep a high standard. When you are in these positions, there is an expectation of you. I do not want to let anybody down, including the young men who play for me. It forces me to get up at four o'clock in the morning and be ready for the day. I feel like the young men that I have coached have such a high regard for me and I cannot let them down.

I have made many wonderful friends through my service with the American Football Coaches Association and hopefully have made meaningful contributions as well. I certainly regard Grant Teaff as a great friend. He was very gracious to participate in this book. As I mentioned, people are always talking about you. Here is an example of how that can be an asset in your life if you are doing the right things.

Grant Teaff, Executive Director American Football Coaches Association

"I first met Joe in the early '90's or real late '80's. I had met him at the American Football Coaches Association convention and have gotten to know him. I was very, very impressed with him. I kid him all the time saying I was more impressed with his wife than I was with him.

"Joe came on the Board when I was Executive Director. I had an opening on my staff and had talked to Joe. He also was head of a committee that I purposely put together. My style of leadership and the mentality that I use is inclusive, and I wanted to make sure that every area of the American Football Coaches Association membership was represented and had a voice. So Joe, early on, became Chairman of the Minority Issue Committee. We worked together on many, many issues. He still serves in that capacity and is a terrific leader. Then of course, he worked his way up to the Board and was our President. He is a great football coach, and a very, very fine man and leader. The thing I have always admired about him is he believes that you should teach more than the game of football. The players see what you are teaching by the way you live your own life. And of course, that is my strong philosophy as well. So we have a kindred spirit.

"I think that the job that he has done there now in Florida is maybe his best work. That program was in pretty bad shape when he took over to say the least. Now, I just think the whole culture has changed, because he brought his style, belief, and discipline to the program. A great football program has a tendency to change other areas of the University. Whereas faculty may have been skeptical of where they were at the time he took over, his commitment to education has probably dramatically changed the feeling of a lot of people about the program. But he has done that, over and over again, everywhere he has been. He is not a one-trick pony. He is who he is, consistently day after day, and he is going to be that way tomorrow, just as he was yesterday.

"Though I have never seen him coach, I am very clear as to what kind of coach he is and how he handles stuff, because I have seen him do that with members of the Board and his committee year after year after year. He and I and several other individuals, several years ago, determined that we would create a way to honor those minority coaches of the past, who because of circumstances that we all recognize, were never really recognized for their greatness. Joe's committee has been in charge of what we call the Trail Blazer Award, and another friend of ours, Oree Banks, has been very instrumental in that as well. It has been really one of the great things that we have been able to do. And some of these minority coaches from predominantly black universities from years and years ago were unbelievable coaches. Nobody was really able to hear about them, like Eddie Robinson and Jake Gaither. They did not get the national publicity even though they had terrific records. The job they did was just like Joe. They went touching and changing lives. So that has been one of the really great things that our association has done. Joe has been the dominant leader in searching out and finding those individuals that need to be recognized.

"He was a very solid leader. The thing that I always look for in leadership is inclusiveness, which I believe very strongly in. Joe was always that way. He always handled himself in a positive way, and was always very firm and solid in his mannerisms, in the way he came across to the association membership. He just did a terrific job, and I think he was one of the really outstanding leaders in the association in the last few years. He continues to lead. He has not stepped away. He is heavily involved. Joe falls in the same category as Eddie Robinson as being someone that everybody listens to and respects. He has been just a solid, consistent, and a positive force in college football.

"One of the things that has always been a virtue of Joe's is that he understands the world. He is not one that comes in with a chip on his shoulder at all. He comes in to every situation determined to carry his part of the load and to be open, constructive, and instructive from his point of view. Those are great characteristics for a leader to have. And I would say because of Joe, and many others of our minority leaders throughout the years, and the openness of the AFCA, we have solved a lot of issues that were there and are not there anymore.

"He has a great ability to get things done in adverse conditions. He has the capacity to go into any situation with an unbiased mind. If you know what I mean, Joe has never come across in any way except very open minded, very sincere, and very firm, which is important as well. He is just a terrific leader and person, and a guy that I have just come to love like a brother. He is just a unique individual."

CONCLUSION

We hope that this chapter is helpful to anyone wanting to begin or enhance their coaching career. It is a wonderful and meaningful profession. It is important to remember that you are building a brand and you have to be careful about what you are building. Going all the way back to high school, it was important that I did things the right way; I was not caught up in illegal things which put blemishes on my record. I was known to be a worker and a real serious guy. I went and obtained my degree, I did not hang out with the wrong crowd, I did not mind giving back, and I did not mind commitment. I sacrificed because I understood the importance of an education and the need to protect my family's name. Once I was in position to help others by coaching, I put in the time. It is one thing to get a position, but you have to understand how to manage it. I believe that had a lot to do with my ascension from a little farm boy all the way up being inducted into three Hall of Fames. I always believe that, "you do your best and the Good Lord will take care of the rest." The promises that He makes — He keeps them. It is up to you to believe and have faith. If you do what is right, right will come by you.

PART II
THE ORGANIZATIONAL BLUEPRINT

This section will discuss the blueprint for our football organization. We believe it is our responsibility to design an atmosphere that is conducive to growth and development for our players. They work hard and we hold high expectations of them. In return, we offer the best environment that will help them succeed in their efforts. Our program is designed in four phases and each phase is designed to create a high performance environment for our players and coaches. We also have a very strong spiritual component with the Fellowship of Christian Athletes. This section is designed to provide guidance and direction for anyone wanting to create a very successful football program which supports the development of young athletes into responsible men.

Chapter 11

THE BLUEPRINT FOR A SUCCESSFUL COLLEGE FOOTBALL PROGRAM

The Head Football Coach at the college level is a CEO running a complex organization. It is a business that has many moving parts. A strong organization alone will win an additional three ball games per year if you know your roles and carry them out. The organization is really the people who are in it. They make up the organization. Everyone, coaches and players must have a clear understanding regarding their roles and responsibilities. When they do, success will follow. We will discuss the specific roles for each coach in our program in order to provide a complete road map for our organization. First, however, let's look at the business side of college football and discuss the essential components that create a winning team and a first class college program.

The head coach is responsible for creating an environment for growth in the program. A program must have the right ingredients to be successful. It is important to remember that our main objective is to help the development of young men into well-educated, responsible citizens who will contribute to society. The educational and moral success of our players is a high priority. We are training college student-athletes. We tell them that they are not, "athlete-students." They are here for an education. Our job is to uplift and transform these kids into men. However, the practical reality is that we will not be around to help these kids if we do not win football games. The football program provides us with an opportunity to touch the lives of these players. So, we have to be successful in doing our job as coaches and win football games if we are going to be around year after year.

THE FOUR PILLARS OF SUCCESS

Given this reality, it is imperative to create the strongest football program possible. In order to do so, four things have to be in place:

1. You have to have a strong academic support system. You have to have academic counselors to make sure that the young men are taking the right courses — the courses that will lead to a curriculum degree. Academic support also includes proper tutoring to help them when they need it.

2. There must be a proper training staff. There are going to be times when there will be some setbacks and injuries. You have to have strong trainers, to rehabilitate your players back from injury.

3. You have to have compliance. There are rules and regulations that the NCAA requires if you are going to function under their umbrella. We need to know what those rules are. We need to have rules and education meetings with the staff and athletic department. You have to have a strong compliance area.

4. You must have a strength and conditioning staff. If you want these young people to go out and compete at the highest level, you have to prepare them physically first and then mentally to take on the challenge.

The President and the athletic administration need to understand that these four areas are non-negotiable. If the President is not interested in providing the financial support to create these components, then you are working at the wrong university. They must be in place to be successful. I think for every 100 student-athletes on the campus there should be at least one full time person in those four areas. If you have 300 athletes, I think you need to have three full time persons in each of those areas. Again, those areas are: academic support; training, strength and conditioning, and compliance. Those four areas must be in place otherwise you are not protecting your investment.

Many people may not realize the business side of college football. There is a significant investment made in each player on scholarship. We provide a twenty-five thousand dollar scholarship per year to provide a free education. That is one-hundred thousand dollars for a four year ride. There are sixty-three full time scholarship awarded at the football championship subdivision each year That is a total of $1,575,000.00 per year. This is a big investment to make in these young men.

Our dividend on our investment is simply this. Once we go out and tell a young man, "If you come to our program, we are going to invest in you with a full scholarship, with the understanding that you are going to come and be a great ambassador." We expect them to be an ambassador by doing the right things in the community, going to class and getting their education, and doing all the things with their trainer and the strength and conditioning person so they are able to show up and convince somebody that he is worthy of buying a ticket to see them play. That is our dividend for our investment. You are going to bring people to the arena with a ticket. Now if we are going to invest in a young player and we are not going to protect our investment, because we do not put those four things in place, that person is going to end up flunking out, they are going to end up sitting on the bench, or they are going to be hurt for four years. They are going to end up being a hospital bill — rather than getting returns on our investment. This is bad business!

Therefore, when you approach the administration, they need to understand, yes it is an institution of higher learning, but it is a business and it must be run like a business. If we are investing, first of all we have to make good investments by recruiting the right people. But once they get here, we then have to protect our monies. It is like we are the FDIC of humans. The administration must understand that!

This has been stressed at every university where I have worked. Even when a new President or AD has come in, I would sit down and have this conversation. As I have previously stated, on an average, we are spending twenty-five thousand dollars a year for a student athlete. That is a hundred thousand dollars over four years. Hopefully, we fill our stadium up to the point where we are getting returns. In fact I tell my athletes all the time, if people are not in the barbershop bragging about how good you are, and can't wait to pay to see you play, then you probably should not be on scholarship because you are a bad investment. You need returns on your investment. That really gives the AD and the President a snapshot of how this works. You cannot bring them here and fail to provide the proper environment. This environment must be conducive to growth and development. If I do not have academic support this guy never gets to be a junior or a senior, then I am really losing out on my investment. That is not what we are in business to do ¬¬— we are not in business to lose money. The contract is the young man comes in, he gets his education, which did not cost him anything, and in return, he is going to provide some entertainment, some exciting play that is going to pack the stadium.

THE RETURN ON INVESTMENT

The football program has an enormous impact on the entire university culture. It sets the tone for both students and alumni. A successful program increases student enrollment because people want to attend and alumni are proud of their university and want to contribute more money. There are many financial benefits to a successful football program beyond filling seats in the stadium.

I remember a University President telling me about the time he really wanted to get his enrollment up and going out to the University of Southern California to speak to their President. The Southern Cal President told him, "Get your football program right." It sets the tone on your campus for whether or not the kids are going to be rowdy or not. If you've got a rowdy football team, the kids are going to follow. If you've got character guys on the team, the school is going to follow. It sets the school year off, because if we've got a good team, everybody is in a good mood and has a good feeling because the team is winning. Alumni will enjoy going to work on Monday's, because they can brag about their team. When they brag about their team, they have a tendency to send more money — the gifts that your alumni give go up. You're going to have a bigger enrollment because people get caught up in that excitement and they want to become a part of that. In addition, when the team is winning, you're going to get a lot of what we call "free publicity," because people want to come on your campus and write stories. We had the New York Times come. We've done documentaries at historical sites on campus. People want to come and be a part of that. The media attention creates more marketing and that attracts more top athletes. The whole entire campus benefits from alumni giving to the student body being excited with a lot more spirit. I know I keep saying that but it is so important to the financial success of a university. It is a business.

THE BLUEPRINT

We have learned over the years what it takes to create a successful program. We have a blueprint that works year in and year out because it is based upon the following core values:

1. Support the growth and development of everyone in the program. Help everyone progress.

2. Demonstrate real love for people.

3. Be obedient to the Lord. Do your part and He will provide all that is needed.

1. Support The Growth The Development Of Everyone In The Program. Help Everyone Progress.

This is the most important part of our blueprint — it is non-negotiable. I once had a secretary, Dr. Jackie Jackson, that worked in the football office. She had a high school degree. Well, I looked up she had a college degree. I looked up again and she had a master's degree. Later she went on to get her doctorate degree. Everybody has to be growing, we do not want anybody around here just checking in at eight o'clock and leaving at five. The involvement and environment must be conducive to growth and development. I tell my coaches that if they are here just for a paycheck, they are at the wrong place. We are looking for a total commitment. I want coaches that are interested in getting better and moving on to become coordinators and head coaches. That is why we have quite a few coaches that played for me or coached with me who are now head coaches or coordinators. We want everybody to be growing. It is a total commitment to growth and development and we want everybody to buy into it. Even the people who clean the building, they are human too. We make sure that they are included. If we are going to have a cookout for the staff or any kind of activity, they are invited too. We all need to be working together. We are creating an environment for success that inspires everyone to go to the next level.

Growth and development applies to me as the Head Coach as well. I have always included a clause in my contract at every university where I have coached, that I am going to attend the national conventions. I do not know how you stay present or get ahead of the curve if you are not putting yourself in a position to see what the new trends are. When we go to these conventions, all of the people that we see who are getting to the bowls are the same guys that are speaking at these conventions. If we want to get to a Bowl, if we want to be successful, it makes sense to go and listen to those who are doing it. A lot of the things that I am talking about, I have learned because I am sitting in the front of a convention session taking notes. I always tell people, if you steal one idea, you are a thief. If you steal a lot of ideas, you are a researcher. I have taken that approach. I want to be considered a researcher. I do not want to reinvent the wheel, we just borrow spokes.

We are one hundred percent committed to helping people. I have been blessed with an ability to look deeper into someone and see potential where others do not. There are many times when my coaches think a young man is not right for our program because of his past behavior. He has been in trouble and created problems. One young man, in particular comes to mind, Herbert Parham. I recruited him; he played defensive tackle and was a starter. Here is a guy whose mom said, "Coach I am so glad you got him because I could not do anything with him." This guy has a Master's degree and is one of the top coaches in America. I saw some things with him. He used to listen to classical music; I thought, "There is something special about that guy." Everybody just saw that mean streak or that little hot head. They all thought he was just a horrible guy. I saw more in this young man and it paid off.

2. Demonstrate Real Love For People

I always tell the guys who handle the equipment, "If you just want to throw a pair of shoes at the guy and say go play, then you need to go down to the local sporting goods store." We do not throw shoes at people. We give the shoes with love. Understand that what you do is going to affect this young man's growth and development. The same way if you are playing, everybody around here when we put our arms around you at the end of our fingertips there has to be some love in it. We are not just coming in here checking in at eight and checking out five. This is about, "I met you, and I am better. You met me and you are better." This is all about relationships.

I am very passionate about depth of love in our program. I have said before that coaching is a ministry for me. My heart and soul is in this work because I genuinely want to help these young men become the best they can be. I do not believe you can fake genuine love for people — they know if you are sincere or not. When I adopted Don Hill-Eley and took him into my family, I was really trying to help and support him. My wife Beverly felt the same way. She treated him as a son as well. Don barely knew his father and his mother was in prison. He needed the guidance and support of a father figure and we filled that role.

We run a tough program and expect a lot of our student athletes. They must be disciplined, attend class, get good grades, and keep high moral standards. If they get out of line, we are there to get them back on track. You have heard some of the stories — it is tough love. But they take it because they know we care, they know it comes from love. That is what makes this program work — our players know we care about them.

One way that I encourage our coaches to demonstrate that they really care about people is to volunteer. I tell them, "you do not ever want to be known as a guy that only serves or gives back when there is monetary gain." There are five things that you can do to add longevity to your life — one of them is volunteering. When you volunteer you are helping a person, but also it is also gratifying to know that you are doing something to make a person feel better. It helps you — it makes you feel better.

3. Be Obedient To The Lord. Do Your Part And He Will Provide All That Is Needed

I have always believed that if you do your best, the Good Lord will take care of the rest. Those promises He makes, He keeps. It is up to you to believe and have faith. If you do what is right, right will come by you. I have always believed that if I build a good program, we will be all right. Minsters say, "Build it and they will come." That has been my experience. When the program is in place, when we create the right environment for our student-athletes, they do not let us down. They play well and the stadium is filled with fans who have bought tickets.

Being a Head Coach is a tremendous challenge. There are peaks and valleys. We have had some losses we should have won. There have been some goals we did not reach, and some folks who did not quite understand what we were doing. When you follow Him, you do not let setbacks get in the way. Reverend Barber always felt that setbacks are setups for great comebacks. Our faith keeps us moving in the right direction with a steady heart. We don't get defensive, explosive or emotionally reactive by the challenges we face. Our faith keeps us humble in victory and persistent and steadfast in defeat. I am happy to say that over the years we have not had too many of the latter.

CREATE THE RIGHT PRODUCT

My job as a Head Coach is to create a program that brings people together. Coaches have to work well together, players have to bond and become a team in which there is a high degree of trust and mutual support. The faculty needs to support our athletes to give them the education they need and deserve. Our alumni, fans, and the administration need to be energized, buy into our program, and provide whatever support is necessary. Every business has a product. That is why the business exists. The successful product justifies the time and expense it takes to make it successful. Our product is people. We are in a people business that promotes the education and development of young men who are disciplined, work together, bring honor and pride to their university, and win football games. You want to create a good product so people will want to come see you. The public does not want to pay to see bad social decisions, students locked up, or fighting in a bar. It's important to have a strong, positive image. The coaches must be the same way, because you want people to come out and buy a ticket to see you play. If you want people to come and watch you, be somebody they can feel good about. If you want people to get onboard and be a part of your program, then they must feel good about you and your program. It's just like anything else. If you have an outstanding product, it's easy to get people to buy in. I cannot emphasize this too much; you must have a good product to have the opportunity to help these kids. Fortunately, we have shown that our program, which successfully promotes the development and growth of character, discipline, faith in the Lord, and academic success, also produces winning football teams.

As the "CEO" I have been given different advice on how to best obtain the proper support for such a program. When I first took over the head coaching job at a division II school in Richmond, VA many people would reach out to me and give me suggestions on how to make this thing work. It was my first real head coaching position. They told me, "You have to go around and find those members on the Board of Trustees that you can befriend. Then, when you need something, that is who you go to." I did try that approach but it did not work for me. I made some appointments, went to their homes, and sat down and talked with them. I was just amazed. First of all, they were not really aware of what we needed to win on and off the field. I became rather confused so I decided on another approach. I said I am going back on campus and I am going to create an environment where these young men are going to be growing, and I am going to speak to all of the Board members, all of the faculty, all of the administration, all of the media through what they see on game day. In other words, I put my emphasis on the players, making sure that they were having a good experience. I found out early in my career that when players are having a good experience, when they are enjoying themselves, they are going to let you know on game day by giving great effort with their play. I just felt like that is the best way for me to talk to or befriend this larger diverse community. We have a product and when we put things in place, the product can grow. A successful product unites all our constituents and creates the enthusiasm for support from all parties.

So I took a different approach, a higher approach where we never bought into the idea that we have to satisfy an individual. Instead, we decided to develop an environment that will produce a product that people could care about. If they like it, they will buy it! In fact when I meet with my AD, and he talks about fund-raising, I said, "I am fund-raising now. I am putting together a product that people want to buy into and that is how I fund raise." It is a successful and viable aspect of our fund-raising. We have been first in our conference in attendance most places I have been. Well that is fund-raising because you have a product that people want to pay and see. When they pay, that is fund-raising!

THE TRIANGLE

The concept of triangle was brought to my attention by a coach that I admire greatly and with whom I coached. They call him Dr. Victory but his real name is Darrell Mudra. One day at a coaching meeting, he explained to us that when you are considering a job on a university campus the support for the football program should be based on the foundation of a triangle. Here is the concept. A regular triangle has the base on the bottom and the apex at the top. If you put the biggest group of individuals, which is the players, on the bottom, next you have the assistant coaches, above that you have the Head Coach, then the Athletic Director, and at the very top the President. Even though the largest number of people are on the bottom, the greatest amount of resources reside at the top with the President. It is commonly understood that the tone and culture of any organization flows from the top down. The values and beliefs of the President influences everyone at every level. This model presented by Coach Mudra explains the importance of "buy in" from the President of a university if the football program is to be successful. This is one of those non-negotiable concepts for success. If you are employed as a Head Coach at a university that does not embrace this model, you will have problems. The President must understand the Four Pillars of Success and be committed to providing the resources to ensure that each pillar is supported.

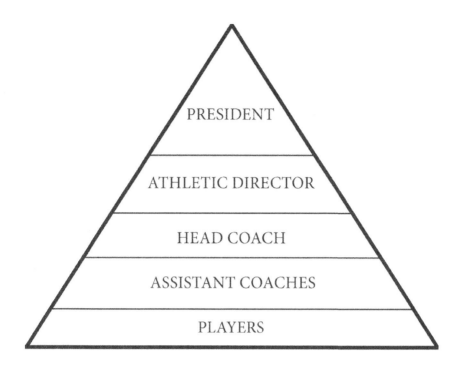

When the President understands the needs of the athletic department, he or she will direct the necessary resources so people can support those under their direct command. Simply put, the President gives the Athletic Director what he needs to give the Head Coach what he needs, so the Head Coach can give the assistant coaches what they need for the players. This is so critical because the President is the one with the greatest resources. Now everybody will get what they need because the resources are being directed from the largest resource area. If the President does not see the value, realistic needs of the athletic department, and need for investment in the program, the Athletic Director will be limited in his or her ability to help, no matter how much they want to. Ultimately, the Head Coach will not be able to provide the proper training and support for his players and the results will show up on the field on game day.

Just to make a point, let's turn the triangle upside down. The entire structure is balanced on top of the President. If he does not stay centered and do his part, the whole thing falls over. One person has the power and responsibility to take care of everybody else. The President must understand the blueprint and support it.

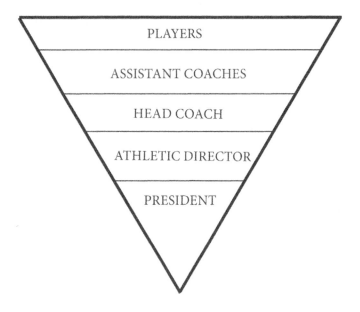

"To whom much is given, much is expected." Success starts with re-sources. Since the President has the most resources he needs to send them up the line so the players will get what they need. If that happens you have a chance to be successful. When you are successful, everyone will get what he or she wants in return. If the resources are given, then you can see how important it is for the players to have the right attitude, right work ethic, right discipline and right behavior in order to justify the large investment in them. Since the coaching staff work hard to secure the right resources to support them, we expect a lot in return. You can see why we place so much emphasis on the de-velopment of the individual in our program. It provides the foundation for our blueprint and justifies our request for resources to be successful.

Since that time, I have always advised coaches when they come to me for advice about a certain job, I always tell them to make sure the position has the triangle approach. If it does, then you have a chance to win because many jobs sometimes are what I call graveyard jobs because they do not have the resources in place. When you go on these college campuses, Presidents want to win, but you have to show them how to win. A lot of them just do not know. The triangle and the Four Pillars of Success provide a great way of illustrating what it takes to win.

THE STRUCTURE

I previously stated that I believe that a good organization will result in winning three additional ball games per year. A proper and well-communicated organizational structure let's everybody know what he or she should be doing and when they are expected to perform. We are not interested in excuses about why something was not done. This is a big, complicated business and we need everyone doing his or her part.

First of all, we clearly assign a variety of roles and responsibilities to each employee in the football department. We make it very clear from the office manager right up to the Head Coach. There is no reason for anyone not to understand his or her role and assignments. A program works when each individual is given responsibilities and he carries out his responsibilities now and in the future. I've always been a guy that believes it is important to put it out there. Write it down. Let everybody know what is expected and develop clean cut objectives. Our philosophy is that our objective and goals must be understood. We accomplish this through the responsibility sheet where we distribute the assignment of each coach. In our organizational chart, we have identified sixty plus areas of responsibilities. Each area is listed under one of the coach's names and equally distributed on a sheet and passed out among the staff. The following is the actual sheet for the 2011 football season.

Responsibility Sheet

Russell Barbarino	William Bennett	Deidre Butler
• Strength/Conditioning • 6 week off season • Summer Manual • Summer Workouts/On Campus • Nutrition/Suggested meals for dinner, pre-game, half time treats	• Video Coordinator • Film practice/games • Film exchange/Dragon Fly • Weekly Hi-light film • Film Athletic Dept. • Liaison w/LRS • Prepare film for SA/Pro Scouts	• Office Manager • Supervisor of Work Study • Facilitate Needs of Office Personnel • Travel (other) Vouchers • P. O. Requests • Other program duties as they are • Identified
Brian Gilmore	**Quinn Gray**	**Earl Holmes**
• Quality Control • Assist/Secondary • Assist w/ computer input • Assist w/ walk-ons • Assist w/ Academic Monitoring	• Quarterbacks/Grading • Admissions • Campus Liaison/Speakers Hostesses • Academic Monitoring • FCA/ Community Relations • Recruit/Miami, Jacksonville	• Defensive Coordinator Linebacker • Grading • Summer Jobs • Pro Scout Liaison • Liaison w/ Trainers/Physicals • Recruit/Tallahassee, Big Bend Area
Reverend Reggie Hutchins	**Steven Jerry**	**Lawrence Kershaw**
• Chaplain • NFL – Necessary for Life Program • Friday Night FCA Program • Spiritual Coach • Movie Selections for away trips • Life Skills Coordinator	• Wide Receivers • Recruiting Coordinator • Grading • Compliance • Press box • Recruit/ Orlando,Lakeland, Daytona Beach, Fort Meade	• Offensive Coord./Offensive Line • Game Planning Accountability • Registration/Summer School • Student Accounts w/ S. Martin • Recruit/Monroe Palm Beach Counties, South GA
George Small	**Aaron Taylor**	**Joe Taylor**
• Assistant HC/Defensive Line • Liaison w/Officials, Game, Practice • Travel Arrangements • Liaison w/Food Service • Recruit/Gainesville, Ocala, Selected Areas of GA	• Running backs/Grading • Film Exchange/ Practice-Games • Summer Camp • Equipment Liaison w/G. Hankton • Game Day Signals • Recruit/Fort Meade, Tampa • Assist w/ Academic Support	• Program Philosophy/On-Off Field • Staff Hiring/ Development Organization • Scholarships/Tickets/Passes • Budget Manager • Staff Responsibilities • Campus/Community Relations • Program Accountability w/ NCAA, MEAC, AFCA, BCA, FAMU

Responsibility Sheet		
Jimmie Tyson	**Juan Vasquez**	**David Hill**
• Defensive Assistant/Secondary Coach • Book Bin • Quality Control/Computer input • Liaison w/ Housing • Recruit/Miami, North Panhandle • Walk-ons • Press Box	• Special Teams Coordinator/Kicking • Assistant Recruiting Coordinator • KO, Punt, Punt Return, K.O.R. • XPT/FG (Block) • Assist. w/ACA Support • Assist. w/ Summer Camp • Recruit/ Panama City & South Miami • Liaison/ SID Office	• Quality Control • Press box • Quality Control/Computer Input • Assist. w/Academic Support • Player Awards • Scouts

You can see it is very detailed and very specific. Everyone knows what to do and who to contact when they need something. This saves a lot of wasted time and excuses.

We also have a very detailed agenda for every day of the week. We want our players organized, focused, and disciplined. We lay it out, day-by-day, hour-by-hour, exactly what we expect and what they need to be doing to be a champion every day, not just on game day. The following is an example of a weekly schedule. I often give the example of a pregame meal. The pregame meal must consist of certain nutrients. If you have been eating junk food all week, no pregame meal will help you to perform better. The same is true about your preparation for winning on game day. If you have not done the necessary things all week, there is no way to win on game day. Winning on Saturday starts with winning on Sunday – Monday – Tuesday – Wednesday – Thursday – Friday. Thus we have our 'Getting Ready to Play Sheet'.

GETTING READY TO PLAY

SUNDAYS

10:00 a.m.	Grade Film
12:30 p.m.	Coordinators
1:00 p.m.	Staff/Grades-Participation
1:00 p.m.	Training Room Opens
2:00 p.m.	Defense Lift
3:00 p.m.	Offense Lift
4:00 p.m.	Game Field/ Russell Barbarino
5:00 p.m.	End
5:30 p.m.	Dinner
6:15 p.m.	Leader Committee Meeting
6:30 p.m.	Awards/Film – Spec. Teams Off 10 situational-Def- 10 situational plays
8:00 p.m.	Coaches Meeting/Film-Opponent Film breakdown, tendencies, Personnel/normal down
10:00 p.m.	End

MONDAYS

Off day for players (No Meeting)

Players
9:00 a.m.   Voluntary Bible Study for Coaches

Coaches
8:00 a.m.   Coaches working on scouting report

4:00 p.m.   Tentative; Scouting report to print

5:00 p.m.   Dinner

6:00 p.m.   Down/Distance/Field Position/
Normal Down
Study Hall

TUESDAYS

6:30 a.m.	Special Teams
7:00 a.m.	Team/Unit Meetings (tentative game plan)
9:00 a.m.	Staff/Injuries-practice schedule- Personnel vs. Opponent Off/Def Opponent tendencies Admin./Program concerns Off/Def Meetings
2:00 p.m.	Segment Meetins/2:30 SPTM
3:30 p.m.	Practice – Full Gear/GL situation
5:35 p.m.	Conditioning/Weight Training
7:15 p.m.	Special Teams
7:30 p.m.	Team Meeting
8:15 p.m.	Study Hall

WEDNESDAYS

9:00 a.m.	Staff/Injuries
	Admin/Program-Recruiting Ticket List Concerns Discuss the Plan (Coordinators) Practice Plan- Full Gear Offense/Defense Meetings
2:00 p.m.	Segment Meetings/2:30 SPTM.
3:30 p.m.	Practice/Full Gear (D/D situation)
5:35 p.m.	Conditioning/WTS
5:45 p.m.	Dinner
7:15 p.m.	Special Teams
7:30 p.m.	Units
8:15-9:45 p.m.	Study Hall

THURSDAYS

9:00 a.m.   Staff/Personnel, Injuries

                     Solidify Special Team game plan
                     Travel squad
                     Admin/Program Concerns
                     Itinerary
                     Coaches tickets
                     Shorts/Shoulder Pads
                     Offense/Defense Meetings/Recruiting calls

2:00 p.m.   Segment Meeting

3:30 p.m.   Practice (5 min. each)
                     Kick Off, KickOff Return, Punt, Punt Return

5:00 p.m.   Extra Point/Field Goal – Block

5:05 p.m.   End — Weights

6:00 p.m.   Team Meeting/Dress List, Itinerary Written Test

6:30 p.m.   Dinner
                     Family Night

FRIDAYS

(Home) Lawn, Haircut, Personal Time

11:00 a.m.	Staff Meeting
	Administrative concerns
	Recruitment
3:30 p.m.	Practice/ 1 hour – Away 7:00 am
4:15 p.m.	End Practice
5:00 p.m.	Hi-Lite Film/Leadership Committee
5:30 p.m.	Dinner
6:45 p.m.	Unit Meetings
7:15 p.m.	FCA
8:00 p.m.	Players Meeting

Chapter 12

FOUR PHASES FOR
PROGRAM ORGANIZATION

Our program is organized into four phases in order to maximize the days leading up to a season. It is very important that we prepare properly. As I have previously stated, it is our belief that organization alone will win you three additional games per year. The following is another component of our plan that has resulted in many successful football seasons.

PHASE I: **JANUARY — MARCH**
  A.   Recruiting of new personnel (coaches/players).
  B.   Program evaluation / on & off the field.
  C.   Off-season program / Spring Ball / Staff Development.

PHASE II: **APRIL — JUNE**
  A.   Exit interview / End Spring Ball.
  B.   Spring recruiting / Staff visitations / Summer Conditioning Manual.
  C.   Revise football notebook / Offense, Defense, Special Teams.

PHASE III: **JULY — AUGUST**
  A.   Follow up on recruits.
  B.   Summer newsletter / Summer Conditioning.
  C.   Staff vacations: Summer camps.

PHASE IV: **SEPTEMBER — DECEMBER**
  A.   Game planning for opponents.
  B.   The success of this phase is directly related to the success of the first three.
  C.   Good Luck!

PHASE I: JANUARY — MARCH
Phase 1 is from January through March. This is where we are recruiting new athletes to replace those who are graduating. Oftentimes, coaches on your

staff will have new opportunities. If that is the case, you have to recruit new coaching personnel. This is where the program actually starts — Everything starts with personnel. That is the biggest part of Phase 1.

Although we are recruiting, the young men returning are in the off-season program. It is important that they are actively involved in an off season program to improve their speed and strength. It is normally six weeks and in those six weeks, three days a week, we have the young men get up and in the gym or on the track at 5:45 a.m. We spend 45 minutes in what we call plyometrics. We are working on explosion, change of direction, and cardio. We are also doing speed school — learning how to run.

The recruiting phase, which normally ends on the first Wednesday in February, is crucial. We have been fortunate, over the years, to land some pretty good talent. As you know, if you hope to win during the Fall, which is Phase 4, you have to win Phase 1 — because the better the athletes you bring in, the better your chances of winning. I often tell people I have never gone to a Kentucky Derby and seen a donkey run. It is all about horses. The better talent you can get in enhances your chances of winning.

Now that the coaches have finished the recruiting, I give them a couple of days off to readjust and make the transition into what we call staff development. The first stage of staff development is when we go back and view the film of each game that was played last season. I always say it is better to plan for war in a time of peace. We go back and we look at our film over a two-week period. We evaluate us in terms of our personnel. We evaluate our schemes. We also look at the opponent and try to understand their personality and their tendencies. We make notes on what we saw on each film, each game. After that two-week period, we go in to what we call staff development, which is based on what the coaches have seen or evaluated from film study the two previous weeks. Each staff member will stand in front of the staff in our staff meetings, and he will teach the staff what he is teaching his segment. The running back coach will talk about some things he wants to do with his running backs and it certainly helps the linebacker coach, which he has to go against. When the offensive line coach talks about his segment, it should also help the defensive line coach. Defense always presents the first week and then offense the second week. Of course, at the end of each week, we talk about special teams with our special team's coordinator. For two weeks, the staff members get up and really enlighten the staff about their segment. It is really a two-week long training clinic that helps all of us to become better coaches. Once that is over, we are normally into spring break. Prior to the young men going home for spring break, they will re-test to see if they have improved. We test them prior to getting started with our off-season training and now we want to measure the results. We do not care what that data is in the beginning, the only thing we are concerned with is improvement at the end of the six weeks — those numbers should be better. If that is the case, then we just won Phase 1.

PHASE II: APRIL — JUNE

We have been off for a week of spring break. When we come back, we are in Phase II — spring football. The spring football is fifteen practices. We now have an opportunity to test the new concepts we adjusted in Phase I, from viewing film. The players should be stronger after the training that took place in the previous six weeks. After spring ball, we have an exit interview with each guy and we talk to them about where they are within the program. Hopefully they are progressing and we can reinstitute their scholarship. However, if they have too much bad data, not doing well academically, did not test well, or missed too many sessions, then sometimes it is unfortunate, but we have to let some young men know they will no longer be with us. Vice versa, there are usually some guys that were not on scholarship, but showed us outstanding data, had good academics, did well in the off-season, and basically had a good spring ball session. If they did not have a scholarship, they just earned one. Since all scholarships are renewable annually, we will pick them up. Phase II is evaluating football, holding exit interviews and letting each athlete know where he stands. Another important part of Phase II occurs in May. The coaches are actually out on the road the whole month. They are evaluating upcoming rising seniors, young men who were juniors in high school. There are 545 high schools in the State of Florida and we try to get to all 545 in the month of May.

When May is over, we come back into the office and transition to our playbooks. We redo and update our offensive, defensive, and special team's notebooks based upon our evaluations in Phase 1. Then we pass that on to the printer and get those manuals ready for 2-A-Day practices.

PHASE III: JULY — AUGUST

In Phase III, we send out summer manuals to our young men. Summer school runs from the end of June through the first week of August. In addition to summer school, there is summer conditioning and we have a summer camp. We make our facilities available to our athletes for strength and conditioning during the summer. According to the NCAA rules, they are allowed to be with the strength and conditioning coach four days a week. Coach Barbarino does a great job of creating an organized workout. These workouts are totally voluntary and the more serious student-athletes will take advantage of this opportunity to stay in shape. Because this phase is voluntary, it does give us an opportunity to discover who is really serious about himself and the program.

During this time, the coaches visit other sites; sometimes they will visit other staffs, talk to the coaches or internship with the NFL, or go to other universities having camps. They might go and work a week or two. We also have each coach write a personal letter to the whole team. It is about the coach's experience as a player, how his life has evolved, and what has helped him to be successful. Each coach takes a week and sends this letter to the whole team. This is all a part of Phase III. During July, the coaches have an opportunity to take vacations. We need to have vacations because the rubber band must return to its normal state if we are to move into Phase IV with the proper energy. We do not meet at all during Phase III. We are, however, in the office and doing follow up work from recruiting and are just preparing ourselves for the upcoming season.

PHASE IV: SEPTEMBER — DECEMBER

This is where game planning for the opponents takes place on a weekly basis after we finish two-a-days. It is called two-a-days because every other day we will practice twice. We have an early morning practice and we have an evening practice. The old NCAA rules allowed two-a-days every day. Now, because of the advent of strength and conditioning coaches, the kids are pretty much in shape year round. The NCAA rules are designed to protect the kids from overload. When I played, we went two-a-day for about three weeks. That was just to get us in shape. Now, the kids are mostly in shape so you go by the NCAA rule — every other day you can have a two-a-day session.

The success of this phase is directly related to the success of the first three. We put our program in four phases so we can evaluate as we go along. Just coming out of Phase 1 for this year, I must say that we are winning, because I thought we had a great off-season, a great recruiting class and the coaching staff certainly has made each other better through staff development. That is why we have these four phases, so that we can evaluate on a monthly basis to see if we are on the right track. As I have said, if you do not have success in Phase I, II, or III, very rarely will you have success in Phase IV — which is a direct indicator of what happened in those first three phases.

Chapter 13
LIFE IS A PARTNERSHIP

All of life's great accomplishments are the result of people working together. T-E-A-M – Together Everyone Achieves More. We accomplish more when we pull together and bring out the best in each other. We see this on the field in all sports. When there is cooperation, trust, and respect great results are achieved.

To be a great coach also requires a strong and loyal support system. Mine starts with my wife, Beverly. We have been married for thirty-seven years. I do believe that in this profession it is important to have a special person in your life and it has to be a special woman, because again there's a lot of hours spent away from home.

ON MARRIAGE

Sometimes young coaches ask, "How do you pick a good wife." They see us together: at the game, in Church, or at the grocery store. Although we are involved together in life, I tell them that your wife needs to have some interest of her own. She needs to have her own career. You definitely do not want to compete with your wife. You want to help complete each other. Now I cannot complete you if you have not started something on your own — where are you going, what are your interests? Your wife needs to have her own separate identity.

I always tell them you have to keep working on your marriage and do not take it for granted. Most importantly, get married for the right reason — know that she is genuinely somebody that you can relate to and can communicate with. I remember one time earlier on in our marriage; she was getting loud about something. So I went over to the radio and I turned it up loud, as loud as it will go. She said, "Why are you doing that? I do not understand what they're saying, it's too loud, its just noise." I said, "Well, when you get loud, that's about the same thing, I do not understand what you said, you're just noise." So, always be ready to share and not always have confrontations. It is not important to always agree. I might hear something she says today and might be Monday or Tuesday before it hits me and make sense. Good communication is a key to a good happy relationship.

Another important aspect of life is, "Do not ever expect more out of her than you expect out of yourself." It is only too common that when we evaluate other people, they have to be perfect. But when they evaluate us we are hoping that they accept us and know that, "we're getting there." Acceptance and unconditional love must go both ways. Do not expect or look for perfection in a partner. I tell people, "At some point you're not going to be able to stand yourself, so you know that sometimes you might not be able to stand somebody else either." Acceptance is very important in the long-term success of a relationship. Do not desire that your husband or wife must be perfect just because he or she is yours. We all have some weaknesses! If you do not realize you have a problem, then you have no chance to solve it — you have no chance to get better. This is so important to understand, because otherwise you lose patience, you get frustrated, you get tired, and end up saying, "Aw, I do not want to take this anymore."

A minister was speaking with me the other day and asked, "What is a gift? How do you determine the value of a gift? Is it because of what it costs, the size of it, how big it is, the weight of it?" To me it starts with, "Is it useful?" If somebody gives me a toaster, at some point I want to toast, you know, it has to be useful. It cannot just sit there. And I think that is the same way with life or your mate. You can do bad all by yourself. You do not need someone else to help you do that. Choose someone that is trying to be a person, who wants to go somewhere, who wants to get something done, who has goals and aspirations, and understands that about life. Pick a partner who is going to add value to your life. Who wants to learn and grow.

I was talking to this 100-year-old lady one time and boy I thought, "To get to be 100 years old you have to have a lot of wisdom." I asked her, "How do you get to be 100?" She had a very simple answer, "Just be like the Florida palm tree. Bend, but do not break. Do not be so rigid that it's always your way or no way. Bend, but still do not lose yourself."

Perhaps the most important thing for young men is, "The wrong head can't be thinking!" You know, so many times that's the key. "Boy, ooh did you see that body?" I want to know what's inside of it? That's what counts! With so many young folks the wrong head is thinking. When they are walking down the street they want everybody saying, "woooo," you know, that's not the reason to get married! If all you want is the milk, you do not need to get the whole cow —milk is flowing everywhere.

My mother told me one time, you need to remember this, "When you're about to get married, marriage is not like an overcoat. You can't just take it off whenever you get ready. Once it's on, it's on." I think it is important to understand that. So, it's important to have a relationship based upon a real commitment. You need to know those inner qualities to make a good choice. See what's on the inside!

ON MY MARRIAGE

I have been very blessed with a great life partner. She is intelligent, articulate, beautiful, gracious, independent, and an asset to me in every way. Grant Teaff, the Executive Director for the American Football Coaches Association, jokes he brought me into that organization because he was so impressed with Beverly.

I always say 1+1=1 because a marriage is not a situation where you are competing with each other but rather you are completing each other. Where I might have a weakness, hopefully she is strong. Where she may have a weakness, hopefully I'm strong and that's really what it should be.

This is a very transient profession. When we move we have to start all over making new friends and creating new support systems, all the way down to finding a new barber. However, your partner has to be at your side. They must be there during the good times and bad. Even when you have successes, it's good to have somebody to share it with you. And certainly when there's adversity present, it is very important to have somebody there to talk with and share. I've had that because of Beverly.

I come out of a close family, one brother, one sister, which are both older. I have always told them that I'm not the baby, just the youngest, and that allows us to talk. We have always been real close. My mom and dad always made sure that the essentials were always in place. So that was not a worry, and that is the same way with my marriage. It takes a lot of time and work to keep a household running. If we need the electrician or the cable man to stop by, she pretty much does it all. Whether it is adding a screen room or building a wall unit or having an ex-terminator to come by. It's a good thing to know that she is there, because again this coaching thing, if its done right, it is 24/7. I am up at 4 or 5 a.m., not just during the season, but pretty much year around. It is a tremendous support to me to trust that I can go into the house and know that everything is functioning properly — that it's peaceful, and that I have someone waiting there that is congenial, at peace and supportive. I know a relationship takes work and you have to attend to it, just like you have to constantly water a plant or tree to keep it growing. But to know that there aren't any cutting issues — that creates a certain comfort zone that allows me to come in and be effective at leading this organization, because it is an organization, it's a business.

A Head Coach, running a college football program, needs a partner that can create a loving and secure home and take care of those other things in your life. That partner has to be there because, we have said so many times that this coaching business is 13 months — I know it's only 12, but that's the kind of consuming effort that goes into it. A coach sometimes is compared to a minister. Sometime we move because we have to, sometime we move because we want to.

Pete Rodriquez was a defensive coordinator at Western Illinois when I was playing. Pete was a guy that moved around. He went from the college level to the NFL. He was known, at one time, as one of the top, if not the top, special teams coach in the NFL. One night he called me and said, "I really am a little jealous, you know, I feel like a nomad. I do not have a home. If the team does well, I stay. If the team doesn't do well, I move on." He's been to at least five or six different teams in the NFL and probably about five or six different college teams before he got to the NFL. This is not uncommon for a football coach — every so many years you are moving. He said, "I miss the neighborhood living, the idea that I know who my neighbor is. My barber, I do not have to go in there and explain what I need — he knows because he has been cutting my hair for years." You know, all of those things create challenges; even with a partner it is a challenge. But I know that the challenge would be a lot greater if I did not have that partner with me — a partner that wants to share and go through it together. It would be really tough.

I have to say — sometimes Beverly went above and beyond the call of duty. When I was at Eastern Illinois, I was the Offensive Line Coach. We had a young man by the name of Clifton Davenport. He played offensive guard. He was a recruit from Washington DC, 6'5" and about 295 pounds. He was an outstanding talent! I actually assigned Beverly to Davenport to make sure that he went to class, had his books, and received any tutoring that he needed. I said to her, "You go pick him up, take him to class, and make sure that he has the books and tutoring he needs. He's your project." Can you imagine that? Beverly was not even on the payroll! Well, I thought that was the right thing to do. Bless her heart, she agreed to do it. I hope you are getting a picture of the type of partner she has been for me. In spite of all the support she gave him, I think sometimes when she dropped him off at the front door to class, he went right out the back door because he still struggled — I think he didn't appreciate the support, he didn't understand the support. Well, we were in a big game. It was a semifinal game of the National Championship. We were in a crucial situation — it was the fourth down. He jumps off sides and instead of being 4th and 1, now it's 4th and 6. Needless to say that play didn't work. I did not blame Davenport and I did not blame my wife. I blamed myself because I created a crutch, and instead of letting him do for himself, letting him develop, and become who he needed to be, I was there. I was there doing it for him. (Beverly was the one doing it, but I am the one who created it.) So I took away the opportunity for him to develop as a man on his own. That taught me a great lesson that has stayed with me throughout my coaching career. Since then, and I'm talking about 30 years ago, I have always let that help me shape my blueprint. The one I talk about to this day! "You can't be a champion on game day and be a butt hole all week!" Well, that came from that experience.

Floyd Keith, the Executive Director of the Black Coaches & Administrators Association, has played an important role in my career — back then he was the Head Coach at Howard. Before I came to Howard, I was the offense coordinator for Virginia Union, a Division II School. Howard was Division 1 AA. He was the head coach who interviewed me. I thought I was going up to Howard to be his running back coach. But a month after arriving, I was the defensive coordinator, and I always thought, that was crazy. But now, I credit Floyd for really helping my career because most colleges, most Athletic Directors, and most Presidents, really do not want a coach who has not coached on both sides. I do not know if you can be a complete Head Coach unless you have coached on both sides. All my life, I had played on both sides of the ball, but that is just playing. As a coach, I was always on the offensive side. So as much as I was reluctant to take that defensive coordinator position, it really helped my career because it gave me an opportunity to go over there and strategically experience what it was like on that side.

After I had been on staff for about a month, Floyd invited Bev and I over to his house for dinner with him and his wife. During the evening Floyd made a statement to Bev why she was there — why we were there. He said he never made a critical decision without letting his wife be involved in the process. I learned an important strategic lesson from him that I believe has helped my career. I always involve her in the hiring process and I do listen to what she says in that vein. I know that when I hire a coach, I'm always looking for the best person first. The Xs and Os do not change — coaching is a people business. You have to be a people person first — which means your interactions and your charisma. You do not always have to have the last word or have the attitude — "your way or no way." It's important that you get good people, because the better the people in organization, the better the organization. I have found out that whomever I have hired, we did not go wrong when she was a part of it. Coaching requires a great understanding of human nature and what makes people tick. Beverly has always been there to help me to deal with that.

In Summary, the coaching profession is very demanding. I think it is very important to have a good woman at your side. Beverly has always been there to support me, raise our kids, and create a warm, peaceful and loving home environment. She is very intelligent and I value her opinion. My son Aaron, who is now an adult and works with me as the Offensive Coach for the Running Backs at Florida A&M University, remembers those early years growing up.

"One thing about coaches, we will always spend more time with somebody else's kids than we will with our own. One part that was tough for me as a kid was sometimes he could not make certain events. But I just pray to God for my mom because even when he was not there, she always spoke highly of what our father was doing, why it was important, and what he meant to the family. I learned from him, if you are going to be a coach, you better find a good woman in your life. I remember he would be gone before sunrise and he would get in after the sunset. But one thing he always did, whether it was twenty minutes or two hours, he would find time for his family. He realized it is a sacrifice to be the family of a coach because of the long hours. But as long as you have understanding, then everything can see its way through."

God has blessed with a great family: a wonderful wife and two outstanding kids. My life is fuller, richer and filled with more joy because of them.

Chapter 14

AN INSIDE LOOK FROM
MY BETTER HALF
Beverly Taylor

I think it takes a special kind of person to be married to a Head Coach. It is a life of dedication to a man and a program. Just as I have seen Joe's student's grow and develop, I have seen myself mature and grow wiser as well. If a woman wants to be a wife of a Head Coach, then, I think she should know what is in store for her. I think I need to start with when Joe proposed to me. We met in college. I was a sophomore and Joe was a senior. So when Joe graduated and went back to DC to teach, he called me my second year during halftime of the Super Bowl and proposed. And he said, "Well Bev, you know, there is no need for us to wait because you can come to DC and go to school and we will just get married." And he said, "Well, what do you think?" And you know, I said, "Well, you know, it sounds good." He said, "Well, you know, Bev, the Super Bowl, this is halftime and the Super Bowl is coming back on." So I just... you do not want to know. Needless to say, Joe has been watching football ever since. Football has been around my life since we were married.

A coach's family moves around a lot. I must truly say each move has been a blessing. I have learned through my own journey that for us it is true — God will not take you where He cannot keep you. There are extra stresses and strains from our lifestyle, but His love has helped us. You have to love each other whether there is a win, whether there is a loss, whether staff members are fired, or whether staff members move on to other staffs. You have to be really at peace with who you are. We are not big enough to do that by ourselves. Joe and I have learned that. We cannot handle that. That is why prayer works. It has helped us through all these years. We have friends whose spouse did not want to move. They just wanted to stay where they were. I was always willing to support Joe, trust in God, and make the adjustment.

One of the first times we left, Joe and I had just bought our first town-house. Our relatives were like, "Guys, you are both teaching and why?" And Joe said, "You know, I want to try this. I think I want to do this." Well, we stepped out on faith. The truck broke down, my brother-in-law helped us move. He is a great guy with lots of wisdom and great faith. He kept saying when the truck broke down the first time, "Are you all sure? You know, is this a sign?" We packed some of the furniture ourselves so it got busted up from moving. When we arrived in Illinois, our apartment was so small that there was no room for my washer and dryer. So Joe and some of the coaches said, "Oh, we will take care of it." So later on, I said, "Well, Joe, honey, you know, washer and dryer? Where are they?" I think they had them in one of the football supply rooms or someplace because there was no room in our apartment. We moved when there was seventeen inches of snow. Each move has been a great move because there were always great people who became part of our lives.

There were so many challenges all along the way. I had to really learn how focused and intense he was with football. You think I would have known that after the marriage proposal! But I learned that I had to be at peace with Beverly. I knew I am interested in teaching. That is something I love. We also had our sons who were active in sports, Little League. We were active in our church. And when I decided that I was not going to be selfish, then the blessings really came. Instead of complaining or being selfish and saying he is never home, I accepted that his job required him not to be home. It was never that he left us out. He is a great dad. We were always involved. But it was different from what I thought it would be. I had to learn how to accept that. When I did, that made all the difference in the world.

Even now it has been interesting. People watch you. When the season is over, we go to 7:30 a.m. service, and then we go to Sunday school. One dear friend said, "You know, Bev, I watch you. I watch Joe and, you know, after a great win, and a great blessing, I do not see Joe in church at 7:30." He said, "And I am praying for him." That Sunday morning, when he leaves the house between 7:00 a.m. and 8:00 a.m., or sometimes earlier depending upon how the game went, that is his quiet time. He goes in to review game film and get ready for the next opponent.

Several dear friends have asked why we chose to coach at Historical Black Colleges and Universities. We have experienced both but we wanted to be in a place where we could really make a difference in young people's lives. The most important thing for us to do as coaches is to make sure we are doing the best that we can do and be the best that we can be, no matter where we are. Joe wanted to be a coordinator and then move into head coaching and run his own program. To him coaching is a ministry — helping to improve the lives of others is the primary purpose for coaching. It has been really rewarding to see football players graduate and become good men, good citizens, good fathers, and good leaders. It has been worth it.

So I saw then, he is okay with wherever we are. There have been people who have snubbed us. We do not get the prime time the way the bigger schools get. But when we realize, we have got players who can go into the pros. We have had players who are Rhodes scholars. We have had players who have productive lives. Then you know what? We are okay with where we are.

First, we really had to be at peace with us and honestly say, "God, is this what you want us to do?" — Because the journey has not been easy. Our sons, when we left Richmond after eight years and moved to Hampton, by that time, they were in middle school. They just felt that they could not leave their friends —"Oh, Dad, how could you leave here?" So for the first two or three months once we moved, I was commuting eighty miles so they could see friends. And after two months, I said, "No more of this. Sorry. Sorry, guys. We live in Hampton." And see, we lived on the college campus so that was different. But my sons found their closest and dearest friends on that campus. So you learn to adjust. There have been great friends everywhere we have been and several of them I still stay in contact with. We have great coaching friends with whom we are still in contact. And when we see them, we are glad to see them. And when we wives are together, we talk about children—we talk about our goals and our aspirations.

I was honored once, in 2005, to have received an award called the First Lady of Football, which was quite an honor. When I received the award I said to the audience, "Once I understood that I am an ambassador no matter where I am — whether I am in the grocery store, whether I am getting my nails done, my hair done, the drugstore, or in church — I understood I am a part of that university and I represent that university. Whether we lost a game or not, whether my husband and the staff get all the support they need or not, I am an ambassador." So what am I going to say when people come to me? What is going to come out of my mouth as an ambassador representing that university? When I understood that the Lord gave me this, I had to be more thoughtful about how I am going to represent the university. I realized that each college that we have been to, each college has a great legacy. They have all stood the test of time. Many of them were established in the 1800's and they have graduated phenomenal people who have done great things. I have had an opportunity to meet great coaches from all over the country.

Being an ambassador requires a certain perspective. Once I was at the altar, we had just got through praying and we were on our way back to our seats. And one of the members patted me on the hand, "Oh, Sister Taylor, it is so good to see you. It is a pleasure seeing you. But I want you to tell your husband that quarterback sucks." I said, "Thank you. I will let him know." I could have really been ugly. But she spoke her mind, she loves her team, and I appreciated her telling me how she felt. Now, I had just prayed. I thought, "It could have been the Lord saying, "Now, what are you going to do with that?" And I said, "All right, thank you. Thank you for telling me." The one person next to her said, "You should not have said that. You should not have said that to her." The person politely said, "Yes, I should have. I told her how I felt. I love my school and they need to know how I feel." It dawned on me. Yes, it is okay, Bev. They love it, and it goes with the territory and it is a great place to be.

When Eddie Robinson came to Hampton and spoke for a banquet, Joe brought him by our house. Just to be in the presence of a man of that legacy was an honor for me, and to meet his wife, Doris a first lady with class among class. I have learned a lot from her, even when it comes to dress and style because I am representing the university. It is important to be in place and to be appropriate. It has all been great.

I have had an opportunity to go to a banquet where the President of the United States was present. I was in awe. Those are things I will never forget — to sit at a table among coaches' wives who were in the Pac 10 and the Big 12 and high school coaches' wives, Division 3 coaches' wives, Division 2 coaches' wives. We were together. It did not matter because when we talked, when we came together, we realized we were all going through the exact same thing. Those experienced wives were able to give us great advice. I never will forget what a wife from Northwestern told me. She said, "Beverly, we have to be friendly even when people are not our friends." I never forgot that. She taught me to be gracious even when you are rubbing shoulders with your opponent. They want the same thing you want, so be kind, be humble.

I had an opportunity to sit at a table at the banquet with the previous coach's wife of Ohio State — wonderful person, very personable. She sat next to me and said, "Bev, you-all had a great season." It is easy for me to say wow, you know, here is someone who is at this big school talking about us. But when you do great things and you work hard and you let your work speak for you, people notice what you do. We know that, based on what Joe has done, he has really made a difference in this country.

I was at a banquet and Joe and I were at Hampton University. And one lady said, she saw my name tag. So she said, "Hampton, Hampton. Is that in the Hamptons?" So that is what I mean about being an ambassador. She had no idea because she was not familiar with historical black colleges. Right then and there was my opportunity to give a geography lesson. We got to talking and she said, "I had no idea." I said, "Yes, we are in Virginia. We are sitting right on the edge of the water, but we are not in the Hamptons." But people do not know and that is an opportunity to teach them rather than sit back in a corner and say people are not interested. I have had an opportunity to be in a room full of women and I was the only woman of color. What did I do? I entered the room graciously, extended my hand, and I said, "Hi, I am Beverly Taylor from Hampton. Hi, I am Beverly Taylor from Virginia Union. Hi, I am Beverly Taylor from Howard. Hi, I am Beverly Taylor from FAMU."

So it has worked for me and I find that if I am truly sincere everything works out fine. There have been a lot of times I have entered a room and said, "Lord, look. Speak for me. Do not let me assume people are being nice to me because they feel they have to be. Let me be peaceful and gracious. Let them see that in me." And a lot of times, in most cases, it is true. When people see that you are okay with who you are and where you are, they are gracious, and they are kind. When they realize that we are not itching to be you because we like who we are. We are proud of where we are because we know that we are representing the university, football players, and we are educating people. And that has been great for me.

I have had an opportunity to meet wives who just got married and they have said, "I do not know if I can do this. He is gone all the time." They are new wives and are not used to a husband being gone more than ten hours a day. So my advice to them is first of all, "understand that this is their passion and they do not have eight to five jobs. They just do not. They work on Saturdays and their new week starts on Sunday. During football season, seven days a week is required."

One of the things that we have here is family night. On Thursday, that means that Joe comes home at 6:00 p.m. Monday and Tuesday, he is home by 9:00 p.m. — between 9:00 p.m. and 10:00 p.m., sometimes later. Wednesday is my bible study night. So Joe knows that I am not going to get home between 8:30 p.m. and 9:00 p.m. So a lot of times, I am meeting him here at home. The good part is he has already had dinner so I do not have to prepare anything. Friday is usually 8:00 p.m. or 9:00 p.m. Saturday, it is game time. What I learned to do is respect family night. I do not make hairdo appointments. I try not to do club meetings. If he says he is going to be home by 6:00 p.m., I appreciate that. I am going to try to be home by 6:00 p.m. because I know he is here waiting for me. If he is going to make that commitment to make that family night, then I am going to make that commitment to be here on family night..

So I had to decide to make our home be as peaceful as it can be. I am responsible for getting the grass cut, paying all of the bills, and doing any repairs that need to be done to the house — painting or anything. I have people to get it done. I take on that responsibility. I love Joe, but do not give him a hammer. He is not a handyman. My husband really is not good at that, and I appreciate him telling me that. So he has said, "Beverly, I am not here to do that so you get the help that you need. If we need to get a plumber, get it."

I have learned that I handle all of that. And there are times when I said, "Oh, I wish you could fix that." And then I realize how blessed I am because some wives tell me their husbands like to repair things, but they want to wait until after the season. They do not have time to get to it. They really, really want to but they do not have the time. So I have said, "Okay, I will get that done."

We have learned to respect our separate interests. Joe can watch football all day long, and I mean total focus. I personally do not want to sit and watch football all day. And believe it or not, I cannot tell you about the plays. Joe would love for me to know more about football so I could sit and watch football with him. So if I know Joe is going to watch football 24/7, there may be washing I may have to do, some homework I may have to do, or some emails I may have to answer. Well, I am at the point where I will say, "Baby, I cannot sit here with you," knowing I have this to do because I have to have a sense of order, for me. So a lot of times, he is in one room and I am in another. And we are not angry with each other; we are just taking care of business in separate rooms.

As a wife, there are things that I enjoy doing. Bible study is one of them. I do that on Wednesdays. I work late; I love teaching. I am passionate about it so I put the hours in. I love storytelling and writing so I spend time doing that. I am active in my church; if they need me, I am there. My relatives are not here, so I check on them. And he has learned and he respects that. I like theatre and art and I like old movies. I like black and white movies that were made in the 1930s. And one day I was watching a Gene Kelly movie and he was singing to his sweetheart. He was telling her how much he loved her. Joe came in and said, "Why does he have to dance all around? Just tell the woman he loves her — all that jumping around! So now, there are not a lot of movies that he will sit and watch with me. He will often say,

"Are you going to watch a movie?" And I will say,

"Yes." So he will say,

"What color is it?" And I say,

"It is black and white." He then says,

"Okay Bev, I am going to watch something else." If I say color, he will say,

"Okay."

If it is a mystery, he will watch it. But it does not bother me that he will not sit and cuddle up with me because we do have those times.

I wanted to see Batman. I am an elementary teacher, middle school right now. So I watch a lot of the movies my students watch. Shrek came out. I go to the movies only two or three times a year and that is good for us. I wanted to see Shrek.

"What do you want to see?" I said Shrek. He said,

"Can't you move it up a notch?" He said,

"Can't you take some of your students and go?" So I said,

"Yes, okay."

We went to see Batman. He said,

"I do not know about this Batman thing, Bev."

I tell you. Well, we got to the movies. A couple of his players were there with their girlfriends watching, they were going to see the movie, to see Batman — so then he was known as a cool guy by the players. You know, Coach is seeing Batman. So when we get in the movie, he's saying, "Bev, this is good, this is good." And I laughed because it was okay.

There is so much I can say about our thirty-seven years together. They have been up and down but we have grown and love each other knowing that we are not perfect, knowing still that there are days when we annoy each other. But I have no doubt that God gave me this man. And because of that, I know that I am going to be there . But even when we disagree sometimes, I am not a nagger. I used to be when we first got married. I am not now.

I learned something from my father-in-law — Joe's father. He used to say people do not always need to know how you feel all of the time. And I used to think that Joe needed to know how I felt, all of the time, about everything. Now, I consider their relevance and think, "Bev, it is important that he hears?" If it is, I know I have to communicate with him to let him know that it is important to me. I discovered that when I said it in the right voice, and in the right tone, it worked, versus raising my voice.

He has a great sense of humor and not everybody sees that. And a lot of times, he can have me laughing about things when we really should be serious about it. But it has really helped me to understand it is really okay. It is not that bad, Bev. We are going to get through this.

Having two sons and having a son on the staff, I have had to be real prayerful. His father is his boss and I do not interfere with that. Whatever decisions that are made in that office are between Joe and his coaches. I am his mom. So that has really helped me when I feel Joe could have said something that I did not think was appropriate or he hurt his feelings. Aaron is an adult, Joe is a coach, and he has decided this is something he wants to do. They both played through high school. Aaron went off to college and Dennis played for his dad. Aaron shocked us at a Christmas dinner with his desire to coach. They both attended practice with their dad during their early years — especially during 2-A-days in August. They saw how football shaped young men through hard work and discipline.

One of the things that as a wife we have to learn, as I said, is that not everybody is going to be your friend. Some people want to be around you because they think there is a fringe benefit. Once I went to a game and a friend asked me for a ticket. "Well, Beverly, do you and Joe have any extra tickets?" Sometimes we do. A family member may not come so sometimes, I do have a seat next to me. I gave her the ticket and the ticket was on will-call. Usually, I get to the game with the team. I am there two hours before the game starts. So I was sitting in my seat and she did not know she was going to be sitting with me. When she got there, she said,

"Is this where you sit?" I said

"Yes."

"Oh, I thought you would sit with the President."

"No, I have been invited to the press box but I prefer sitting with the wives of the staff."

Sometimes when you go to a game, some people have had too much to drink, or they are angry that we are not winning, or they are upset we are not winning by these many points, or they are not satisfied with offense or defense, or they think we need to run the ball more.

But it is a journey and I would not ask the Lord to take it from me. I know He is in the midst of this. It is truly the best is yet to come and it is great to come home and say Joe, "How was your day?" And he will say, "Well, Bev, you know, we got this done and I got a letter from this player and you know, this player is eligible. And strength and conditioning, the guys are working out, and the guys are going to class, and coaches are feeling good, and administration is working with us." That is a blessing. Do we always have days like that? No. But it lets us know that if we are doing the right thing. If we are focused on what we are doing, if we are learning to step out on faith, if we believe in someone who is bigger, and someone who can handle it better than us, then, we are going to be okay.

I hope this gives a perspective from the feminine side and is helpful to new coaches and wives starting a career.

PART III
FOOTBALL 101

Chapter 15
SEVEN COMMANDMENTS

We have reached the final section in this book, Football 101. We have discussed in Part I what it takes to prepare and develop young men so they can compete on the football field and win in life. It takes a physically strong, emotionally healthy, mentally alert, and spiritually devoted man to succeed in our program. We demand a lot of our players because that is what life demands. We do not want our players to be hurt in this very physical game. They must have a strong work ethic to prepare themselves for the battle they will experience on the field and to be successful in the classroom. Our playbook is very detailed and thorough. If our student athletes cannot master the educational material presented in the classroom, how will they ever master the material we present to them for plays and strategies? We are confident that our program prepares them and gives them the best chance to succeed in life and in sports.

Part II discussed the blueprint for our football organization. We believe it is our responsibility to design an atmosphere that is conducive to growth and development for our players. They work hard and we hold high expectations of them. In return, we offer the best environment that will help them succeed in their efforts. So we have prepared them, created the necessary organizational support, and now it is time to play. It is game day! They are mentally prepared, physically strong, and ready to play.

Part III will now take you onto the field and give you an inside look into the game. There are many subtle aspects of the game that are probably not understood by most fans. As a fan in the stands or at home watching the game in HDTV, you cannot see the same things that a player will at the line of scrimmage. Also, there may be some aspects of the game that are not commonly understood. This final section is for anyone who loves the game and wants to have a greater understanding of what players and coaches know and use everyday. We hope this section will deepen your understanding and appreciation of football.

Some people may think football is just a bunch of big, strong guys hitting each other. While that is true and it does happen on every play, there is much more going on as well. For example, there may be a common misconception that the fastest players should be on offense. Common sense tells us that these men need to run fast to make touchdowns. We see wide receivers and running backs breaking away to score. However, the opposite is actually true.

The fastest players need to be on defense. Defense needs the fastest and most alert players. The offense knows what the play is going to be. Defense has to react to keys to stop the play. Also, defense has to run faster in order to catch the offense. The defensive players perhaps deserve more credit than the average fan may give them. There are additional important inside facts that we will share in the upcoming chapters. We will discuss defense, offense and special teams — the three phases of the team. We will discuss the philosophy behind each phase and the ways each can be most successful.

Before we begin that discussion, we want to share the Seven Commandments for playing the game. We already have one opponent, that is enough! It is imperative that we do not beat ourselves on the field. With regards to actually playing the game, here is what we need to do in order to win.

THE SEVEN COMMANDMENTS

1. No Breakdown In Kicking Game: (Often the determiner of outcome)
The kicking game is critical because it creates great field position for the offense and the defense. The kicking game often determines the final outcome because there are 4 or 5 plays that decide the outcome of a game — those 4 or 5 plays are found in special teams play.

2. No Missed Assignments: (Study playbooks/Practice hard)
The team that makes the least mistakes is usually the team that wins. If we execute our plays correctly and work together as a team effectively, with everyone doing his part, then we have the best chance to win. It is only through long hours of hard practice and a thorough knowledge and understanding of the playbook, will we be able to avoid mistakes.

3. Play Great Goal Line Offense/Defense: (Be Physical)
In order to win we need to score and keep our opponent from scoring. It gets very physically at the goal line. We need to be at our best where it counts the most. I believe that you develop your team with great practices in the red zone. You find out how courageous your team is with how competitive you are in the red zone.

4. No Foolish Penalties: (Play Smart)
Too many mistakes will lose a game. We train our young men to be smart in the classroom so they will play smart on the field. Mental errors, which result in penalties, can cost us the game. You must stay out of your own way — be disciplined.

5. Allow No Long Touchdowns: (Pursuit/Tackling)

Proper tackling technique is a basic skill in this game. If you have an offensive player in your gap, you cannot let him spin out or break away for the long touchdown. We have to be able to catch them and bring them down. A long touchdown gives our opponent too much confidence and energy. We want them to work hard for every point they make and wear them out in the process. We want to break their will and demoralize them in the process, play after play.

6. Must Hold Fumbles, Interceptions To A Minimum: (Protect the football)

We do not want to make it easy for our opponent to score. If we fumble and allow interceptions, then we are giving them too many opportunities to score. The team who holds possession of the ball the majority of time, has the greatest advantage to score and win. The fact is you must have the ball to score, so don't ever give your opponent extra opportunities to defeat you.

7. Enthusiasm And Persistence – Mind, Body, Soul In A Spirit Of Never Giving Up: (Commitment to the cause)

This game lasts 60 minutes. The team with the strongest will and most determination has the greatest chance to win. Many games have been won or lost in the last seconds. The team with the greatest heart and soul often becomes the victor, even against a bigger and stronger team.

Winning teams win because they master the basics. Blocking and tackling are the single most important factors in deciding the outcome of a ball game. Know your alignment, assignment, and be disciplined in your responsibilities. Execute each play to be best of your ability for the full sixty minutes.

Finally, we think it is important to understand the basic difference between offense and defense. Offense is constructive. Defense is destructive. It is like building a house. It takes a lot of construction to build a house. You have to lay a foundation, build the floors, build the walls, build the ceilings, and finally the roof. That is constructive and it has to be a step-by-step process.

Defense is destructive. After that house has been built, which took you six months to a year to complete; one swing of a big steel ball can knock that house down. It's a different mentality. It's aggressive and competitive. Offense is competitive, a quiet storm. It has a different approach. You must have both on your football team to be successful. You have to construct a good foundation, but you also have to be able to destroy the opponent.

Chapter 16
DEFENSE

We have prepared. We've been through Sunday, Monday, Tuesday, Wednesday, Thursday, Friday, and now it is game day. What are we going to do with all of that prep we've gone through? What do we need to do to be successful once the game starts? As a fan sitting up in the seats, our program always starts with defense. All the great coaches over the years who have been successful, who have been consistently successful, understand the importance of defense. I think that you have to understand the importance of defense, whether it's wrestling, baseball, or basketball. It all starts with defense and sometimes my players and coaches, especially on offense, do not quite understand when I tell them our best players must be on defense — the fastest, the strongest, the most competitive players must be on defense. We have a philosophy that is in the playbook. It's in the first ten pages of our playbook because we have to play good defense if we hope to win. Here is the sheet we give to our players on defense. We will discuss it in detail.

DEFENSE

- Winning starts with Defense – Failure to understand this fact results in inconsistency. Good defensive play requires an attacking mode. Running and hitting with great intensity starts with speed and minimal thinking. Knowing defense (keys) is a simple way of asking each guy to look at individual movement. The helmet on offense tells you where the ball is going. That is the reason you see offense running more counters, boots and play action passes. They are trying to create a bad first step/ Speed on defense is the best counter to counters. Great defenses have boring practices. You cannot work triangle enough, you cannot work fundamental techniques enough, and you cannot work coverage enough. Blitzing is for an adrenaline rise. Familiarity creates a comfort zone of less thinking – greater reaction. Too much thinking creates paralysis by analysis.

- Great defenses thrive on sudden change – another opportunity to take the will to win from the opponent.

- Great defenses bleed slow/ every yard gained by the opponent must be tough – Eliminate the big play

- To be a great defense: #1 in scoring
  #1 in turnover ratio
  #1 in 3rd down conversions
  Must sell 3 and out

- Every offense has a personality – they have role players and go- to guys. Film study will determine the personality and who must be stopped. Paying attention to the difference makers dictate the game plan. Multiple formations and motion by an offense is an attempt to take attention away from the playmakers. The number of touches and stats will take you to the leading receiver or runner. Rarely at this level will there be multiples.

- The greatest characteristic of an outstanding defense is that they are great tacklers. Flying to the football with the entire unit is a 5-minute period daily. I once heard a coordinator speaking at a clinic about his scheme. He was very convincing until a coach in his same conference stood and said that the speaker's defense gave up 500 yards per game. The speaker replied – it wasn't the scheme – we just couldn't tackle – do not put the cart before the horse.

The importance of defense was proven to me some years ago when in one game we scored 7 points on offense and won. In another game, we scored 56 points and lost. The difference was defense. My philosophy is always that our best players must be on defense. Let's go through our philosophy as shown on the sheet.

GOOD DEFENSIVE PLAYS REQUIRE AN ATTACKING MODE

Running And Hitting With Great Intensity Starts With Speed.

When we do our testing, we find the guy who runs the fastest forty yard dash and the guy who has the best bench press. These guys are a candidate for our defense. It is important to get the right player for the right position — everything starts with personnel. I have been in ballgames where we run a blitz, which assigns an extra guy to the quarterback. So instead of four guys rushing the quarterback, we send five. That fifth guy has to be someone that understands the concept behind blitzing, which is — you need to have minimal thinking and great reactions. This is why you must have your best players on defense.

Read the Keys

The offense knows where the ball is going before it snaps. On defense, you do not. Everything is reaction. There are some keys but you have to read them quickly. There are some little subtle things that tell you what is happening. If you are the defensive player, you watch the offensive lineman's helmet — that can tell you something as to where the ball might be going. For example, if you are defense looking at the tight end on offense and he blocks down, then that tells you, the defense, there's probably a run coming. If he comes up, there's probably a pass coming. Since you do not know, you have to read keys. When you read these keys, now you have to be able to react quickly and get to it. The helmet on offense tells you where the ball is going. That is the reason you see offensive running more counters, bootlegs, and play action passes because they are trying to give the defense a false key as to where the ball might be going. They are trying to make it more difficult for the defense to pick up where the ball is going.

The Counter, Bootleg and Play Action

Let me explain more so you can see how the offense is trying to confuse the defense. A counter is a play in which the ball starts one way, but it has a cutback possibility, the fullbacks takes three steps to his right only to plant that right foot and then come back to his left. That is considered a counter play.

A bootleg is where the quarterback's going to open in one direction. He will take as many as four or five steps in that direction before he rolls back to his backside. Those are very prominent plays on offense. You see it more and more because defenses have become so much faster, so much more athletic. You almost have to run a counter play to force the defense to make a wrong step. That is the idea behind offense as running counter to boots.

Play action is simply giving the appearance that you are going to hand the football off to the running back. As you approach the running back, you pull the ball at the last moment and you set up as a quarterback and try to throw the football over the heads of the oncoming linebackers. All of those have become very prominent plays on the offensive side of the ball because the defense usually has the fastest players, most competitive, and strongest players.

DEFENSE MUST HAVE SPEED

If you have a situation where you can recruit nationally and get everybody you want, it is good when everybody's fast. But, if you are in a situation where you are limited, you do not have all that you would like to have, or if you are in a high school setting and you have to take what comes to you, then those best athletes must be on defense because they have to react to what they see, and then in most cases turn and run to where the ball is.

If you are a slow guy, if you are not competitive, you do not have a lot of the desire, you really cannot play defense. I have always said it takes a special guy to play on defense. In fact, on offense they make all kinds of jokes — if you are on the offensive line they call that the last stop before the bus stop. If you cannot make that position you are on your way home. Defense is where those top players must be, because sometimes you may think the ball is someplace, only to discover that the offense has done a good job of faking or camouflaging, and you find yourself completely out of the play. But, if you have that speed, you can make a false step and now have the ability to get back into the play and probably run it down. The defense has to be fast because they do not always know where the football is.

ASSIGNMENT FOOTBALL

To play good defense, once you get the personnel in place, you must have what I call, assignment football. Every guy on that defensive line will be assigned a gap — the A-gap, B, C, or D on both sides of the center.

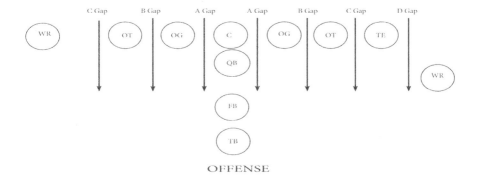

We label that so that they have an area to protect. On defense, you must always protect your home area first. However, once you determine where the ball is, you then have to pursue it. If I am a defensive tackle and playing over top of the offensive guard, I have the gap between the guard and the center and that is called the A-gap. If that is my responsibility on that particular play, my teammates must be able to trust that I will take that A-gap assignment. Now, again, once I see that there's no threat in gap A, I can pursue to the football. Most of the time, defensive practices are boring because no matter what happens, you always have to protect home first. When you get that down, by doing a lot of walkthroughs, somebody's got B-gap, somebody's got C-gap, and somebody's got D-gap, so the gaps should be canceled because no matter where that football is going, you have somebody in every gap. In fact, when we put our defensive players in those gaps, we call that gap cancellation. In other words, if you are in there, there's no longer a gap. Now, if everybody is in their gap, you are building a wall, and when that wall is built there's no place for the offense to go.

The challenge as a coach is to get guys to understand the principle of the Gap and be disciplined because every once in a while somebody going to try to guess. "I thought the ball was coming this way." Oh no, do not guess! You had a gap. So go to A-gap, if it was going to C-gap, your linebacker has gap C. You must make sure you take care of your own assignment. That is what good, strong defenses do. They get the best personnel and give them their gap responsibility and then practice whatever play they call. Sometimes you will change it up and the tackle might have B-gap and a linebacker gets A. But the important thing is to always make sure that on every play called by the defense, every gap is accounted for. When that happens and they can trust each other to get to their gap, then, they can play with a lot more confidence and a lot more movement.

Another important thing in defense is that if you are on the end of the line, you can never have your outside arm hooked. You have to keep it free because, again, the object of the defense is to keep the ball inside of them. If the offense ever gets outside of the defense (break containment), good things are going to happen, but it's all going to be for the offense. That is why you sometimes see people run sweep plays to get outside and run up the sideline. The defense can never allow the ball to get outside of containment. Somebody always has to be assigned the responsibility for containing the offense. In other words, keeping the offense inside of them.

READING THE KEY: WATCH THE HELMETS

A fundamental way to read the key for each play is to watch the helmets of the three men in your area. We refer to these three men as the triangle. Whenever I see the offensive tackle helmet come straight up, he is telling me automatically that it is a pass because he is in pass protection mode. So reading a triangle means you have three helmets to watch on defense. Everybody on defense has three helmets to read, and those helmets are broken down and assigned, so that by the time we finish, all eleven helmets on offense have been accounted for.

This is how it works. When the offensive tackle's helmet comes up, that means he is setting up for pass protection. If his helmet goes straight ahead, that means it's a run. So the helmet is going to tell the defensive player what's going on offensively. And, each defensive player normally, like I said, has three helmets to read and those helmets are normally side-by-side. You might have the center and both guards.

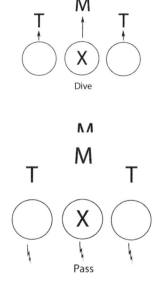

The center and two guards is the simplest one to explain. When I am the linebacker and I am watching those three helmets, if I see the center block back, which means block down, and I see the right guard block back, normally a trap play is coming. On a "trap play," the running back attacks the area of the down block. If the helmets come forward. It is a dive play straight ahead. If that helmet sits up, that means, now I can get into a back pedal because, chances are, a pass play is coming.

That is why I say defensive practices are boring because all we do is watch helmets. But those helmets tell a player what is about to happen. You have to believe what you see. Those helmets are not moving by themselves. They are attached to heads and bodies. If I see the helmet pop up, I have to know it's a pass. I cannot be wondering if it's a run. No, the helmet movement will tell what it is. That is why the offense will try to create a wrong first step by the defense with misdirection in their offensive packages.

THE POWER OF FILM

There are very subtle things we can learn from observing our opponents on film that will help us on game day. The fans in the stands may be too far away to see these things, but they are very important keys that help the guys on defense read the play. When we look closely at the film, if a guy has his weight on his hands and kind of rocked forward, that tells you that he is coming off to make a run play. If you notice that his hands are free flowing, there's not a lot of weight on his hands, so he is probably going to sit up for a pass. Running backs try not to do this but it's kind of instinctive. They should be looking straight ahead, but they will come to the line and if they are going to run the ball to the left or to the right, you will notice them peak to see who's over there. Well, he is giving away the play. A wide receiver, if he is going to catch a pass, a lot of times you will see him more in a sprinters stance. But if he is got a block and he is not going to go for a pass, you will see him more upright. As a coach, you try to teach your players not to give away those kinds of things. By watching the film, you can tell when a guy is very disciplined. He is strong with his fundamentals when you cannot tell the difference between a run or a pass.

Watching film also gives you specific information about individual players, so you can make a game plan, and design your offense and defense. They might have a guy on that defensive line who is outstanding. He is a good player. Well, do you run away from him? Do you double-team him, or do you try to give a lot of misdirection? We want to find out who is their best player on defense. We want to have a plan, so when we go at him, we are probably going to double team him — put two on one. Or, we might want to just go away from him because he is ferocious — I mean he is just tough.

THE BLITZ

Every once in a while, as part of a good solid defense, you want to blitz. Blitz means bringing more than the offense can handle. Normally, if you have a four-man front, you have three or four linebackers that are going across the line of scrimmage. Every time you bring five or six across the line, that is a blitz. Usually, when you do that you are going to create a big play. You are going to make a tackle behind the line of scrimmage — you are going to sack the quarterback. Well, that is what blitzing is for. When that happens, it raises the adrenaline in the defense. They get all excited. They jump up and down and high five. Well, every so often you got to do that because you want those guys to be having fun out there and that certainly creates fun for them. Sometimes you even end up in a fumble/recovery, a take away. That is good because we want additional opportunities to score with our offense.

The reader might be wondering, how do you decide when to blitz? Good question. First of all, if the offense is methodically moving the ball down-field, you have to do something to create a change — a blitz might do it. If we are playing a team that is pretty good, we cannot allow them to do whatever they want. We want this team to get out of rhythm. We want the quarterback to throw the ball before he is ready. If we just let them do what they want, they will probably win. A blitz is a good way to shake things up. In some game we might usually blitz thirty or forty percent of the time. However, in other games we might blitz sixty to seventy percent of the time — six or seven plays out of every ten. It all depends on the opponent. For example, if we know they like to throw the football, we would blitz them probably sixty, seventy percent because we want to make them throw before they are ready, before their receivers can get in and out of their cuts.

KEEP IT SIMPLE — KEEP IT FAST

When you have a playbook that looks like an encyclopedia, it looks good for the board of trustees, but it is not worth a dime for your players because the more you think the slower you are! If I am recruiting and I have never been to this kid's house, even though I have the directions, it's going to take me a little longer to get there because I am unfamiliar with the area. I have to think about the streets and the turns. However, once I go there, the next time I will get there a lot faster. Well, that is how we want our players. We want the defensive practices to be boring, to be doing it over and over and over again until it becomes a comfort zone. Our goal is to make them more comfortable because they are thinking less. The less they think, the faster they are going to play. We do not want them trying to analyze everything because it will slow them down. If I see a guy running the 40-yard dash in 4.3 seconds, that guy's fast! But if I get him thinking too much, now he is running 4.8. I just slowed him down because I put too much on him — keep it simple to keep it fast. In fact, there's another thing about KISS — keep it simple and stupid. The truth is, less is best — the less thinking, the faster we are going to play. Too much thinking creates paralysis by analysis. If we have them trying to analyze too much, we will just paralyze them. So we fight to keep it simple because the more simple it is for us, the more difficult it will be for our opponent.

DEFENSE THRIVES ON SUDDEN CHANGE

This is a concept I picked up when I was coaching at Eastern Illinois. Every once in a while, your offense is going to turn the football over and most of the time the players on defense are going to think, "How could you do that? How could you put us in this situation? We just gave you-all (offense) the ball back." As most people know, this is called a turnover. Well, since this is a part of the game, we have to practice this so the defense does not get mad when it happens. This is part of the mental training for defense. We prepare our defense to think like this. "I am glad the offense turned the ball over because now that is another opportunity for me to go out and hit somebody." Well, that obviously is not really the way they feel, but we have to coach that way because, otherwise whenever a turnover comes, it's going to really hurt your team's morale — it's going to hurt their energy level. Our coaching approach is to train them not to be too emotionally reactive to the turnovers. It is hard not to have any reaction to it, but we try to minimize it. I always fight hard to make sure that my offense does not turn that ball over because I know it's devastating, it is demoralizing. But, we have to practice turnovers, over and over again, so that when it does happen, the defense is ready to take on that challenge, rather than wanting to kick the offense in the butt. I have seen guys come to the sidelines and some guys say, "Man don't worry about it. That's okay. We'll get it back." I have also seen guys actually throw water bottles at a guy because their attitude was, "How dare you turn that ball over." So you have to practice and prepare for it, so they do not have an adverse reaction when it does happen, and turn against each other. We are going to make sure they say, "Okay, it's a part of the game, it's unfortunate but look, let's go get it back again."

When the defense can go out and recover the ball after a turnover, it does demoralize the other team. If they can create a fumble, then that is another sudden change that takes the will to win right out of the opponent. The other team is thinking, "Man, we had a great opportunity and we just gave the ball right back to them!" Now you are playing some winning football when defense can do that.

Well, like I said, it is important to prepare for this because it is a part of the game. Yes, it is unfortunate, and if we had to write the script, we would never fumble or turn it over, but it happens. That is why we practice for it. We practice on the minus three-yard line. We do not ever want to be in a game and be on the minus three-yard line, but it's going to happen — it's reality. So, we practice on the minus three so that when we get in a ballgame and we are on the minus three, our anxiety level will be a lot lower.

BLEED SLOW

It is essential that defense makes the opposing offense struggle for every yard they get. The theory held by most people is that after the offense runs about six or seven plays, they are normally going to self destruct. So if we can just make them bleed slowly, if we do not give up the big play, but just give up a yard here and there, then sooner or later they are going to turn the ball over. They are going to self-destruct. However, if we are letting them get twenty yards every time they have the ball, man, then the tourniquet is broken — the blood is flowing. Heck, we are just letting them get all the momentum they need. So good defense makes every yard tough to get — do not give up those big chunks of yardage.

THE STATS

To be a great defense, there are a lot of stats that people look at but these are the only ones that I believe matter.

- # 1 in scoring.
- #1 in turnover ratio.
- #1 in 3rd down conversions.
- Must sell 3 and out.

If you are number one in scoring, that means that you are keeping folks out of the end zone. If you are number one in turnover ratio, that means that you are taking the ball away. If you are number one in third down conversions, that means you are really getting off the field and letting the offense take over to score. If you are taking the ball away and your offense is on the field more than the other offense, then you have a great chance to score. Finally, every time the defense goes out there, you want to make sure that you are making the opponent punt the ball — three downs and they are punting. At the end of the year, if you are leading in these four areas, your are in good shape. Some people say, "I want to give up no more than eleven first downs," or "I don't want to give up more than two hundred and sixty yards," or "I don't want to give up more than a hundred yards rushing." Well, all that sounds good, but these are the only stats that result in you winning ball games.

STOP THE BEST

Every offense has their go-to guy for passing or running. During the week when we look at the opponent's film, there's usually somebody on that team that is probably catching the most passes and is carrying the ball the majority of the time. We need to identify their go-to guys — the guys they like to use for those plays. So, once we discover who they are, we make sure that we keep our eyes on those guys. We want to make them beat us with somebody else, not with the guys who have the best stats. We need to take away their best players. Most running backs make anywhere from twenty to twenty-five runs per game. You have about sixty-five plays per team. So if a team has twenty-five of the plays going to one guy, he is probably their spark plug. Well, we want to make sure that we shut him down. The average team is throwing about forty times, and out of those forty times, one kid will make fifteen catches. Well, we need to put an eye on him. We need to develop the plan so we shut him down, because if he catches fifteen balls, he is probably going to have a pretty good day. We will put our best guy on him or double team him, but we cannot let him have a good day. So we are looking for those play makers and then we are trying to take them out of the plan.

Film study shows a lot of things: who's getting the most touches, who's their lead receiver, who's the play maker, and how many different formations do they use. A lot of times a team will use different formations in order to camouflage so they can get the ball to that same guy in different ways. We have to make sure we know who their lead receiver is and who their lead running back is. We have to make sure that we do not let those guys beat us even if it means putting two or three guys on them. We do not want their main guys beat us. Make them —force them to use somebody else to beat us. If we do that, we will probably have a pretty good chance to win.

OUTSTANDING DEFENSE MUST BE GREAT TACKLERS

I went to a clinic one time and this guy was a giving a presentation about how great his defense was. He was going on and on about his awesome scheme (his lineup) and telling us that we all needed to try it. Well, there was a guy in the back of the room, in his same conference, who said, "Well coach, if your defense is so good, why did you all give up five hundred yards a game." He said, "Yeah. Well, it wasn't the defense. We just couldn't tackle." Well, hell, that is what defense is! So do not put the cart before the horse. You have to tackle on defense. That is why I have said those guys have to be quick. They have to be strong, and they have to be competitive because we can have the best design for defense, but if you are there to make the tackle and the guy on offense just ran over you, or gave you a quick fake, then you lost that play. Your defense broke down — the only way to tackle is to tackle!

Everyday you have to have your defense making tackles. Each segment on defense — every day of practice they must have a period where they are practicing how to tackle, because there is nothing worse than to be right there to make the play, and you miss a tackle — that could mean a first down, it could mean a touchdown. They will not be good unless you practice tackling. The better tacklers you are, the better defense you are going to have.

This is the thing. The scheme is really less important. I was saying earlier, however you line up, you have to have accountability for A-gap, B-gap, C-gap, or D-gap. So the scheme does not matter. I do not care how you line up, whether there is a four-man line and three linebackers or three-man line and four linebackers. The key is however you lineup, you have to be a team that tackles well.

Justin Durant now plays with the Detroit Lions although he was originally drafted by the Jacksonville Jaguars. This is his sixth or seventh year in the pros. He was a sure tackler at Hampton. Once he found that football and went to it, there was normally no further movement —forward progress was stopped. He was a great tackler and he is in the NFL, probably an undersized linebacker, but he is a great tackler.

CREATING THE GAME PLAN

Game plans come from trying to find the most vulnerable players. I always ask my players, what are the opponents seeing when they see you on film? Are they saying, go at you because you are weak and your fundamentals are no good? I always tell them, watch what you are putting on film, because you are letting people know whether you are going to be a tough competitor or you are going to get run over because you are doing some things that are not very sound. So you have to be careful.

We always watch film to see, if we are going to throw the football, which of those four guys, back there in the secondary, is the guy that we want to pick on because he doesn't turn his hips, he has a weak back pedal, he doesn't close, or he doesn't tackle well. That is the information on which we develop a game plan. We look at the opponent and see who is the weak link. Sung Tzu, in "The Art of War," advises, "Find the weakest and attack them." If they have two over there who are weak, then it's like, "Ooh boy. Man, we are in real good shape now." When we are sitting there on Sunday, Monday, and Tuesday trying to decide what we are going to do to win, that is what we are looking for.

We do a lot of research on personnel, our team and the opponent, because that is the key or first step in creating a successful game plan for Saturday. The "Getting Ready to Play" sheet is part of the process. We included that in Chapter 9 if you want to refresh your memory. In that sheet, we tell all our players and coaches what we are going to work on every day of the week: Sunday, Monday, Tuesday, Wednesday, and Thursday. Because when Saturday comes, everybody wants to know as much as we can about the opponent. This is what I tell the players, "If you do not know yourself and you do not know your opponent, you have zero chance of winning. If you know yourself, but do not know your opponent, you got a fifty percent chance of winning. But when you know yourself and you know your opponent, you never leave the field defeated."

We take the pictures out of our opponent's program and put them in our game plan. We want our players so see the guy's face, to know who they are coming up against. We put his height, weight, and position in our game day scouting report. We even want them to know what hand he is going to use when he is in his stance. That is how the game plan is created.

KNOWLEDGE IS POWER: KNOW WHO YOU ARE

As I have previously stated, "When you know yourself and you know your opponent, you never leave the field defeated." Let's take a closer look at the process of acquiring that self-knowledge. We previously discussed the Four Phases of our program in Chapter 10. During each phase we are working to find out who we are and what kind of team we have. We are up at 5:00 a.m. and doing plyometrics to find out who we have and who we are. Spring ball — we are trying to find out what kind of team we have. Summer ball — we are trying to find out what kind of team we have. Now, once we get that figured out, when we get to the season, now we are trying to find out each week what kind of opponent we have. That is why we watch so much film. For instance, this year we have Oklahoma coming up. Well, we know that is going to be a tremendous challenge, but we know that now. So we continue to get to know who we are so that when we get there, we'll know our strengths and weaknesses. It does create a comfort zone when we know who we are.

COMMITMENT

When I first came to Hampton and Florida A&M University, they would practice at 3:30 p.m. in the off-season, which lasts from January to March. NCAA rules allow eight hours a week of practice in the off-season. However, when I arrived at both those campuses, we started practice at 5:30 a.m. instead of 3:30 p.m.! This was a shock to some of these young men. I did this because I am trying to find out who is really committed. Let's face it, at 3:30 p.m. in the afternoon it is easy to make practice because you are already up. But 5:30 a.m. in the early morning, when it is still dark, is another thing. Another reason I do this is because you cannot have any excuses for not showing up at that hour —there are not any classes in session and there are not any campus offices open. If you miss a practice, it does not take me long to get the message — you are not really committed.

So the first thing we want to find out it is: who is really committed, who really wants this thing. Who really loves this game and has the passion to play. The next thing we want to know is that once you show up and get here, how hard are you willing to work. If you do not mind being in the back of the line when it comes to sprints, chances are you are probably going to get beat up on game day. If you have the best bench press, and we have a guy here at FAMU now benching five hundred and twenty pounds, you are letting us know that you are a competitor. The same goes for the classroom. Some people think that it is all right to be a good athlete, but not a good student. Well, let me tell you, you have a lot of things to remember on each play. Just as you go to the weight room to develop your physical muscles, you have to go to class to develop those three mental muscles; cerebral, cerebellum, and medulla. The fact is, if you do not think that is important, you will make mistakes on the football field because you are going to forget your assignment. We look at a young man's behavior on the ball field and in the classroom to determine if he has the level of commitment required to play at our level.

GET THE DATA

We work hard to make informed, fair, and intelligent decisions. We do not play favorites; we play those who have proven we can trust them. We have ten tests that we use. After our six weeks of off season conditioning, we test every guy on these measures: the vertical jump, the broad jump, pro agility, three cone drill, the 60 yard shuttle, the 40 yard sprint, the match bench press, the 225 bench press, the power cling, and the back squat. We post all these scores so everyone knows how they are doing and how much they need to improve to compete with the top guys. The strength and conditioning coach gives me the results of the top ten guys on each one of those ten tests. I take the data home and see how many guys excelled on all of those ten tests. This one guy, John Ojo for example, performed very well in the vertical jump — he is a defensive back. It was pretty obvious to me that he is going to be one of our captains because he is a guy that is competing in everything. And I was not surprised at his outcome he never missed a morning workout. These are the kind of things we find out. Another example is James Owens. He had a vertical jump of 37.5. That means he has tremendous power in his lower legs. Although he has not played a lot, when we want somebody to block an extra point or field goal, it makes sense to put him on that special team because that is all about get off — explosion. We had a guy at Hampton. In fact, it was Tim Benson's brother. His name was Malcolm Benson. This guy, every time we got near the ten-yard line, we put him in the game. We knew this by looking at his vertical jump. His data let us know that he had real strong legs, and at the goal line, that is very important. Well, he probably had less yards gained of any running back, but he had the most touchdowns because, based on the data we collected from these tests, he was the guy to be in there near the goal line. We have another guy here at FAMU, Travis Harvey who is from California. He is on the team but has not played much. We have noticed that his grades have gotten better. He runs a 40-yard dash in 4.3/8, which was the fastest on the team. Well, he is telling us that he is ready to play. It will be interesting to observe him in practice. It looks like this guy is now going to help us win because he has his mind focused. In fact, he finished in the top ten on these six tests.

We are evaluating ourselves the entire year. We are constantly looking at the data. ¬¬We look at how many times they have not missed practice, have their grades improved, are they punctual, the way they walk around campus, and how they dress. All this tells us a whole lot about — can we trust this guy? That is really what it comes down to. Can I trust you? I have a saying. "If I cannot trust you to go to class, I cannot trust you on 4th–1 to make the play." As I was saying earlier, when you get up at 4:00 a.m. to be at a practice at 5:30 am, if you are there, you are letting me know when it's 4th – 1, and the game is on the line, I can trust you to compete.

CONCLUSION

The guys who were here last year they should be bigger, faster, stronger, smarter, and be making more plays. I believe you do not get better with age, you get better because of what you are doing while you are aging. We are just like GM, Verizon, Sprint, but our product is people. We also measure to see how our product is doing. We have a design and a blueprint that results in growth and development in all areas: mental, physical, spiritual, and emotional. If our student athletes follow the program, they will emerge stronger, smarter and more productive citizens at the end of their four or five years. Everything we do, every day, is designed to help these young men grow and develop. We challenge these guys to do something every day to make themselves better as a person, as a student, and as an athlete. Well, I always tell our players that we have a thirteen month program. I know there's only twelve months in a year, but we have something designed for them to do every day of the year, so that when it comes time to actually get on the field and compete, they are prepared to compete at their highest level.

We believe we are preparing them for life because that is what life is all about. If you want something in life, you have to compete for it. If somebody just gives you something, it is probably not worth much. So you want to compete. I even tell them, if you are the only one in the world that wants your girl, there's something wrong with her. You have to compete for everything that is worth anything: your girlfriend, your wife, your car, your house and your job. So we are teaching these young men how to be a competitive person, because in my mind no matter how intelligent or how strong you are, the people who win in this society are the ones who are competitive. In those early mornings 5:30 a.m. sessions, we have ropes and we play tug-of-war. We have eight different groups and we put the groups against each other. We want to see who is going to compete, who wants to pull that rope and pull their opponents across that line. Everything we do is designed to improve a man's competitive spirit. We do all kinds of things to get to know who we are. The ones who excel, these top ten guys, chances are they are going to be the guys who you will see playing more — because they have shown that they are competitive. We have two or three records here. Padric Scott benched two hundred twenty-five pounds, thirty-eight times straight. That is a record here. It is obvious he is going to be one of our leaders. John Ojo, 41.5 inches in the vertical jump. That is a new record here. That is a great jump even by NFL standards! He is going to be on the field. James Owens, our running back, he runs the 40-yard dash in 4.3/8 and had a vertical of 38.5 inches. We are talking about explosion here! My God, I do not see one guy being able to tackle him. I just do not. All that data gives us some idea on who we can count on when it's on the line. Those are the guys that are going to be out there.

Chapter 17
OFFENSE

The offensive philosophy was kind of built over the years. Being an offensive player myself, I always thought that was the side of the ball that was the most fun because you can be creative. It is almost like playing chess. You are trying to outwit someone and put together some strategy to beat the other guy. The most important rule of offense is not to beat yourself by giving away the ball — don't turn it over. A good offense must run and pass effectively. There are usually a hundred and thirty plays in a ballgame. That is sixty-five plays for each team. Winning the give away take away (turnovers) gives us sixty-five plus ten or fifteen of the opponents. The advantage becomes obvious. If I am not turning the football over and my defense is forcing the other team to turn it over, then we are going to get our sixty-five plays plus whatever we can get from the opponent. I have been in games where we had ninety-five plays. The other team ended up with about thirty-five. It is obvious who won that game because when you turn the ball over, it is like being in a war and giving your weapon to your opponent so he can shoot at you. So, first of all, a winning offense does not turn the ball over.

Here is the sheet that we hand out to our players. We will discuss it in more detail.

OFFENSE

- Don't beat ourselves – Must be able to run and throw the ball effectively and don't turn it over. There are usually 130 plays in a ball game. We get 65 and the opponent gets 65. Winning the give-away take away ratio gives us 65 plus 10 - 15 of the opponents

- An effective running game creates toughness and ball control. An effective passing game gives you explosive plays that turn into scores and it allows you to run effectively (getting people out of the box)

- Move the chains is a moral buster for the opponents' defense and a confidence builder for our offense. In a 60 minute game – the ability to average 40 minutes of possession time, keeps our defense fresh and the opponents offense out of sync.

- Multiple formations and motion are key busters as stated before when you shift strengths and attach weak and strong. Most defenses are set with a strength call.

- The use of a scheme to personnel is more effective than personnel to a scheme. Know your personnel and design scheme according to talent.

- When you have too many mistakes, turnovers or zero plays – It is a lack of understanding for the concept or we didn't rep the play enough – means the same

- The run game should feature a power scheme (inside/outside zone) misdirection, option and a perimeter scheme (sweep, toss).

- The pass game should feature the vertical pass game, intermediate curl to hook to come back, the quicks, slant and stops. Boots, play-action, screen and draw are complementary packages.

- Time is a premium – use it wisely in practice – should be as game like as possible to work on timing, blitz pickups, assignments, audibles, huddle vs. no huddle, signals, and personnel groupings.

- Must practice the 4 minute offense when ahead — the 2 minute offense when behind

- Penalties account for nearly a loss of 1,000 yards yearly must become more fundamentally sound.

RUN AND THROW

It is important for an effective offense to be able to run and throw the ball. Why is that? Well, some games you are going to be able to run the ball because the opponent is a little weak up front. There are some games you are not able to get too many yards on the ground because they are tougher, but they may be vulnerable in their secondary. Your opponent determines what you are going to do. All those hours spent in watching films helps to assess the other team and determine what you do. You have to be able to do both because you don't know which one you will have to use in a given game. If you just practice the run all the time, and then you come up against a team that is stiff against the run, no matter how much you have perfected your run, you will be through. The same holds true for the passing game. If you only practice passing the football, and you have a team that is really pretty good with their secondary, and they do not let you pass and they force you to run, but you do not have that part of the game, you are through again. So you want to practice fifty-fifty. You want to be able to run and throw effectively.

In the years where we won the statistical plaque from the NCAA, we had 5,000 yards of offense. We had 2,500 yards running and we had 2,500 yards passing. Well, it doesn't get any better than that. Of course, there were some games we ran more and some games we threw more. But at the end of the season, we were able to have 5,000 yards and that was a fantastic season. We were able to do it all: running, throwing, and not turning the ball over. It is important not to give away your opportunities to your opponent. I always say, "There's only one football and as long as we have it the other team can't score." I love this saying. It is real down home wisdom. So we practiced not turning the ball over and all that practice paid off.

RUN AND BE PHYSICAL

If your offense can run the football, you are going to win a whole lot more games than you lose. Running the football makes you a more physical team. There is a prerequisite for every play in the playbook — "You have to be physical." Joe Gibbs, former Head Coach for the Washington Redskins, made that statement. I don't care if it is an offensive play, defensive play, or special team's play. There is a prerequisite — you must be physical. Teams that run the football are tougher. There is a lot more contact when you run the football. I always say if you want to be a champion on game day, you have to be a champion everyday. So, if you want your defense to stop the opponent's running game on game day, you have to make your defense stop the run all week. That means they have to stop their own team, the offense, all week in practice. This gives the offense a lot of practice on the run. This is great for practice because both sides need to win. If they can win all during the week, they will win on Saturday.

Let's look at the 2012 Super Bowl. It is obvious that the New York Giants are a much more physical football team than the New England Patriots. They run the football. They have two big running backs and they just pound you. Then, if you look at their defense, their front four linemen are really tough. Tom Brady (New England Quarterback) caught hell because the Giants ran the football and they played great defense. I remember 1992 when Alabama won the national championship under Gene Starlings. They had the number one defense and they ran the football. Alabama, this past year against LSU, they ran the football and they played great defense. It does not take a Philadelphia lawyer to figure out how to get this stuff done. If you are a running football team, you create a much tougher team. When the offense can keep making first downs, it demoralizes the opposing defense. A strong, tough, consistent running offense will take away the opponent's will.

KEEP POSSESSION FOR 40 MINUTES

The key to winning is having possession of the ball. In a sixty-minute game, if our offense can maintain control of the ball for forty minutes, it accomplishes a couple of things. First, if we can run the football for that time, it keeps our defense fresh and it keeps their offense out of sync because they are on the sideline. In this past several years, we were either first or second in possession time — somewhere around thirty-four or thirty-five minutes averaged per game. The biggest game we had last year was against South Carolina State. We had not beaten them in ten years. We had the ball forty-four minutes, which means they only had the ball sixteen minutes the whole game! While it is possible to win a game with lesser possession time, it is not very likely. We just consumed the clock. Our offense was out there controlling the clock and our defense was on the sideline resting. When they did come on the field, they were ready to play because they were so fresh. That is why possession time is an important factor in the game.

USE MULTIPLE FORMATIONS AND MOTION TO BUST KEYS

We already spoke about defense's need to be fast and read the Keys in order to pick up the play. The best way to make that tough for them, and add more frustration to the opposing defense, is to use very few plays but have multiple formations. Multiple formations and motion are key busters. I always say "motion causes emotion." If I take your key and I move it, you will get frustrated. Motion does that. This is one way I explain this to my staff. "If I go in my house and I put my keys down in a certain place, I expect for those keys to be there when I return. If they are not, I am frustrated."

We want to keep forcing their defense to adjust. We want to confuse them. If they are looking at a wide receiver and he moves from one position and goes across the formation to the other side, you just moved his key. He gets frustrated because now that key became a lot harder to read — it was not the same key that was in the film. It was not the same key his coach drew up on the board. So now he has to think a little bit more. I already spoke about how thinking slows a man down. We want to force them to think more and not just react to what they have been expecting from their week's preparation.

So whenever you see offenses moving around before the ball snaps, they are trying to move the keys of the defense in order to take them out of their comfort zone. It is very common for the offense to do a lot of movement, even though they are only running two or three plays. All that movement by the offense is an attempt to get the defense out of their comfort zone.

ATTACK WEAK AND STRONG

Most defenses are set with a strength call, which means everything has to be either strong or weak. The strong side is generally determined by the position of the tight end or three receivers.

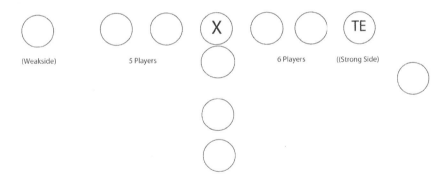

(Weakside)   5 Players   6 Players   ((Strong Side)

Wherever the tight end is on offense or the three receivers are positioned, that is normally the strong side. The opposing defense, base their calls on where the strength is because they also have a weak side and a strong side blitz. Now get this. Before the ball snaps, we are in a certain formation. The strength is to the right side. My tight end is on the right. Well, if I back him off the line and I now send him across the formation, I just shifted the strength from right to left. The defense now has to make a call to shift their position because our strength is no longer to their left — our strength is to their right. The beauty of all this is when you are in motion, you are taking their defense out of their comfort zone — You are making them think more. And the more they think, the slower they play. That is exactly what the offense wants to accomplish — slow down the defense because they are the fastest, they are the strongest, and the most competitive. We want to make them think so that 4.5 – 4.3 guy is now a little bit slower — to 4.7 to 4.6. That is why we use multiple formations.

Here is another way to think about this. I am not a hunter but I know people go out and hunt deer, rabbits, and squirrels. If I was in the woods hunting, and I saw a rabbit standing still, I am pretty confident that I can hit him. But if he takes off running, I know I am not going to hit him. I do not have any confidence. Well, that is the same thing we try to do with offense. When offense goes in motion, the defense should have a little less security about being able to hit us because they do not know exactly where we are. That is why we like to use a lot of different formations and a lot of motion, but very few plays.

ADJUST YOUR SCHEME TO YOUR PERSONNEL

Another important aspect in creating a successful offense is to use a scheme (a lineup and plan) that fits your personnel, rather than forcing your personnel to fit a scheme. It is important to know personnel and design schemes according to them. In other words, some people are so bullheaded they will just run off tackle no matter what. They just know that is the way to do it — and that is all they know. Well, your personnel might say spread it. You might have more speed so it makes better sense to use a speed formation. In the old days, everybody was lined up and just played "mano a mano," you know, power football, a big old slugfest. Now it is more wide open.

I am looking at our current FAMU stats here and I see a bunch of guys running 4.3 forty-yard dashes. Well, it makes sense that we should probably spread it out and run more speed stuff. The smart thing to do is to look at your data, find out what you have, and then match your scheme according to your personnel. I think that is real coaching because it all starts with personnel. If you have the right personnel on the field, then you have a chance to win.

Once you have them out there, you have to call plays that they can successfully execute. I would not want a speed guy running up between the tackles because that is not his thing. Buck Rogers, the successful baseball coach who focused on "Making the Adjustment" in "Bouncing Back: How to Recover When Life Knocks You Down," would probably love hearing about all this. He reminded me of the importance of adjusting to the current conditions and situation, because I know I have some old school in me where I just love to run that football up the middle. Sometimes, it is easy to get so attached to a certain way of doing things that it is tough to make the adjustments. Well, I think over the years, if you are still winning, it is because you do make adjustments. I believe in what he is saying. You have to be like the Florida palm tree. You bend but you don't break — sometimes you just have to make some adjustments.

AVOID ZERO PLAYS

When we have too many mistakes, turnovers, or zero plays, it is a lack of understanding for the concept or we did not rep (practice over and over again) the play enough. It means the same. When we make a bunch of mistakes, I do not get on the players, I get on the coaches. If we are turning over the ball, we are not locked in. Every Sunday, I come in and watch film. I look to see how many of those sixty-five plays went for zero yardage. I cannot stand zero plays. Give me at least one or two yards, don't just give me zero! I believe if we are getting too many zero plays, we either have too many plays, the kids do not understand the concept, or we have the wrong guys out there. Whatever it is, it all means the same. So look, let's get it done. The other day when we were on the track, somebody was telling me that it takes ten thousand hours to get to be good at anything. Well, that means I can't be doing a thousand things if it is going to take ten thousand hours just to get good at one thing. However, if I am doing fewer things, I might have a chance to get the ten thousand hours. If the offense is having too many turnovers, they are doing too much. They have to take something out. If they have too many turnovers, the kids are not comfortable. The run game should feature a power scheme, misdirection, an option, and a perimeter scheme. That is all you need.

BASIC PLAYS

Power Scheme: A power scheme means running off tackle where you have to lead block. You are bringing somebody from the other side of the center to the play side so you can load up. Woody Hayes, Vince Lombardi, all those old coaches, believed in the power game. They would have a tight end and fullback in the game and just come at you. There was no mystery. They would just be telling you, this is what we are going to do. Until you stop us, we are going to keep doing it. Because it is totally about power, you have to be committed. Down on the goal line in tight proximity, there is not a lot of room. It is not about trying to fool anybody. Somewhere along the line, you have to button your chinstrap and say, "Whose will is stronger?" You have to have that as part of your game.

Misdirection: In this play, you make a step one way, only to come back to the backside, so that you can force the opponent to commit to the initial step.

Options: In this play, after the ball is snapped, your quarterback can either keep it, hand it to a fullback, or he can pitch it to a running back. The option game is used to slow down very aggressive defensive lineman because, they do not know who is actually going to be carrying the football. The option means all three have an opportunity to carry the ball solely based on the movement of the defense.

Perimeter Scheme: The important thing about the perimeter scheme is that you have to be able to get outside. You have to make the defense run. Sometimes you have to go right at them or go off tackle. Sometimes you have to option, or run a wide sweep play. You have to make the defense cover the whole field, get them tired so that in the fourth quarter, you might be able to go at them. A football game is like a boxing match. Every play is a jab. If I jab you enough, in the fourth quarter, maybe I can give you an old haymaker and knock you out. The legendary boxer Jose Torres said that a great boxer wins with intelligence, not just brute strength. It is the same with football. The offense tries to mix up the plays and outsmart the defense in at attempt to wear them down. It is like the "rope-a-dope." Every time I come off the ball, I want to break down some of my opponent's will. That's a jab. I might not get a whole bunch of yards in the first quarter — maybe only two or three yards. But, if I keep jabbing you for three or four quarters, then in that fourth quarter, I might start getting eight or nine yards. I might even be getting a touchdown. So the idea is to make sure that you make them run, make them cover the whole field, and wear them down. Don't let them just gang up on you because you are only running in one area. You have to run in the A-gap, the B-gap, the C-gap, and the D-gap.

PASSING GAME

The pass game should feature the vertical pass, the intermediate curl, the hook, the comeback, the quick, slants and stops, boots, and play action. The screen and draw are part of a complimentary package.

Vertical Pass: I think it is important to throw the ball vertical, which means deep passes, because I want the opponent's secondary to back up and think, "Look, they will throw the ball, so we better not get too close to the line to try to stop the run." So you have to have a vertical game.

Intermediate and Other Passes: You have to be able to push the defense deep but then throw crossing routes. Those are the intermediate to curls and comebacks. In other words, you have to make sure that you can throw all of the passes, so that you are prepared for whatever they give you in a game. You don't know, they might not be a good underneath coverage team. Well, your underneath passes would be better. They might be slow, so you might be able to get behind them and throw a drop ball. It is important to work on that vertical game. They might be a zone team and play really far off. Well, now you have to have some quicks, you have to have some slants, and you have to have some stop routes — make them think you are going deep but stop after five yards and catch the ball. You have to practice all the different routes because you don't know which ones are going to be most effective in a game. If you can run them all, then you will be able to take advantage of what the secondary's giving you.

Complimentary Packages: The bootlegs, the play actions, and the screen game, all of those are just counter passes where you are going to start one way and try to roll away from the play and get the defense out of position. Screens are useful when you have a defense that really comes at you with a lot of blitzing. Sometimes, the only way to slow them down is to throw a little screen pass over the top of their heads.

PRACTICE LIKE GAME DAY

Practice should be as game-like as possible. So it is important to create similar situations that you will have in a game and work on them in practice. We work on the sudden plays, we go to the plus five-yard line, we go to the right hash mark of the field, and we work the left hash. If you visit a high school, look at their practice field. There is grass everywhere but right in the middle on the fifty-yard line, because they practice on the fifty-yard line every day, all the time. They always stay in the same place. But the game is not played on the fifty-yard line. You have to move the ball around and practice the same way you will play on game day. You have to practice different situations to make it realistic. Go to the twenty on the right hash and run four or five plays. Let your team know what you are thinking. When we are in this particular situation, on this yard line, what do we like to do? We will go to the left hash and maybe the plus forty. There are some plays that are better. Your team gets familiar with what the coach is thinking because you place the ball in practice, for five minutes all over the football field, and you run certain plays. You are getting used to all the areas of the field and the players are learning what the coach likes when we are in this area. It just makes sense to move the ball around in practice so that you are using the whole field.

I do not believe in doing anything in the game that I have not done in practice. So you have to break it down and make sure that you are doing it in practice. For example, work on the blitz pickup and know what the assignments are. Work with the audibles which signal a change in a play at the line of scrimmage. In other words, everything you do in the game, you have to do in practice, so that you are not just working on the physical part of the game, but you are also working on the mental part. In addition, you must practice the four-minute offense. This is where you are ahead and you don't want to lose. The two-minute offense is when you are behind and need to score quickly. When you are ahead, you do not want to be out there throwing the ball around and running high risk plays — just hand the ball off and run the clock out. Well, if you are behind, the two-minute offense is where you don't huddle up. You are trying to march the ball down field as quickly as possible and you throw a lot of out routes (this is where the receiver steps out of bounds after catching the ball) to stop the clock. You do not want to waste the clock so you do not huddle up at all. You just run the play and get right back to the line of scrimmage.

In the last Super Bowl, in the first quarter, the Patriots got a flag for twelve men on the field. That was their first mistake. Penalties account for a loss of nearly 1,000 yards a year. They are a real killer! I cannot say it enough about this. You have to practice everything and make it game-like. During our practice, we want everybody on the sideline. We are going to run in and out the same way we would during the game, because you cannot just say, "Get it right." You have to practice it right. You have to rep it. You have to put the time in; otherwise, you are stuck with paralysis by analysis. I have seen a lot of coaches, smart as hell in the classroom, really smart. That stuff looks good on the board, but they are the only ones who understand it. Once the team gets out on the field, they cannot execute it. That is just not a very smart way to coach. There is nothing worse than going out there on first down, calling the play, picking up five yards, only to look up and see somebody's off sides. Somebody was holding. Then it is second down and fifteen. You are going backwards. You have to stay out of your own way. Nobody is so good that they can hurt themselves and still expect to win. Let your opponent beat you — do not help him to beat you. This is where we started with offense and it seems like a good place to end. Don't beat yourself — avoid the penalties and keep possession of the ball. These are the fundamental of offense.

Chapter 18

SPECIAL TEAMS

The Special Teams consist of the following players:

- **Kicker**: He is often called the placekicker and handles kickoffs and field goals attempts.
- **Holder**: He holds the ball for the placekicker.
- **Long Snapper:** This is not always the regular center because the ball needs to be snapped much further on punts.
- **Punter:** The player who kicks the ball down field usually on a fourth down.
- **Punt & Kick Return:** These players catch the ball and return it after punts or kickoffs. They are usually the fastest players on the team.
- **Upback:** Typically used to make line calls and protect the punter.
- **Gunner:** This player is designed to quickly get down field in order to tackle the kick returner. He usually lines up near the sidelines to have clear access downfield.

We also have a one sheet hand out for the Special Teams that we give to all our players. The following is the actual page which we will discuss in more detail.

SPECIAL TEAMS

- Create great field positions.

- We always utilize the best personnel on the team for special team. Linebackers and defensive backs have more scholarships than any other segments for this reason. These two segments should operate better in open space with support from other segments where necessary

- Extra point, fields goals, extra point/Field Goal Block will decide the close games – fundamental skills with an understanding of importance is paramount.

- Onside and hands are no longer just used in obvious situations. They are looked upon as tempo plays in modern day football game plans.

- We will continue to start our practices with special teams to promote its value (1/3) to winning. In every game, there are 4-5 plays that will determine its outcome – they are usually found in the kicking game.

I have a very high regard for the Special Teams. I have discovered over my coaching career that Special Teams are really just as important, if not more important, than offense and defense. You have to have all three. There are always four or five plays in a game that will determine the outcome of the game. All of those four or five plays involve a Special Teams play. We talked earlier about how we want the defense to play tough and force the offense to go six or seven or eight plays before they score. Well, there's nothing worse than our offense going eight or nine plays and finally scoring, only to have the opponent take one play to score on the kickoff return. Our plan is to wear our opponent down — this is not a part of the plan.

We start every practice with Special Teams. We do that because we want the team to understand the real value of solid Special Teams play. Some coaches do that at the end of practice and I think that's a bad time, because players might tend to think the practice is over. There are some coaches, and I personally do not do this, stop in the middle of practice and work on Special Teams. Your team has to internalize the importance of great Special Teams play.

At the conclusion of any game, you can go back and see if there was an extra point missed, a field goal blocked, a field goal made, or a punt returned that made the difference in that win or loss. Our philosophy for Special Teams is, "Be the reason we won, not the reason we lost." Special Teams are really designed to create great field position. It is important that they execute their role effectively. We always tell our team, "Don't ever leave the field without a kick," which subtly means, "Don't turn the ball over." If you can't get a first down, punt, and if you get into field position and can't score, at least get a field goal. When you do score, get the extra point. It's all about field position.

FIELD POSITION

The punt is so important, because it changes field position. If we are driving, but we stall, and we punt, we want to get as many yards as we can for our defense. It's a lot better playing defense when the opponent has eighty yards to drive, versus getting a punt blocked or trying to go for the fourth down which may result in our opponent now only having to go thirty or forty yards for a touchdown. It's about creating better field position. A coffin corner is a kick that ends up just a few yards outside of the end zone. It is something now that people are doing instead of taking the ball into the end zone, which results in the ball being brought out to the twenty-yard line. If we can practice punting the ball and it rolls out on the one-yard line, now the opponent has ninety-nine yards to go to score. It is a lot better as a defensive player to look behind you and see ninety-nine yards to defend versus eighty. So a great punt is all about field position.

UTILIZE YOUR BEST PLAYERS

We always utilize our best players in Special Teams. We normally take more linebackers and defensive backs on a road game, because they are more familiar with open field tackling. They practice it all the time. They are more familiar with open field than any other segment. So most of time we're going to have those guys. We tell our starters, if you are a starter on offense or defense, you have to be on at least two Special Team units, either punt, punt return, kickoff, kickoff return, or a field goal block. That's important because I'll tell them, "If you look at a high school kid coming into college, chances are he's not going to start on offense or defense in his first year. But where he can probably help this football team is on a Special Teams unit." Well, it's the same way if you're leaving college and going to the NFL. Very few kids go from college to the NFL and start on offense or defense. But the pro scouts always want to know, "Did he play Special Teams?" If he did, that's going to enhance his chances of getting drafted or being a free agent, because if he can play Special Teams, he has an opportunity to help the team win. So, that can help a player from an NFL standpoint — whether or not they are going to get selected. There's nothing like seeing a wide receiver on kickoff going down making most of the tackles. Certainly the return game is all about skilled guys.

Your philosophy must state the use of personnel, because a lot of times coaches want to protect their players on offense and defense and they don't want them to play Special Teams. The rationale is that they are going to get tired. I am not going to keep a guy off of Special Teams because of that. That just means he will have to run more in practice to be in better shape. I'm not going to save a guy on offense and defense and not let him play on Special Teams, because Special Teams can get you beat just as much as the offense or defense. You have to be careful that you are not sacrificing talent in order to play good, solid offense and defense. You cannot let your Special Teams suffer because they do not have the same talent as offense and defense. Any coach that is winning understands this. He doesn't allow backups to always play Special Teams. Most of the time they are going to be found in the linebackers and defensive backs.

These two segments should operate better in an open space, because they play in space. They cover the pass and the run. Extra points, field goals, and extra point field goal blocks will decide the close games. It is very important to understand the value of these fundamental skills. Coaches and football programs in the past did not give scholarships to kickers. They always wanted them to be walk-on players — they did not think they were that important. Bobby Bowden, the retired football coach from Florida State, right across the street, could write a book about the importance of kickers. He lost games to Miami in the early '90's and in early 2000 because his kickers were walk-on kids. In contrast, we provide three scholarships at this level. We only have sixty three to give but three of them are definitely going towards Special Teams: the punter, the kickoff and the extra point guy. In addition, one good snapper or two snappers might get a half scholarship each.

I remember being in the Meadowlands Giant Stadium. We were playing Grambling in 1997 or 1998. We were ahead 27-20 and Grambling came down and scored in the waning moments of the fourth quarter, which made the game 27-26.

Malcolm Benson, Tim Benson's brother, blocked the extra point, which kept the game at 27-26. We had the ball again but kind of sputtered. Now they had the ball and drove down again but didn't score. However, they are now in field goal range. Malcolm Benson blocked the field goal — two blocks in a row! A Special Teams play made the difference. We ended up winning the game 27-26 on a blocked extra point and a blocked field goal by the same guy. Why was he there in that position? We had looked at some stats and saw that he had explosive power because of his vertical jump. He blocked two very crucial kicks, and we won it by a point.

We place a high value on the Special Teams and use the data we collect and the stats on these kids to find the best players for these positions. For example, when we go ahead for spring ball based on stats, a guy like Roderick Cromartie is 37.5 in the vertical. Then he ran a 4.3 forty-yard dash. He is number two with a 10.2 in the broad jump. Somebody on the defense has to come off and we are going to put him in, because he's going to block some field goals for extra points. That's what the data tells us, and this is a chance for him to contribute to the team in a very significant way.

In conclusion here, I have seen Special Teams make a difference in a one-point win or a one-point loss. I know that onside kicks (instead of a kick off going deep into the end zone, it must go at least ten yards and can then be recovered by the offense) are no longer just used in obvious situations, like when you are behind and want to try to get an onside kick to maintain control of the ball. The New Orleans Saints were in a Super Bowl a couple of years ago. They started the second half with an onside kick and won the Super Bowl. So the goal is to put your team in situations to win by being aggressive. Special Teams have become a real weapon. We continue to start our practices with Special Teams because we want to promote its value. We always said it is one third of our game plan because we know those four or five plays will determine the outcome. We tell them, "Be the reason we won, not the reason we lost." But, of course, you cannot just say that, you have to actually put the time in to accomplish it. That is why we start every practice with Special Teams, every meeting with Special Team, and every walk through with Special Teams.

EPILOGUE

Well, now you have it. We have laid out our entire blueprint from beginning to end. As you can see, it is based upon the development of the individual who will be a champion everyday for the rest of his life. We work hard to create an environment that provides the best support in all areas of our players' lives: academic, physical, emotional and spiritual. It is not an easy program, but no great victories are ever achieved without effort. We hold our players to a high standard and when they falter, we are willing to confront them and bring them back on track. We believe in love and discipline, respect and honor, and pride and humility. Our blueprint is based upon service and obedience to the Lord's word. We have been fortunate to see the deeper potential in our young men and have been able to help them achieve great personal victories on and off the field. We believe our program brings greater respect to the Universities where we reside, and uplifts the entire student body. We serve as mentors for future generations of coaches and educators. We are grateful that we have been blessed to help others and share this work.

We have shared everything about our blueprint. We invite you to use whatever aspects of our approach and program that speaks to you and apply them to your life and work. This book can be your first step in taking your life to the next level — whether you are a player, coach, parent, teacher, or businessman.

My desire is to mentor more coaches so we can share what we have learned over the years with more people. I am available for keynote speaking engagements and seminars at universities, colleges, professional organizations, professional sports organizations, and corporations.

In addition, we have a select group of coaches that I have trained who are available for individual coaching for players and coaches at the college and professional level. Individual coaching is a powerful way to speed up your learning and development.

We are also developing a collection of online products and services, which can be found at www.coachjoetaylor.com. We also invite you to "like" our Facebook fan page at http://www.facebook.com/successisaninconvenience.

Please contact me if there is anyway we can help you or your organization.

Best wishes,
Joe Taylor

AFTERWORD

TONY DUNGY
NBC Football Analyst
Former Super Bowl Winning Coach

The Making Of A Champion is an important contribution to the body of knowledge about coaching football and being successful in life. As you have read, it is not easy to be a champion on the field and create a successful life, family, and career. Many people do not realize the amount of time, sacrifice and dedication it takes to be the best that you can be. Striving for personal ex-

cellence is a lofty goal. Coach Taylor and I share similar values and faith in the Lord Jesus Christ, which has helped us both to overcome obstacles, provide inspiration to thousands of young men, and create championship teams with men of high character, integrity, honor, and valor.

Joe Taylor has been a very successful coach at the high school and college level for over forty years. During that time he has won numerous championships and sent many players to the NFL. But I would say his greatest accomplishment has been helping his players grow as men off the field. This is where Coach Taylor has really been a champion. He has been a great role model to not only his players, but to those of us in the coaching profession as well. I know you will enjoy this book and, in reading it, you'll get a glimpse of how he showed everyone he came in contact with how to win in life.

Coach Taylor's presence on any college campus provides an inspiration and incentive for everyone to strive to be their best. We all realize the power, influence, and importance that a college football program has to uplift the entire campus community. Joe Taylor has been an asset everywhere he has coached and has positively influenced the athletic, spiritual, and academic culture on those campuses.

This book is important because it provides a roadmap for success on and off the field. Anyone who wants a resource and guide to help young men deepen their spiritual faith, integrity, responsibility, and dedication to excellence will find great value in this book.

Tony Dungy

ABOUT THE AUTHOR

I was born in 1950 on a family farm in Sussex County, Virginia. My mom and dad were farmers in the 40s and the 50s, but the farm went bad and my father moved the family to Washington D.C. I was eleven years old when we moved. I was in junior high school. I ultimately finished my formal education at Cardozo High School in Washington, D.C.

Prior to that time, my sport was baseball. Football was not even popular then, it was all track and baseball. Bob Headen was the football coach at Cardozo High School. He came up to me in the hallway and said, "Listen son, I think you need to come out for football." I really did not have any great interest to play football because baseball was my thing. However, there was a whole different life in the inner city. There was not any baseball around to play.

I did get into the football program but my family really was not real excited about it. I have an older brother (Leroy), and an older sister (Mary). After school they all worked —it might have been in a hotel, a restaurant, or wherever, but they worked. My mother and father felt like I was just out there playing around, that I really was not doing anything beneficial. According to Mary, my mother's sister was the one who was responsible for getting my birth certificate and all the paperwork that I needed to get into playing football. It was my mother's sister who did that. My mother did not want me to play football because she was afraid I would get hurt. Because of that, they never really saw me play until I was afforded a scholarship in my senior year to go out to Western Illinois. I had some other opportunities, some other scholarship offers, but I really wanted to see more of the world. I knew how we lived in our neighborhood, but I always felt like there was more. And so I went a thousand miles away from home to a completely different culture. In fact, Western Illinois, at that time, probably had about a 16,000 enrollment, and there were probably only about thirty African Americans. I was one of them!

It is an interesting story how I ended up at Western Illinois. Cardozo was playing Good Council High School in Wheaton, Maryland, which was north of the city in a Catholic area. That game was one of my better games in high school. Harry Fritz, the Athletic Director at Western Illinois, was in town visiting a friend. The friend said, "Listen, we are finished with our business. Let's go to this game." He was talking about my high school game. Well, they were sitting there at the game and I made twelve tackles, unassisted! I am playing offensive guard, fullback, linebacker, and I am on all of the special teams. I am having one of my better games. When the Athletic Director went back to Western Illinois at the end of the weekend, he said to the coach, "Listen, there is a guy at Cardozo High School. I know you do not recruit that far away, but you have to see him." So, you know, all of that is the Lord's work. When I graduated from Cardozo, I went up to Western Illinois. That is how I got there. James Cox, a guy who I was introduced to through Bob Headen, was instrumental in the follow up and paper work process. He was truly a Godsend and blessing in my life at the time.

I was playing football there but it was not until my second year that my parents saw me play for the first time. It was a homecoming. I was so excited they were there, I did not even realize I had a couple of fingers that were broken in the game. It was Monday, after they had left, and all of the excitement was over, that I felt it. They had come and I knew they were in the stands. It was one of those feelings, you know, that there was no way that I was not going to play. It did not happen until the third quarter. This ring finger is bigger than the other one because this knuckle has been broken several times. It never really went back to its normal size. I was so excited because my parents were there — I did not want to be hurting, but I was. Afterwards, we all had a very nice time together. I stayed out there for four years and graduated.

I had promised my high school coach, Bob Headen, I would come back to D.C. Each year, between my freshman and sophomore, and then my sophomore and the junior years, he would hire me. We would move around in the city and put on structured activities for inner city kids. This was called The Mayor's Youth Program and Mr. Headen was in charge of it. I used to help him all the time. He was always the coach for the all-star game, because the coach that won the city championship was always the coach for the summer all-star game. I was there, helping him.

When I first went to college I wanted to major in business. But I realized that I was at the gym for most of my day for early morning workouts. I started at 5:45 a.m. and then I would come back to lift weights during the day. And then I had practice in the evenings. So I said, "Well, I am going to be smart. I am going to major in health and physical education, so I do not have to go way up on campus, and then turn around to come right back down here." There was also my coach back home, Mr. Headen. I was getting involved coaching with him during the summer. Like I said, it was not a dream to coach, but it became obvious that was my direction — my head coach is employing me every summer. I am coaching with him. I am playing and I am in the gym all day. I always tell people, "The good Lord chose me for this profession. And so He will probably let me know when it is time to get out of it." Everything just looked like it was pointing in that direction.

I really appreciate those days because I know that the organization and the blueprint took shape in my college days under Darrell Mudra. In fact, Darrell Mudra was not there when I got there. I was recruited by the A.D. The A.D. fired the coaching staff my first year there and brought in Darrell Mudra.

You had to prove yourself all over again! An incident happened at the end of the first month. We were out there doing some drills — the offense going against the defense. I came off into my assignment with good contact. I kept my feet moving and he ended up falling back and hitting his head — He had a concussion. He was advised by the doctors never to play again. Well, I guess that was instant credibility. You know, this guy here can help us win, because that is that brute sense of what football is. I had to pass that guy going across campus to classes for four years. I did not really feel like it was my fault just because I kept my feet driving and he did not. I was disappointed for him because that ended his career. But boy, everybody started saying that is the guy that…. You know how that goes — so my reputation spread. I have always been a real serious, no nonsense guy throughout life.

All I ever wanted was to know the rules. Once I found out what they were, then that is what I followed. For me, that makes life a lot more manageable. I tell these players all the time, "These are the rules around here. If you were not at the table when they were made, they probably do not care how you feel about them. Find out what they are and follow them! You are not here to resist and break rules but to obey them — it's called discipline." That is the way I have always been.

I did not like getting up at 5:45 a.m. to practice. But I do not know where I would be if I had not done it. It is important to realize that the things we are now doing in the program are not stuff I just read about. Our program is based upon my personal experiences. Sometimes I was stretched to the point where I wondered if I could make it. I know that if I had not listened, if I had resisted, or if I had been one of those guys with an attitude towards leadership, I would not be here today. There are so many kids today who have an attitude — they know it all, "I know what is good for me." That is not the right attitude for success.

I finished in four years, mainly because every year when I returned to D.C., even though I worked during the summer, I always went to Howard University for courses. When I did graduate, I returned to Washington, D.C. because I had promised Coach Headen that when I got my degree, "I am coming back to help you." I felt like I was indebted because of all he had done for me. First of all, he got me out of the hallways and involved with football, and then I end up with a scholarship. In addition, during the summer, he always gave me a job. I do not know where I would be without him. In fact, when he retired, of all of the guys he had coached, I was the only one he invited back to speak at his retirement. He still lives in D.C. He is a great guy. He sent many young men to college. As I kept coming back and working as a coach, it became evident that I was supposed to pursue coaching as a career.

After graduation, I came back to help him but I could not get in right away. He was working on a new project. There was a new high school in D.C. called H.D. Woodson. It had elevators, escalators, and a pool, an indoor pool! It was just opening up, but you almost had to be a veteran teacher to get over there. It was the flagship school.

I was working at Alice Deal Junior High School but I knew I was not going to stay there long. It was up in northwest Washington. The students that went there were senators' kids — government figures. If I told them to line up so I could call roll for the physical ED class, they would keep running around and act like they couldn't hear anything. One day I remember they were playing with the basketball and I am trying to call roll. I went over there and acted like I was playing with them. You know, I threw the ball up on the backboard so someone had to go get it. When one of the boys came down, he landed on my foot that I had lifted to kick him in his you know what. That was on a Friday. I back came to school on Monday and the principal said, "Are you still here?" I thought, "Oh, Lord, I got fired already." But that wasn't it. Something better was in the works.

They had made arrangements for me to be transferred over to H.D. Woodson. I know Bob Headen had been working on that. This is how he did it. I had to have something they needed. And again, as the Lord would have it, this principal wanted to start a wrestling program in his high school. But there was no wrestling in the whole city. Well, fortunately, my offensive line coach at Western Illinois, Bob McMahon, was the head wrestling coach. He made all of his football players in his segment wrestle. Bob did not know I wrestled while I was I in college; not on a high competitive level, our coach just wanted to keep us in shape. But I did learn some things. So when Bob told me to go to the library and read up on some wrestling terms so we can talk about this program, I was ready. That is why, and any of my coaches will tell you, when we are recruiting a player, and I find out he has a wrestling background, I get very excited about that young man.

Let me tell you why I think wresting is so great. In team sports, if I am a great running back, I probably made a few people miss on my way to the goal line — that lineman did not necessarily have to block anybody. But I made him look good because I ran for a touchdown. And so when we get to the sideline, all eleven guys coming off will get a high five. This guy probably did nothing. But in wrestling, it is only you and that opponent. Everybody is sitting up in the stands and they are looking at you two guys. Whatever you are doing, you do not have to tell anybody, they can see it. To me, it takes a very high level of competitive spirit to be a great wrestler, because that is the longest six minutes in America.

I am known as the father of wrestling in D.C., because we took that team and won championships for five years. We used to go out in the suburbs to get competition because there were no teams in the city. Each year we would add two or three schools in the city and eventually got to about ten. Darrell Mudra, who coached me in college, kept calling me to get me to work with him, the same way my high school coach kept calling me when I was in college. I said to Darrell, "I just started and I made a commitment to my high school coach to work with him. We had just started the sport of wresting and I am just not ready to move to the college level."

He was at Florida State for about three years when he got fired. In fact, the day he was fired, he had just left my house. At that time, I was the assistant football coach at H.D. Woodson. I was also the head wrestling coach, the assistant baseball coach, and I taught adults at night. When I arrived at school, I had FCA (Fellowship of Christian Athletes) in the mornings at 7:00 a.m., and then taught all day. We practiced year round: the first of the year was football, then wrestling in the winter, and baseball in the spring. I was coaching all year. I was working in what was called the Community School. The school was open to everybody — kids during the day and their parents took classes in the evening.

Since I was working year-round, I could not see moving when Darrell first called me. I always tell my coaches and players that hard work does not go unnoticed. Darrell Mudra is known as "Dr. Victory." He would take fledgling programs and just turn them into champions with the same blueprint we pretty much use. Playing for Coach Mudra really helped to shape my approach to this coaching profession.

Meanwhile, Eastern Illinois was doing well with their sports program except for football. Mike Mullaly was the athletic director. Mike flew down and convinced Darrell to come out of retirement and come take the job at Eastern. Well, Darrell called me again. I had been at the high school for five years at this point. It was in January of 1978 and I decided I wanted to go to the college level. I told Darrell that I would work with him on one condition — I had to finish my wrestling season. In retrospect, I should have gone earlier because that was the only championship I lost. I guess mentally I had already shifted to Eastern Illinois. This just shows how important focus is in winning. So, we went on to Eastern Illinois, and that year we won the 1978 national championship for NCAA Division II football. We beat Harold R. "Tubby" Raymond and the University of Delaware Blue Hens.   Eastern Illinois is where I met guys like Mike Shanahan. Mike was hired by Darrell as the offensive coordinator and now he is the Head Coach of the Washington Redskins. He has been at Denver, San Francisco, Los Angeles and Oklahoma. Along with Vince Lombardi, Don Shula, Chuck Noll, Jimmy Johnson and Bill Belichick, he is one of six coaches with back-to-back Super Bowl championships. John Teerlinck was the defensive coordinator and line coach, and I was the offensive line coach. They tried to blackball John out of the NFL because in one year he had broken something like six or seven quarterbacks' legs. He thought the best play in football was to sack the quarterback. And he taught it! He said, "We will pick up the runner on our way back to the quarterback." He did a good job of that. Mike hired John and Denver won two championships — two Super Bowls! They had Elway, which gave them a good offense, but their defense was not there. Once they hired John, he fixed that. We used to invite him down to run my clinics. We still talk, but we do not talk as much because everybody's plate is so full.

So, I went to Eastern after the second call from Darrell, and that is when it all started. I went from being born in the country on a farm, to the inner city, on to undergrad at WIU, and grad school at EIU. After two seasons at Eastern Illinois, I came to Virginia Union. I had an opportunity to go out to California, because after we won a national championship everybody had opportunities. Cal State Fullerton was calling. But I had never been a West Coast guy. In fact, now I think I am too far away and I am just south of home, but to go all the way over to the West Coast, oohh, that was too much.

So we decided to come back this way. We came east to Virginia Union as the offensive coordinator. I had an opportunity to go to either Hampton or Virginia Union. Well, as an offensive coordinator, you always want a strong defense, because you do not have to score as many points to win. At that time, Hampton was giving up a lot of points. However, when I was at Eastern, we noticed that Virginia Union always ranked at the top of NCAA stats. So I said, "Well, I am going to go to where I know there is a strong defense." I came to Virginia Union, but the head coach told me, "We won a championship last year, but we lost most of our offensive people. The best we can go this year is about 500." I said, "Hell, I didn't leave Illinois and come all the way to Virginia to go 500." We had a great defense and we started eight freshmen. We won a championship. I tried to initiate some changes in the weight room, the organization, and a lot of things. I suggested things that were a little different than what they were used to. And they always said, "Well, you know, you are at an HBCU now, things are different." And I said, "What does that have to do with anything? Organization is organization. Structure is structure." I went in there and tuned out all of that stuff. I just kept working and it really became a platform to further my career.

After a couple of years as the offensive coordinator with Virginia Union, I had an opportunity to go to Howard University. It was a Division 1 — AA program. The pay was a little better and it was a step up. I was enjoying Virginia Union, but I wanted to take the opportunity that was presented.

So I went up there. Howard did not have all the resources that you needed to have but I thought they had a chance to win. To make a long story short, the Head Coach at Virginia Union, Willard Bailey, had an opportunity to return and work for his alma mater, Norfolk State. Bailey had been very successful at Virginia Union, but his alma mater called him and off he went. Now, all of the kids that I had coached at Virginia Union, before I went to Howard, were now seniors. They told the President of Virginia Union that if you all do not hire Joe Taylor, we are all going to transfer. So, that was my first real Head Coaching job at Virginia Union. I got it because Bailey went back to Norfolk. I came back and we were champions by the third year with an undefeated season.

When I was there, I ran the weight program and the academic support program. I was in there with the players. I lifted with them, I ran with them, and I was there for study hall. I helped them with everything. My door was always open. I have always had an open door policy. I always tell coaches, "If a kid gets up his nerve to come from across campus to see you, find time for him. Because, you know, for him to get his nerve up, he might not do it the second time. Do not turn him away. Make time for these athletes." And that has always been my policy. They all knew it, so when the job came open, they pretty much told the President who they needed to hire.

I was at Virginia Union for eight years. We had a lot of success. Hampton was in the same conference as Virginia Union. One year after we beat Hampton, their President walked into my huddle after the game was over. I would always kneel down with the guys and we would end with a prayer. The President walked right into the huddle and said he wanted to talk to me. I came back to Richmond knowing that I pretty much had the job at Hampton. Since it was in the same conference, some people said that was a lateral move. I saw it a little differently. Hampton was known first for its high academics. They did not have resource issues and they had a president that wanted to win. Darrell taught me that a long time ago — "wherever you go as a coach, understand one thing, if it is important to the President that you win, it is a good job. If he does not care, that is not a good job."

Presidents that do a great job at their universities know how to get the students involved; how to get enrollment up. One president said to me that, "The front porch of your school is your football program. Make sure that it is attractive." Most presidents who understand that do well with the alumni. Why? — Because it starts the year off right. If you are at a school that has some issues, look around and see what the football program is like. Now a lot of folks do not want to hear that. Faculty members often do not want to hear that. However, I was at an opening school ceremony and they had invited the President, Harrison Wilson, from Norfolk State to speak. He told the faculty, "If you want to learn how to improve your retention, talk to football coaches;

they have a way of keeping players around. They monitor their players. They are going to find out what those kids are doing."

The retention rate for athletics and especially football is probably higher than the regular student body. I believe this is so because we teach, "nobody cares for you more than you care for yourself. Nobody should love you more than you love yourself." So if that is the case, then do what you need to do. Do not say, "I love myself, but then do all kinds of things to hurt yourself." Be real! I believe we teach these kids to care about and value themselves, which includes getting a good education. The faculty does not always want to hear that. They believe the football team is a bunch of barbarians that wear wire on their face. But if you have a great tradition, and a strong football program, the university tends to function better.

Virginia Union was good training and preparation for me. I sincerely believe that the Lord is always preparing you for the next move or the next step. Sometimes we ask, but we may not be ready to receive. Sometimes we need to experience something first. I had the opportunity to gain a lot of experience at Virginia Union. We painted the field and the locker room. We bought the equipment and put our own media guide together. We had to get ads for the poster and even sell the tickets. We had to do it all. That prepared me for anything else that came along. I did not just paint the field. I had to go buy the lime to put on it. Some of these things you had to actually experience because, if you just heard it, you would not believe it. But it was great preparation for what was to come. In 1992, I went down to Hampton and was there sixteen years. We won thirteen championships. That lets you know that the resources were in place.

The kids at Virginia Union were really disappointed that I left. I went back to the first graduation after my departure. Forty guys graduated. That was a great accomplishment. In addition, I had a relationship with those kids. I was not just a "playing coach." It was much more than that. My philosophy and experience is, "Because I met you I am better. Because you met me, you are better." That is what I believe in and it was and continues to be real. It was exciting and meaningful. Every day we looked forward to showing up and seeing what else we could do. It was powerful because we knew that the thing we were doing were great. It meant a lot to all of us and so it was hard leaving those kids.

We had thirteen championships at Hampton; sometimes it was multiple championships in the same year. You know, it could have been a conference championship, but also SBN, which is the Sheraton Broadcasting Network. We were also invited to a few classics and we got trophies for that. But for all those years, it shows that when the ten steps are really supported, great things can happen. It is not miracles. We have the blueprint and it works when you follow it. Success is an inconvenience. You do have to work for it and it is not always easy, but the hard work always pays off.

We really enjoyed our relationship at Hampton. The campus and the town were great. In fact, I was part of a six-person group that was like a subsidiary of the city council. We were selected to be liaison between the community and the local government. If a little brush fire was brewing, because the community did not always trust the city to do the right thing, whether it was law enforcement or just legislation, we would be called in to talk, and be the intermediaries between the two. That was a great experience. We brought a lot of great notoriety to the school and to the community. I know the President and the A.D. got on a lot of NCAA committees because they knew you could not do things all by yourself.

I thought I would retire down there. I was happy. I was fine in all aspects. I did not have any problems. However, I did want to help my assistant coaches a little bit more. Assistants talk from staff to staff. They wonder how is it that we are wining all of these championships in the conference; we are beating up on these teams every year, but they were getting paid more than we are? Well, at some point, you have to stop saying it is going to get better, you know, it has got to be better. I felt that I was just being obedient to the Lord's will in moving over here to FAMU. A lot of people left there with me. When I left, I brought half of the staff with me and we were able to do more for them here at FAMU. I did not want my coaches to worry about how they were going to pay their bills and take care of their families. There was another aspect to it. I was intrigued to have the opportunity to come and try to revive a very storied tradition. I knew Jake and what he stood for, and we knew what we were getting into. We wanted the opportunity to resurrect one more program.

And so that brings us to where we are. And that is from childhood to where I am right now. There is a lot more to be said about our program, how it works, and why it works. It has been a long road and a great one, a really very blessed one.

Made in the USA
Middletown, DE
07 September 2024

59929772R00156